ifacs

STUDIES IN A CHRISTIAN WORLD VIEW
Sponsored by the Institute for Advanced Christian Studies
Carl F. H. Henry, Editor-in-chief

Available

vol. 1: Contours of a World View, by Arthur F. Holmes
vol. 2: Christianity and Contemporary Philosophy, by Keith E. Yandell

In preparation

vol. 3: Christianity and Psychology, by Mary Stewart Van Leeuwen
vol. 4: Christianity and Economics, by Brian Griffiths
vol. 5: Christianity and Natural Science, by V. Elving Anderson
vol. 6: Christianity and Eastern Religions, by John B. Carman
vol. 7: Christianity and the Arts, by Nicholas Wolterstorff
vol. 8: Christianity and History, by Robert Eric Frykenberg
vol. 9: Christianity and Contemporary God-Concepts, by Alvin Plantinga
vol. 10: Christianity and Literature, by David L. Jeffrey

The Institute for Advanced Christian Studies is a non-profit corporation dedicated to the development of Christian scholarly writing for our times. Mailing address: Box 95496, Chicago, IL 60690

CONTOURS
OF A
WORLD VIEW

by

ARTHUR F. HOLMES

WILLIAM B. EERDMANS PUBLISHING COMPANY
GRAND RAPIDS, MICHIGAN

Copyright © 1983 by Wm. B. Eerdmans Publishing Co.
255 Jefferson Ave. S.E., Grand Rapids, MI 49503

Library of Congress Cataloging in Publication Data:

Holmes, Arthur Frank, 1924–
Contours of a world view.

(Studies in a Christian world view; v. 1)
Includes bibliographical references.
1. Civilization, Christian. I. Title. II. Series.
BR115.C5H56 1983   230   82-21096
ISBN 0-8028-1957-5

CONTENTS

Preface vii

PART ONE: SETTING THE SIGHTS 1

1 *Wanted: A World View for Today* 3
2 *Contemporary Humanism and the Secularization of Values* 15
3 *The Anatomy of a World View* 31

PART TWO: CONTOURS OF A WORLD VIEW 55

4 *God and Creation: Theological* 57
5 *God and Creation: Philosophical* 71
6 *Persons in Contemporary Perspective* 92
7 *Persons in Christian Perspective* 107
8 *Truth and Knowledge: Theological* 127
9 *Truth and Knowledge: Philosophical* 138
10 *A Theistic Basis for Values* 155
11 *Society and History* 174

PART THREE: A WORLD VIEW IN ACTION 197

12 *Human Creativity* 199
13 *Science and Technology* 207
14 *Work* 214
15 *Play* 223

Conclusion 235
Index 237

PREFACE

Today's world is ravaged by dehumanizing barbarism and torn by ideological conflict. Its barbarisms are outrageous violence, a terrifying nuclear standoff, extremes of poverty, wanton abuse of natural resources, and usurpation of political power for sectarian ends. Our ideologies are partly to blame. They come from both East and West, but the dominant tradition is a secular, naturalistic humanism that approaches human existence without the theistic basis for human values on which Western culture was built. Art and science have indeed made tremendous strides, giving us new art forms and new thought forms, with new concepts and theories and technologies to match. But they, too, are penetrated by the ideologies of the day whose values and presuppositions permeate society, shape the spirit of our times, and affect both thought and action.

Toward the end of World War II, when civilization faced the mammoth task of reconstructing a world ravaged by another barbarism and torn by other conflicting ideologies, Oxford professor Arnold Nash envisioned a worldwide order of Christian scholars enlisted, among other things, "to work towards an intellectual synthesis for the twentieth century which, as an interpretation of human life and destiny, can be set over against the positivistic, the Marxist, the liberal humanitarian *Weltanschauungen*."[1] A similar vision was evident in Catholic circles when the distinguished Jesuit scholar John Courtney Murray spoke in 1955 of integrating the

---

1. Arnold S. Nash, *The University and the Modern World* (New York: Macmillan, 1944), pp. 292–93.

whole of human knowledge under the primacy of the word of God into an organized Christian view.[2]

To rekindle and disseminate that vision is of strategic importance today. Christianity has vitally important implications for every area of life and thought, implications that need to be developed; but to live and think Christianly in today's world, with meaning and hope, does not come easily. It means ferreting out the influence of non-Christian assumptions and bringing distinctively Christian presuppositions to bear in their place. To identify and articulate these distinctives systematically in relation to the world of ideas is to develop a Christian world view.[3] Moreover I am convinced, for reasons that will appear as we proceed, that the most persuasive case for Christianity lies in the overall coherence and human relevance of its world view.

The present volume is merely an introduction. It talks about the importance and nature of world views and sketches in broad strokes the overall contours of a distinctively Christian world view in relationship both to the history of ideas and to the contemporary mind. Working at the intersections between theology and philosophy, it outlines a Christian view of things as a live alternative to the naturalistic humanism of our day. Subsequent writers in this series will contribute the more specialized task of uncovering the presuppositions at work in their particular fields and of addressing those fields in greater depth from a Christian perspective. My own task is more preliminary, generalized, and suggestive: an integrative overview of what I believe it means to think Christianly today. It leaves unargued many of the theological and philosophical issues that arise. Yet such an overview is important because it sets the parts on a common foundation.

Of course, Christianity as a theistic faith has much in common, at the conceptual level at least, with Judaism and other forms of theism: I shall not pursue that comparison. Moreover, alternatives to theism exist other than the naturalistic humanism of today. My approach, however, is not exhaustive but selective, and for good

2. Quoted by Father Richard O'Brien in *Commonweal*, Jan. 21, 1977, p. 43.
3. The beginner might look at two books by James Sire, *The Universe Next Door*, subtitled "A Basic World View Catalog" (Downers Grove: Inter-Varsity Press, 1976), and *How to Read a Book Slowly* (Downers Grove: Inter-Varsity Press, 1978); also Harry Blamires, *The Christian Mind* (London: S.P.C.K., 1966).

reason. The purpose is simply to set a Christian world view in contrast to representative forms of contemporary humanism, and in doing so to both draw on representatives of the past and point directions for further inquiry. The result will not be some kind of mathematical-type proof, but rather a proposal and an invitation: a proposal as to the shape that Christian thought takes, and an invitation to pursue its implications further because of the intellectual credibility and the human appeal of its claims.

Two misconceptions must be avoided from the outset. On the one hand, it is by no means the case that a Christian view of things will differ from other views at every point. We live in a common world with common human needs and experiences; frequently agreement will occur, and we will often make common cause. Yet even then the basic presuppositions from which Christian thought and action stem will contrast starkly with those of nontheists. On the other hand, it is not the case either that just one and only one Christian view of many particulars is possible. The overall parameters of biblical theology leave considerable room for variance, and we shall see how significant is the influence on Christian thought of additional historical and intellectual factors.

Part One of this volume orients us to the task at hand. The first chapter suggests four reasons why a Christian view of things is important at this time; the second looks at different forms of the major contemporary non-Christian alternative, naturalistic humanism, and the third chapter identifies variables that shape a world view and asks how world-view beliefs may be justified. Part Two then spells out the major themes of a Christian view in historical perspective and in contrast to naturalistic alternatives. Finally, Part Three tries to operationalize these themes in regard to four kinds of human activity.

Much of this material was developed piecemeal and in simpler form for faculty workshops and lectures in Christian colleges and elsewhere across America, in pursuit of a constructive integration of faith and learning. Now it takes fuller and more systematic form. I am indebted to faculty colleagues in all those places and to both their students and my own for stimulating dialogue, and more specifically to those who have read and criticized the manuscript, especially Galen Johnson, Dallas Willard, Keith Yandell, Carl F. H. Henry, and James I. Packer. Mrs. Roz Shaw patiently typed and retyped the manuscript, for which task she too deserves thanks.

PART ONE
SETTING THE SIGHTS

CHAPTER 1

WANTED: A WORLD VIEW FOR TODAY

A BASIC HUMAN NEED

The quest for a unifying world view that will help us see life whole and find meaning in each part is as old as humankind. Ancient religions played this role, as well as the more theologically oriented faiths of subsequent times. Anthropologists find that contemporary primitive cultures also have world views that interpret their experiences and guide their activities. Western culture has been so influenced by science and technology that some now say we have a scientific or even a technological world view: science and its uses shape our thought and focus our lives.

Philosophers throughout the centuries conceived and debated philosophies to live by. Aristotle said that philosophy begins with wonder, wonder about the "what" and the "why" of things, about the hints of order and unity we find around us. And ordered unity, he believed, gave purpose to life. Philosophy in fact began in ancient Greece with a search for the one that unifies the many, a search whose persistence through twenty-six centuries of inquiry bears testimony to a driving human need. What is it that ties everything together, matter and mind, life and death, art and science, faith and learning, and makes this a *universe*? That seems to be what humans need to know. What can unify our vision of life? To see things interrelated as a whole is to get one's bearings on the map of life, to know one's way in the confusing interplay of ideas, to find relatedness in what we do.

The perennial quest for a world view goes further: it is also a

3

quest for a life that is good rather than bad, for purpose in life rather than emptiness, for something that promises hope rather than despair. World views differ in this regard. Some are more optimistic and some more pessimistic, some are deeply ethical and others only incidentally so. Not all satisfy the human longing equally, nor all in the same way; but all express a deeply rooted human need. Aristotle also asked about man's highest good, a *summum bonum* that gives everything else its value and purpose. The need for a unifying *summum bonum* is the need for a world view.

In the final analysis, the biblical writers would insist (and many of the great minds of the past would agree) that it is not how or what we think that promises hope, but God himself. God the Creator and Lord of all must be the unifying focus of life and thought, and his action in Jesus Christ restores purpose and hope to humankind. Augustine's classic words sum it up: "Thou has made us for Thyself, O God, and our hearts are restless until they rest in Thee." Or the Westminster Shorter Catechism: "The chief end of man is to glorify God and to enjoy him forever." The living God is our highest end, our *summum bonum*; and a Christian world view unpacks the implications of this belief for all our thought and action.

A world view is also needed as a guide to thought. A world filled with things to think about and arrayed with a multitude of ideas and theories on everything under the sun compels us to be selective. Nobody can possibly consider everything or consistently accept every theory. And for any particular world view, some topics have more interest or importance than others and some theories more promise than others. We have to set priorities. What, then, will determine our priorities and guide our selectivity?

In a recent book[1] Nicholas Wolterstorff distinguishes between "data beliefs" and "control beliefs." He claims that the selection, evaluation, and construction of theories in any discipline are influenced not only by what we believe to be the relevant data, but by other theoretical beliefs one holds as well. A person's control beliefs can be scientific theories or religious beliefs or anything that goes to make up a world view. They will affect his selection of theories in any field: in art criticism, in historical explanation, in psychology, in philosophy, and even in biblical interpretation. The devel-

1. Nicholas Wolterstorff, *Reason Within the Bounds of Religion* (Grand Rapids: Eerdmans, 1976).

opment of a world view requires that we identify our control beliefs and explore their consequences.

But a world view is also needed to guide action. Amid the endless things to do, endless places to go, unnumbered kinds of political and social action, and unnumbered possible vocations, however does one decide? A world view is needed to rank possible activities and to set priorities for possible actions within any particular activity. Career decisions, moral decisions, time utilization, financial management, family life—all of these are affected. My world view influences how I vote, how I spend my money, what I read, what I do.

In biblical terms life is a sacred trust, and our choices must be made in relation to proper purposes. But that calls for a world view. Not all kinds of activity nor all particular actions may be morally legitimate: we need an ethic to guide action. A world view facilitates this by mandating certain tasks, providing overall purposes, giving basis for moral judgment.

The human need for a world view, then, is fourfold: the need to unify thought and life; the need to define the good life and find hope and meaning in life; the need to guide thought; the need to guide action.

A TROUBLED AGE

When things go topsy-turvy and the accepted foundations of life are upset, when meaning seems lost and we wonder if there is any ultimate hope, then the need for a clear and reliable world view is especially acute. Ours is just such a troubled age. It has so lost its religious moorings that some call it "post-Christian." Education has been thoroughly secularized, where once it conveyed a religious view of life; a scientific mentality shapes the popular world view, where once the most formative influence was Christian; moral decisions in medicine and scientific research are too often determined by what technology makes possible, rather than by ethical principles rooted in the sanctity of God's creation; business and politics too often operate on the Vince Lombardi motto that "winning is the only thing," rather than in the interests of economic or political justice; the arts reveal an underlying loss of religious perspective; and a purely "secular religion" has made its appearance.

The confusion is aptly captured by such ominous book titles as

The Abolition of Man by C. S. Lewis, *The Technological Society* by Jacques Ellul, and *One-Dimensional Man* by Herbert Marcuse. Lewis writes of a rhetoric textbook that outlawed value judgments and value terms, both moral and aesthetic, by claiming that language must be strictly descriptive, objective, and logical, or else it lapses into meaningless emotion. But when values are thus reduced to feelings, people either become manipulators or are manipulated. A world without values is a world without respect for persons. Lewis accordingly speaks of "men without chests," dehumanized.

Ellul, a prominent French sociologist, describes how technology controls people in business and industry, politics and law, and even controls our moralities and the way we reason. Insistence on efficient technique enslaves us: it saps freedom of inquiry and reflection on the meaning of life; it undermines good judgment; it eats at the roots of responsible liberty.

Marcuse, a neo-Marxist philosopher, laments the effects of an advanced technological society on the human person. Whereas work should enrich one's self-awareness, the productivity principle reduces people to economic tools; imagination and play are repressed. Work has an alienating effect, and life is dehumanized.

These critics describe a crisis of human values in a secular society. Since they wrote, the moral revolution has gone further, and technology offers still more advanced possibilities for good and evil. A nuclear holocaust still clouds scenarios for the future; a self-indulgent society cries out for far more than its share of dwindling energy resources; poverty and starvation continue; and narcissistic individualism pharisaically passes by on the other side.

Emil Brunner observes that the character of a civilization is determined by three things: natural factors like geography that are the external givens, physical and spiritual qualities of humankind that are inwardly given, and culture-transcendent factors, religious and otherwise, that speak to underlying questions about the meaning and purpose of human existence.[2] It is not surprising, therefore, that many features of our troubled age are perennial. We have new secularisms, new rationalisms, new relativisms, and new self-interests: all old "isms" in new garb. The basic problems on the minds of our contemporaries are not new: problems of scarcity, problems of violence, problems of morality, problems about hope and mean-

2. Emil Brunner, *Christianity and Civilization* (London: Nisbet, 1948), pp. 10-11.

ing in life. The questions asked and the alternatives faced are common to humankind. In this troubled age, then, whose need to find the highest good is ageless, it is to culture-transcending possibilities that we must turn. A Christian world view, transcending cultural differences as it does, is at least a viable alternative worth considering.

A BIBLICAL MANDATE

The monotheism of ancient Israel involved a theology and an ethic that affected every kind of human activity. It begins with the creation story and is spelled out in the multidimensionality of the Mosaic law; it finds vivid expression in the poetic books, and the prophets held it before the people and their leaders. One who is alert to its world-viewish dimension finds in the Old Testament history and literature the makings of a biblical world view for our day as well.

Consider how deeply ingrained this world view is in the biblical literature. Abraham's departure from Chaldea for a promised land was more than just another migration; it was an act of faith in a God who called him to a markedly different view and way of life. Nor was Israel's exodus from Egypt a political and economic liberation alone, nor an attempt to preserve a particular form of religion in some narrow sense; it represents the preservation of a distinctively monotheistic world view. Subsequent conflicts of world views arose between the Israelite faith and Canaanite religion or the worship of Baal and Moloch, whose wanton anger had at times to be appeased by sacrificing human victims. Sadly lacking was the concept of an altogether wise and just deity, ordering his creation for moral ends. Even more familiar is the disparity between Israelite and Babylonian views. A Babylonian creation myth saw all things in the context of a cosmic conflict: the god Marduk slew the monster Tiamat, forming the cosmos from her dismembered body. Thus any notion of creation out of nothing by the free act of one omnipotent God was entirely alien.

Analogous observations stem from reading the New Testament account of the early church in a Greco-Roman world. St. Paul's Colossian letter, for example, confronts differences between a consistent theism on the one hand, with its clear-cut distinction between God and creation, and on the other hand the emanationist view that a hierarchy of intermediaries stretches between God and this world. The resultant mysticism tried to find salvation by escape from physical and earthly involvements. A dualism of flesh and spirit further confused the meaning of good and evil, affecting attitudes toward marriage, toward work, and toward social relationships in general. The apostle contrasts such a philosophical tradition with beliefs, attitudes, and values that are consistently Christian. Here again are the makings of a contemporary world view.

A HISTORICAL TRADITION

There is still another reason for our project, in what the history of ideas reveals about the resources a Christian world view brought to one crucial juncture of history after another.

The early church, for example, faced two typical expressions of the Greek mind, one a dualistic view and the other monistic. Dualism saw two eternal realities, spirit and matter, the one good and the other evil; monism saw one all-inclusive reality out of which every particular emanates. For dualists (such as the Manicheans) the good was always limited by the evil, the spirit was impeded by matter. For monists (such as the neo-Platonists) evil was due to finiteness: it is a privation of good, an unavoidable necessity in the process of emanation from the One. In both cases, asceticism was advised and frequently a mystic path of escape was sought; but in neither case was there any hope that good would triumph in this world.

That hope was distinctive to Christianity, for Judeo-Christian theism affirms belief in an altogether good Creator who calls things into existence out of nothing. No eternal "other" limits what he can do. No eternal necessity causes evil. Rather, God remains entirely sovereign, free to act as he will in his creation. The Christian, therefore, has a firm basis for the hope that good can and will triumph in the end. Nor are we left with asceticism or mysticism as our only resorts, for it is God who acts to accomplish for us what we cannot do for ourselves. The early church thus provides a convenient and helpful paradigm for developing a Christian world view, in contrast to current alternatives,[3] that may be summarized as follows:

3. On this paradigm in Christian thought see J. Langdon Gilkey, *Maker of Heaven and Earth* (New York: Doubleday, Anchor Books, 1965); and the article "Christian Philosophy" by the present author in *Encyclopedia Britannica*, 15th ed. (1974).

DUALISM	MONISM	THEISM
(1) Creation out of eternal matter (*ex materia*).	Creation out of God's own being (*ex deo*).	Creating out of nothing (*ex nihilo*).
(2) God is limited by conditions he did not create.	Creation is a necessary process which God does not choose.	God is free to create or not to create, and to continue acting in his creation.
(3) Evil is inherent in the eternal reality of things.	Evil is necessary to the world process.	God allows evil to occur, but for good purpose.
(4) We are inescapably involved in eternal conflict between good and evil: no ultimate hope.	Our finiteness is itself a lack of good: no ultimate hope.	We are involved in evil, but have hope in a living God who acts to vindicate the good.

In effect, then, a Christian world view conceives everything in terms of a transcendent God's creative activity in the world: theism's doctrine of creation provides the overall framework of reference—

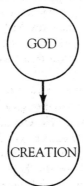

not dualism,

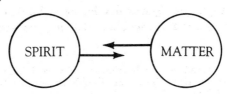

and not monism.

ONE
BEING

In the Middle Ages, God was accordingly acknowledged as our highest good, and implications of this and of the doctrine of creation were more fully explored in relation to persons and society, to law and morality, to art and science and history. Christian philosophers, like Augustine and Aquinas, adopted the Greek view that objectively real universals order the world of our experience, and that God created in accordance with them. On this basis they constructed a metaphysical understanding of creation, which they applied to man, morality, and grace—an all-inclusive world view.[4] The Reformers took a somewhat different route. Martin Luther, for instance, talked more directly of God's vocation for us in any walk of life, rejecting the medieval tendency to elevate religious over secular callings. And John Calvin's theology made its keynote the sovereignty of God in all of creation and in every area of life and thought. He, too, envisioned an overall world view:

> There cannot be found the least particle of wisdom, light, righteousness, power, rectitude or sincere truth which does not proceed from Him and claim Him for its author: we should therefore learn to expect and supplicate all these things from Him, and thankfully acknowledge what He gives us.[5]

In measure, it was this Christian heritage in Renaissance humanism that stressed the value of the individual and his liberty in contrast to the absolute authority of church or state. Eighteenth-century thought, however, combined this individualism with mechanistic science's all-encompassing causal explanations, and with Enlightenment rationalism's overconfidence in the rule of reason. The result in religion was deism: belief in a transcendent creator who rules his creation by fixed laws and therefore does not act in supernatural or redemptive ways. The result in politics was the ideal of a society ruled by rational laws to which all individuals consent.

4. See the writings of Etienne Gilson, esp. *The Spirit of Medieval Philosophy* (New York: Charles Scribner's, 1940).
5. *Institutes of the Christian Religion*, trans. John Allen (Philadelphia: Westminster Press, 1949), vol. I, p. 52.

Nineteenth-century evolutionary optimism extended these themes: nature and society alike are ruled by laws that guide their destiny.

When Romanticism turned to a more organic and vitalistic outlook, however, deism's transcendent God of reason and law was replaced by a wholly immanent God struggling creatively like the rest of us to be completely free. The biblical hope in a transcendent yet living God who can act freely in his creation was laid aside, yet optimism about human nature and history persisted. The human person became wholly part of nature, his meaning and hope found there, rather than in the transcendent God.

Emil Brunner sees the three centuries from 1650 to 1950 as progressively undermining the dignity of persons created in God's image, an idea he finds fundamental to Western civilization.[6] The trend may be traced in literature. Alexander Pope's *Essay on Man* portrayed in optimistic terms the rule of reason in a mechanistic universe, but Alfred Tennyson's *In Memoriam* is not as confident:

> "The stars," she whispers, "blindly run;
> A web is woven across the sky;
> From out waste places comes a cry,
> and murmurs from the dying sun;
>
> "And all the Phantom, Nature, stands . . .
> With all the music in her tone
> A hollow echo of my own
> A hollow form with empty hands."
>
> And shall I take a thing so blind
> Embrace her for my mortal good;
> Or crush her, like a vice of blood,
> Upon the threshold of the mind?

Matthew Arnold felt the impact of this "thing so blind," and in *Dover Beach* he laments:

> The Sea of Faith
> Was once, too, at the full, and round earth's shore
> Lay like the folds of a bright girdle furled.
> But now I only hear
> Its melancholy, long, withdrawing roar,
> Retreating, to the breath
> Of the night wind, down the vast edges drear
> And naked shingles of the world.

6. Brunner, *Christianity and Civilization*, pp. 2–3.

And both Tennyson's "hollow echo" out of "waste places" and Arnold's "let us be true to one another" are eloquently picked up by T. S. Eliot:

> We are the hollow men
> We are the stuffed men
> Leaning together
> Headpiece filled with straw. . . .

And the world ends . . . "not with a bang but a whimper." All hope is gone, for a Christian world view is lost.

Our twentieth century indeed despaired. The playwright Ibsen looked in *Hedda Gabler* and *The Master Builder* for a romantic hero-savior to arise. Beckett hoped against hope in *Waiting for Godot*. Jean-Paul Sartre, the French existentialist, speaks of man as a bubble of consciousness in an ocean of nothingness, bobbing around until the bubble pops. We are adrift in a boat without rudder or compass on an ocean that has no bounds. It makes no difference which way we row. There is no exit, no ultimate hope.

And consider the moving confession of Bertrand Russell in "A Free Man's Worship," as he considers what meaning life has for us in a purely physical world:

> That man is the product of causes which had no prevision of the end they were achieving; that his origin, his growth, his hope and fears, his loves and his beliefs, are but the outcome of accidental collocations of atoms; that no fire, no heroism, no intensity of thought and feeling, can preserve an individual life beyond the grave; that all the labours of the ages, all the devotion, all the inspiration, all the noonday brightness of human genius, are destined to extinction in the vast death of the solar system, and that the whole temple of Man's achievement must inevitably be buried beneath the debris of a universe in ruins—all these things, if not quite beyond dispute, are yet so nearly certain, that no philosophy which rejects them can hope to stand. Only within the scaffolding of these truths, only on the firm foundation of unyielding despair can the soul's habitation henceforth be safely built.[7]

Yet hope springs eternal in the human breast, and the contemporary mind tries with Russell to build its habitation in a purely

---

7. B. Russell, "A Free Man's Worship," in *Mysticism and Logic* (New York: Doubleday, 1929), p. 45.

physical world. In the next chapter we shall look more fully at this contemporary naturalism in its various forms and at its humanistic ideals. But even while old hopes dissolved and new humanisms arose, Christian thinkers continued to stress the essentials of a Christian world view.

At the turn of this century, the Scottish theologian James Orr claimed that pessimism was the logical result of the demise of the Christian faith. In *The Christian View of God and the World*, he addresses the overall character of a Christian view of things. The main design, he announced, was to show

> that there is a definite Christian view of things, which has a character, coherence, and unity of its own, and stands in sharp contrast with counter theories and speculations, and that this world-view has the stamp of reason and reality upon it, and can amply justify itself at the bar both of history and of experience.[8]

In the Netherlands, the neo-Calvinist theologian and statesman Abraham Kuyper developed a world view around the sovereignty of God and his law over every sphere of creation; he initiated a tradition within Reformed thought that remains influential to this day. Among Roman Catholics, Jacques Maritain drew on the resources of Thomism, writing about theism and humanism, about human rights and political justice, about education and art; and Teilhard de Chardin developed an evolutionary idealism that pictured Christ the Logos as both Alpha and Omega, the beginning and the end of a cosmic process alive with hope. Meanwhile, Protestant writers, such as Archbishop William Temple, addressed both philosophical and social issues from a markedly Christian standpoint, and Emil Brunner and Reinhold Niebuhr tried to articulate a Christian understanding of persons, history, and society against the background of Enlightenment, Romanticist, and twentieth-century misconceptions. Karl Barth called on the modern mind to stop and listen to the Word of the living God.

American evangelicals also were active. While their energies were too predominantly absorbed and diverted by the fundamentalist-liberal controversy, some of them correctly saw that certain aspects of that debate involved the difference between a consistently

8. Orr, *The Christian View of God and the World*, 5th ed. (Edinburgh: Andrew Elliot, 1897), p. 16.

theistic world view and the nineteenth-century preferences to which we have referred. During the nineteenth century, Scottish realist philosophy played an important part in their thinking, and in the first half of the twentieth century some evangelicals used the general framework of personal idealism. By the 1950s, some writers, such as Gordon Clark, Carl Henry, and others, were addressing world-view topics directly: science, education, politics, and so forth. A variety of evangelical scholarly organizations arose, publishing journals and giving strong evidence of the continued relevance of a Christian view. By the 1970s a new generation was actively involved in all the major academic disciplines and working creatively in the arts, in law, and in social action.

Other hopeful signs are present, of course, which are related to the Christian sources of our values: the surge of interest in value education amid a moral revolution, the emphasis on human rights in an age of dehumanization, the attention to environmental concerns and bioethics amid seemingly unbridled technological advances. But a more widespread renaissance of Christian thought is of critical importance: its influence must extend into business and politics, into literature, art, and science, into education, the family, the moral fabric of life in general, and most of all into the university world. An overall world view is needed if this is to occur, and if Christian principles are to be a significant influence in shaping the twenty-first century.

Charles Malik, former President of the United Nations, puts it thus:

> I am worried about the humanities—about philosophy, psychology, art, history, literature, sociology, the interpretation of man as to his nature and his destiny. It is in these realms the spirit, the fundamental attitude, the whole outlook on life, even for the scientist himself, are formed and set.
>
> . . . Believe me, my friends, the mind today is in profound trouble, perhaps more so than ever before. How to order the mind on sound Christian principles at the very heart of where it is formed and informed . . . [that is the issue].[9]

9. Charles Malik, *The Two Tasks* (Westchester, IL: Cornerstone Books, 1980), pp. 28, 32.

CHAPTER 2

CONTEMPORARY HUMANISM AND THE SECULARIZATION OF VALUES

Throughout history, a theistic world view has challenged other alternatives. In the days of the early church, Greek viewpoints were pervasive. In the eighteenth century, deism vied for the faith of thinking people. In the nineteenth century, Romanticism with its pantheistic leanings captured the imagination and influenced the rise of liberal theology. Now, in the late twentieth century, a variety of naturalistic alternatives are to the fore: in fact, at least among Western-influenced peoples, Christian theism and naturalistic or secular humanism are the primary options of the day.

We have noted a basic human need to find overall meaning in life, and humanism offers to meet that need. We also underscored the troubled character of our age, and humanists are well aware of its characteristics. We have pointed to a biblical mandate to address the whole of life, but the humanist view implies an overall mandate, too. We have a historical tradition of Christian theism, but secular humanism also goes back at least to ancient Greece. In addition, the presuppositions of humanism, its basic tenets, are the presuppositions of our age which guide its thought and shape its action.

In preparing to address a Christian world view to the contemporary scene, then, it becomes imperative to understand the essentials of humanism, along with its various formulations and the source of its appeal. Our purpose in this chapter is to look at contemporary humanism, to glimpse the tradition from which it arises, to distinguish its current formulations, and to identify the basic points at which it either concurs or is in tension with Christian theism. Subsequent chapters will address these tensions more fully.

WHAT IS HUMANISM?

In the broadest sense, humanism is any view that recognizes the value and dignity of persons and seeks to better the human condition. Like Western culture generally, it has roots in both the Greco-Roman and the Judeo-Christian traditions. On the one hand, Socrates, turning from the more speculative inquiries of his predecessors to focus on questions about values, declared that the unexamined life is not worth living. "Know thyself," he advised, and by his death as well as his life he urged the pursuit of high human ideals such as wisdom, loyalty, friendship, and justice. The Roman Stoics similarly encouraged a rational rather than emotive approach to life, whether in religion, politics, or private life, seeking the highest good of which humankind is capable. Partisan interests and narrow nationalisms must bow to univeral law and to the responsibility of being a citizen of the entire world. On the other hand, however, the Jewish and Christian Scriptures placed immense value on the human person made in God's image. Individuals have a worth that derives from this, for God is no respecter of persons. The law and the prophets insist on it, and Jesus' life and death endorsed what his teaching affirmed. Justice and love for all are of paramount importance; finding wisdom and truth is essential to life's highest good.

During the Middle Ages these two traditions combined. Some medievals, following Augustine, attempted to infuse the Christian ideal of sacrificial love (*agapē*) into Greek humanistic ideals. Some, like Aquinas, supplemented Greek ideals with Christian virtues. Some adapted the Stoic concepts of natural law to Christian ethical and political thought. In each case the result was a Christian humanism that sought a Christian culture informed by Christian thought. The role of reason was recognized as well as of revelation, and the law of God as well as his goodness was traced in nature and society alike.

With the breakdown of this medieval synthesis (or syntheses, rather, for many versions of it developed by the fourteenth century), attention turned back to the Greco-Roman tradition. Italian Renaissance humanism exalted in nature and human freedom and tried to recapture the creativity of the classical mind. Equating Greek ideals with religious values, it tended to erode any distinctively Christian contribution. A secularizing trend had begun. Gradually the Judeo-Christian and the Greek strands fell apart, leaving a humanism devoid of a theistic basis.

The two basically different types of humanism that emerged persist today, the one theistic and the other naturalistic. Jacques Maritain speaks of them as theocentric and anthropocentric respectively, and argues that only the former can be an integral whole and truly humanistic.[1] Geddes MacGregor relabels the naturalistic kind "hominism," for it denies any essential uniqueness to humankind. Persons are wholly physical, a part of nature, and whatever is different about them is quite incidental, their nature and destiny essentially that of every other physical thing.[2]

Theistic humanism was nourished by the Reformation with its stress on the individual, by Reformed theology with its cultural mandate, and by the sacramental view of nature and human existence that characterizes Catholic, including Anglican, thought. Anthropocentric or naturalistic humanism was nourished instead by the growing scientific mentality of the Enlightenment, by the rise of deism, and by the evolutionary naturalism of the nineteenth century. It came to regard medieval thought as irrelevant to human concerns, and the Reformation as a lamentable set-back for the human intellect.

Contemporary secular humanism as a world view is of the second kind. It views persons as a part and product of the physical world, and it limits values to what has value for humankind. In Protagoras' famous dictum, man is the measure of all things. This is both a *naturalist* (rather than theistic) and an *anthropocentric* (rather than theocentric) view, and it stands in contrast to theistic humanism over the very nature of reality, the existence of God, and his activity in human history. It denies any theistic basis for human worth, for values in general, and for hope and meaning in this life. The secular humanist's source of hope is entirely immanent in nature and humanity and cannot transcend their limitations, rather

1. Jacques Maritain, *Integral Humanism*, trans. J. W. Evans (New York: Scribner's, 1968).
2. Geddes MacGregor, *The Hemlock and the Cross* (Philadelphia: Lippincott, 1963). Cf. Paul Kurtz, *A Secular Humanist Declaration* (Buffalo, NY: Prometheus Books, 1980).

than being located outside of nature and man in a transcendent God.

Paul Kurtz, one of America's most articulate humanists, defines these two basic humanistic principles. In an essay entitled "What Is Humanism?" he describes the first as a rejection of the supernaturalist world view that sees God as the ultimate source of all existence and value, in favor of the naturalistic view that persons are a part and product of the physical world, their existence and destiny to be explained solely in that way.

> There is no break between the human mind or consciousness on the one hand and the body on the other, no special status to personality or "soul," and no privileged or special place for human existence in the universe at large. All claims to unique human immortality or eschatological theories of history thus are held to be an expression of wish fulfilment, a vain reading into nature of human hope and fancy. Nature, for the humanist, is blind to human purposes and indifferent to human ideals.[3]

The second basic humanist principle is "that value is relative to man and to what human beings find to be worthwhile in experience."[4] This follows from rejecting theism's transcendent source for value. To state it more positively, humanists believe that people must achieve for themselves a good life, satisfying their individual dreams, developing a just and harmonious society, and fulfilling their creative potentials. Not all are equally optimistic about it; some are pessimists. Not all hold the same values, nor need they, for they see values as relative. Man alone is the measure of all things, and like Prometheus he must create his own life.

To these two principles, naturalism and anthropocentrism, Kurtz adds two others on which some but not all humanists agree. One of these we shall call *scientism*, the view that *scientific knowledge* can be applied to the solution of all our problems, as well as to the testing of all human beliefs and moral judgments. This is the contemporary version of the rule of reason, enthroned during the Enlightenment. Early in the seventeenth century, Francis Bacon said that knowledge is power; but his claim had a theistic basis: the creation and its processes are the work of a rational God who man-

3. Paul Kurtz, ed., *Moral Problems in Contemporary Society: Essays in Humanistic Ethics* (Englewood Cliffs, NJ: Prentice-Hall, 1969), p. 3.
4. Ibid., p. 4.

dated us to search out and employ its powers for human benefit. The Enlightenment went further and asserted two natural powers to human reason independently of special help from God: the power to understand both nature and human beings and their varied functions, and the power to follow the laws that govern nature, human beings, and society alike. Contemporary humanism has inherited this twofold confidence in reason, and Kurtz transfers to it the methods of scientific reasoning. The methods and findings of science, therefore, are our source of hope.

Kurtz' remaining principle, on which many but not all humanists agree, is a commitment to *humanitarianism*, defined as an obligation to further the welfare of all humankind equally. The humanist ethic is therefore consequentialist, guided by empirically observable consequences. Deploring equally the dehumanization of the person in a technological society and the tragic effects of war, poverty, and disease, it seeks rational means for resolving the problems we face. But what constitutes human welfare is a matter of conventional wisdom. So consequentialism combines with a conventional ethic that can even draw on some New Testament ideals.

Two decades earlier, Corliss Lamont wrote that humanism is a philosophy of which man is the center and the sanction. It employs the methods of reason, science, and democracy in serving the greater good of all humanity.[5] Lamont lists ten central propositions, of which the first is a naturalistic metaphysic as against supernaturalism, the second is that man is entirely a product and part of nature, and the third is that human beings have the power to solve their own problems by reason and scientific method. Our highest end is this-worldly happiness, freedom, and progress for all mankind, and to this end humanism "assigns to man nothing less than the task of being his own saviour and redeemer."[6]

Similar statements appear in what is perhaps the fullest expression of naturalistic humanism as a world view, a book of essays edited by Y. H. Krikorian and entitled *Naturalism and the Human Spirit*. Its contributors included such influential figures as John Dewey, Sidney Hook, J. H. Randall, and Herbert Schneider. In a final chapter on "The Nature of Naturalism," Randall, too, contrasts it

5. Corliss Lamont, *The Philosophy of Humanism* (New York: Frederick Ungar, 1949), chap. 1.
6. Ibid., p. 283.

with supernaturalism, includes persons wholly within nature, and appeals to scientific knowledge to resolve human problems.

> Thus naturalism finds itself in thoroughgoing opposition to all forms of thought which assert the existence of a supernatural or transcendent Realm of Being and make knowledge of that realm of fundamental importance to human living. There is no "realm" to which the methods for dealing with Nature cannot be extended.[7]

"The faith we need," he concludes, "the faith that alone promises salvation, is the faith in intelligence."[8]

In the preceeding chapter we contrasted Christian theism with monistic and dualistic world views that the early church faced. Now it becomes evident that naturalistic humanism is another monistic view. While it is not our purpose to engage in any extensive critique, plainly, naturalism faces problems analogous to those of monism in general. Monism's perennial problems concern human individuality and the overcoming of evil. In the first place, if nature is a causal process of which persons are wholly a part and their lives a product, then on what basis can we ascribe value and responsibility to individuals, and what significance has their apparent freedom? Does the naturalistic basis of contemporary humanism cut the ground from beneath its own hope that we can create and sustain the kind of life we want?

In the second place, if evil is necessitated by natural processes, then how can finite beings who are themselves a part and product of nature hope to avoid and wholly overcome evil? Maybe we can accelerate the outgrowing of some problems and devise means to solve others; but as long as nature and human beings continue to generate evils, any hope for lasting deliverance seems destined to disappointment. Yet while naturalism faces these problems, the strength of biblical theism partially resides in its handling of these very same issues.

But contemporary humanism is varied, and it is not always either optimistic or scientifically oriented. Four types may be delineated, each having its own characteristics but all of them sharing the two basic principles Kurtz identifies, namely, philosophical naturalism and the human basis for values.

7. In Y. H. Krikorian, *Naturalism and the Human Spirit* (New York: Columbia University Press, 1944), p. 358.
8. Ibid., p. 382.

(1) *Scientific humanism* is well represented by Kurtz himself as well as by Lamont and Randall. Its distinctive characteristic is Kurtz' third principle, that scientific reasoning is the key to solving all our problems. It can be traced to Francis Bacon, to the Enlightenment's rule of reason, and more particularly to Auguste Comte's delineation of three stages in the evolution of thought: from a superstitious and religious stage, through a speculative metaphysical stage, to a positive scientific stage that approaches everything empirically. Thus the scientific humanist not only rejects supernatural religion but also discards speculative metaphysics in favor of empirical methods.

This insistence on scientific method received a strong impetus from John Dewey. In his *Reconstruction in Philosophy*, for instance, Dewey extended experimental methods of inquiry to all spheres of life. Science has given us control over natural processes; now its methods can guide human and social conduct and greater human progress can thereby be assured. Dewey's pragmatism (experimental thinking, he called it) accordingly pervaded the humanist movement and encouraged confidence in scientific knowledge and controls. Sometimes this method is labelled "scientism," meaning that only scientific approaches to problems of knowledge and action are countenanced; sometimes "technologism," meaning that technological advances hold the solution to our problems.

Underlying Dewey's commitment to scientific methods, of course, lay the naturalistic view of the human person. Dewey pushed its implications: not only is the human race a biological product of natural selection but society also is involved in evolutionary adaptation. Humans have learned to adapt successfully by thinking, and science is simply an extension of ordinary reflection on problem situations. Its success is measured pragmatically: does it work in practice? Does a scientific approach in fact help solve society's problems?

Dewey's pragmatism has been one major influence on scientific humanism, and it has stressed human values more than has another line of influence from analytic philosophy. Here attention has focused rather on our empirical knowledge, thence on reinforcing naturalism with a purely scientific picture of persons. The "physicalism" of Wilfred Sellars is a good example because of his interest in an overall world view. Philosophy aims, he says, "to understand how things in the broadest possible sense of the term hang together in the broadest possible sense of the term." It helps one to know his way around among such different though related items as "numbers and duties, possibilities and fingersnaps, aesthetic experience and death."[9] What, then, is the key to such a world view? The key is scientific knowledge. "Science is the measure of all things, of what is that it is, and of what is not that it is not."[10] The scientific picture accordingly supersedes the commonsense picture of persons and minds, just as science supersedes the commonsense view of nature. Consciousness is to be explained in terms of brain processes; the private states of individual consciousness can be described as an "inner speech" analogous to overt verbal behavior. No human soul is then needed as a seat of consciousness, nor a "mind" (other than the brain) to do the thinking. Persons are entirely a part of nature and are describable in purely scientific ways.

D. M. Armstrong similarly insists that only in science can we reach substantial agreement about what is the case. So what better authority have we? It is the "scientific vision of man," he continues, "and not the philosophical or religious or artistic or moral vision of man, that is the best clue we have to the nature of man."[11] And this means a physicochemical account.

A primary objection that philosophers have raised to physicalism concerns the privacy of conscious states, in the sense that each of us has privileged access to his or her own ideas and feelings, in contrast to the public nature of verbal and other physical behavior. "Inner speech" hardly describes it. Nor do neurophysiological descriptions get at the dimensions of inner experience that literature, religion, and the arts perceive. The scientific picture helps less there than with overt behavior. As Ludwig Wittgenstein asks, when I deliberately turn my attention to my own consciousness, is this produced simply by a brain process? And is there not something uncanny and odd in saying that all the people around me are automata, and all the liveliness of children mere automation?[12]

9. Sellars, *Science, Perception and Reality* (London: Routledge & Kegan Paul, 1963), p. 1.

10. Ibid., p. 173.

11. D. M. Armstrong, "The Nature of Mind," in *The Mind-Brain Identity Theory*, ed. C. V. Borst (New York: St. Martin's Press, 1970), p. 69. See also *A Materialist Theory of the Mind* (London: Routledge & Kegan Paul, 1968), and, by a scientist, Carl Sagan, *The Dragons of Eden* (New York: Random House, 1977).

12. Wittgenstein, *Philosophical Investigations* (New York: Macmillan, 1953), § 420.

But a more basic issue is the tendency to "empire building." If science explains everything, and no other kind of insight is allowed, then we have a reductionism that dehumanizes persons of what is distinctively human. Is "scientific humanism" then a contradiction of terms?

Plainly, a Christian world view must face this concern. Are there limits to the scope of scientific knowledge? If more needs saying about persons than science can say, then what about that religious and artistic and moral vision with which the scientific humanist disagrees? From a Christian point of view, what is lacking in neurophysiological accounts? And what of the scientific humanist's confidence in the rule of scientific reason? To what extent does technology provide hope? Questions like these are crucial.

(2) *Romanticist humanism* is, in large measure, a reaction against scientism and the technological mentality. Its roots lie as far back as Greek Cynics who, like Antisthenes and Diogenes, repudiated the corrupting influences of institutionalized society in favor of an innocent state of nature. The same theme keeps reappearing. Nineteenth-century Romanticism is usually traced to writers who, like Rousseau, espoused the virtues of a free spirit and a self-reliant soul, because human nature has been alienated from its essential goodness by the artificiality of an externalized culture. The American transcendentalist Thoreau regarded men and women more as a part of nature than as members of society, and advocated communion with nature as the necessary means to clear-minded self-reliance. The value of life is in the experience. Nineteenth-century Romanticists generally reacted against value-free scientific objectivity and the analytic mind. "We murder to dissect," wrote Wordsworth. Natural instinct, intuition, and feeling, rather, are value-laden and more to be prized.

In recent psychology the work of Abraham Maslow reflects similar concerns. Standing as a "third force" over against the two dominant trends of behaviorism and Freudian psychology, Maslow offers a more humanistic approach, one concerned with being fully human and with human values. His emphasis is on self-fulfillment, for as evolving beings men and women are capable of wider and more intense consciousness than is yet manifest. Self-fulfillment means perceiving the intrinsic values of being (B-values, he calls them), the consciousness of which characterizes our highest moments: truth, goodness, wholeness, aliveness, completion, effortlessness, and so forth. To perceive life as value-laden, we must give up the habit of "desacralizing" people and things, of treating them objectively in a purely factual way. We must learn to "resacralize" life—to see it as sacred and its experiences as symbolic of the values we seek. Maslow describes peak experiences of ecstasy and bliss in which we see life thus as "secularized religious experiences" that can equally be produced by sex, by athletic success, by watching an artistic performance, or by philosophical insight.[13] Thus it turns out that, as with earlier Romanticists, the value is in the experience, and the experience has purely natural and psychological sources. It is a naturalistic and anthropocentric approach that romanticizes experience and at times even approaches a nature-mysticism.

In pop culture, parallel developments are evident in the "Hippies" and "flower children" of the '60s and in other counterculture movements. Even environmental concerns at times are expressed as a desire to shed the technological trappings of an industrial society, though we easily forget how needful technology is: solar energy requires it, and even farming is now a complex industry. Modern life is unavoidably entwined with science and social institutions.

Yet the principle point of tension with a Christian view of things is not this, which is a question of possible methods and strategies for preserving human values. The point at issue here is not intellect *vs.* feeling, nor technology *vs.* the environment, nor an individual's inner resources *vs.* civilization's external constraints. It is, rather, the assumption that civilization and its institutions corrupt the lives of people who are essentially good. Both kinds of humanism, the scientific and the romanticist, obviously share the same basic premises: that as persons, we are a part and product of nature, and that all values depend on us. Both place their hope in human resourcefulness with nature's resources, whereas for the Christian the basic problem is with the person himself, even if corrupt institutions have played a part.

(3) *Existentialist humanism* developed in reaction against both scientism and Romanticism. On the one hand, scientific objectivity ignores human values and a technological society dehumanizes us.

---

13. See Abraham Maslow, *The Farther Reaches of Human Nature* (New York: Viking Press, 1971), and *Religions, Values and Peak-Experiences* (Columbus, OH: Ohio State Univ. Press, 1964). For a resounding critique of humanistic psychology and its "selfism," see Paul Vitz, *Psychology as Religion* (Grand Rapids: Eerdmans, 1977).

On the other hand, the romantic vision is unrealistic, too optimistic about life and progress. In identifying persons with nature it fails to reckon with nature's indifference to us and our values. We live our lives alone in a world that is alien to our concern. Existentialist humanism arose with Friedrich Nietzsche, whose ideas are echoed by such novelists as Thomas Mann, Herman Hesse, and Andre Gide. In *Thus Spake Zarathustra* Nietzsche pictures an old man traveling the towns and villages of Eastern Europe, telling the news that God is dead. "Whatever shall we do?" people ask. To which the old man replies, "Let your will now say, man shall be the meaning of the earth!"[14]

The anthropocentricity in this is plain: all values and hope depend on us. And its blatant rejection of theism is in favor of naturalism. Appealing to the biological basis of psychology, Nietzsche finds a creative force pervading nature, surging with energy that overcomes the static and the weak. So it is in man and history: a will to power dominates human life, the strong-willed struggling with the weak-willed. Yet progress is possible only through struggle: even our ideas are what we will, and our arguments turn out to be rationalizations. Philosophy, religion, ethics, and art are all part of the game.

Although not all existentialism is pessimistic, and some existential writers have even been Christian, Jean-Paul Sartre and Albert Camus remain gloomy. As Sartre puts it, the world constantly negates my will to become what I will, so I must master my world. But there are no guarantees, no overall hope in life, no divine providence at all. Sartre quotes Dostoevsky, "If God is dead, then anything is possible." With God eclipsed, only my will remains; but that freedom is dreadful.[15] In Sartre, humanism has lost hope.

One crucial factor merits closer attention. The world, for Sartre, is utterly indifferent to us and our values. Nothing in earth or heaven supports the human quest. The bleakness of this outlook is underscored by science, for the existentialist sees science as objective and empirical, operating in a world of bare facts. Mechanistic science with its causal explanation of everything created this pic-

14. Nietzsche, *Thus Spake Zarathustra* (New York: Macmillan, 1902), pp. 1–10. See also his *Beyond Good and Evil*.
15. This theme, expounded in *L'Existentialisme est un Humanisme* (1945), is dramatized in Sartre's plays and novels, of which the best known is the play *No Exit*.

ture. Positivism with its insistence on empirical verifiability reinforced it. Fact and value thus are divorced. Whatever our place in
nature, neither nature nor science support the values we pursue.
The world is neutral to all our weal and woe.

This is indeed a bleak house in which to make a home. While
the scientific humanist thinks science can tell us how to do it, the
existentialist has misgivings: whatever we do, death and despair will
forever threaten to destroy. Plainly we must address this fact-value
separation in our times. Does nature support the values we as humans pursue? Is the bleakness of our home really the fault of the
house or of its occupants? Is there any objective basis in this world
or beyond for value and for hope?

(4) *Marxist humanism* has since the 1960s attracted a considerable following in the West, as well as in Third World countries.
It is to be distinguished from Communist politics, with which it
may or may not be associated, by its greater dependence on the
early writings of Marx and on such exponents as Adam Schaff and
Herbert Marcuse,[16] who are critical of socialist as well as capitalist
regimes. Not surprisingly, its humanism has engendered a Christian-
Marxist dialogue.

Concern focuses on the problem of alienation. Creative human
activity would naturally bring joy in living and a sense of freedom,
for by their labor people create the world they inhabit and they
shape their own lives. But constructive creativity is thwarted by
corporate greed, and the compulsion to amass wealth alienates
workers from their own labor. They lose their self-determination
and are shaped instead by economic forces they did not create.
Inevitably conflict has ensued, and liberation is needed.

Schaff therefore writes of

> the need to transform this inhuman world, in which things rule
> men, into a human world—a world of free human beings who
> are architects of their destiny and for whom man is the supreme
> good.[17]

Marcuse likewise complains of

16. See Adam Schaff, *Marxism and the Human Individual*, ed. Robt. S.
Cohen (New York: McGraw-Hill, 1970), and Herbert Marcuse, *One-Dimensional Man* (Boston: Beacon Press, 1964). Ernst Bloch's *Man on His
Own*, trans. E. B. Ashton (London: Herder & Herder, 1971), clearly exhibits the tangency of Marxist humanism to Christianity.
17. Schaff, *Marxism*, p. 8.

a pattern of one-dimensional thought and behavior in which ideas, aspirations, and objectives that, by their content, transcend the established universe of discourse and action are either repelled or reduced to terms of this universe.[18]

Yet human life can and ought to be made worth living: the realization of human values is in fact possible.

Marxist humanism is greatly influenced by Ludwig Feuerbach's book *The Essence of Christianity*, which turned Hegel's attempt at theism on its head: instead of man and history being a finite manifestation of the Absolute Spirit, God became a projection of the human spirit, an expression of human ideals. Denying a transcendent God, man asserts that he himself should be regarded as the supreme being, and world history becomes the creation of man through human labor and the development of man for man.[19] Naturalism and anthropocentrism again prevail.

Liberation, meaning in life, a free spirit, human progress— these are the ideals of contemporary humanism. They are implicitly interrelated, and we meet them in various combinations. A Christian world view must take them seriously, addressing the human needs they manifest. But their twofold root, naturalism and anthropocentrism, is the point of basic difference. For contemporary humanism, people create their own world. For Christian theism, people are discoverers of God-given possibilities in the world, and thus of God-given possibilities for themselves. For contemporary humanism, we are our own lords, our own highest end, and the measure of everything else. For Christian theism, we remain God's servants; our highest good is God; it is God who is to be Lord, not us. The difference between humanism and theism is the difference between these two highest ends, and it is immense.

SECULARIZED VALUES

Naturalism and anthropocentrism are the basic presuppositions of contemporary humanism, and their consequences can readily be traced in the secularizing of human values.

18. Marcuse, *One-Dimensional Man*, p. 12.
19. See *Writings of the Early Marx on Philosophy and Society*, ed. and trans. L. D. Easton and K. H. Guddat (New York: Doubleday, Anchor Books, 1967), p. 314. Also Robert C. Tucker, *Philosophy and Myth in Karl Marx*, 2nd ed. (Cambridge: Cambridge Univ. Press, 1972), p. 12.

We have glimpsed the consequences for religion in Feuerbach and Maslow. Once the existence and supernatural activity of God are laid aside, doctrine and worship and sacrament no longer have significance. Instead, religion is a concern for human values. According to S. P. Lamprecht,

> . . . multiple interests and diverse values are brought into effective and organic unity through central allegiance to some integrating ideal.[20]

And that integrating ideal, being independent of the will and providence of any divine being, is the value of humanity itself. John Dewey sums it up:

> The things in civilization we most prize are not of ourselves. They exist by grace of the doings and sufferings of the continuous human community in which we are a link. Ours is the responsibility of conserving, transmitting, rectifying and expanding the heritage of values we have received. . . . Here are all the elements for a religious faith . . . that has always been implicitly the common faith of mankind.[21]

In view of this kind of religious humanism, the death of God theology of the 1960s was hardly new. Its "religionless Christianity" did without a supernatural God and the associated forms of religion. Such a deity had supposedly lost all relevance to the contemporary mind, and God-talk seemed a dead language. The new element was that it was inspired less by the pragmatism of the thirties than by the positivism of the fifties that insisted on confining itself to purely empirical facts. God was out. But Jesus and his values, the values of humanity, were still in. It was a thoroughly secular religion.

Secularization is apparent in ethics as well. Kai Nielsen writes of ethics without religion. In a world without God we still prize the happiness life offers, along with emotional peace, human love, creative work, and aesthetic satisfaction. These human ends are sufficient to provide purpose and meaning for persons. Nor can the Christian object that the value of persons depends on Christian doctrines: Kant's ethic of respect for persons was established quite

20. S. P. Lamprecht, "Naturalism and Religion," in Krikorian, *Naturalism*, p. 20.
21. John Dewey, *A Common Faith* (New Haven: Yale Univ. Press, 1934), p. 87.

independently of religion. "Even if God is dead," Nielsen writes, "it doesn't really matter."[22]

The English Catholic philosopher Elizabeth Anscombe went so far as to claim in 1958 that the law of God has been systematically excluded from ethical theory.

> To have a law conception of ethics is to hold that what is needed . . . is conformity to divine law. Naturally it is not possible to have such a conception unless you believe in God as a lawgiver . . . every academic philosophy since Sidgwick [d. 1900] was written in such a way as to exclude this ethic.[23]

Since she wrote, philosophers have given renewed attention to so-called divine command theories of ethics and to natural law, but Anscombe's complaint surely applies to the welter of utilitarian and other consequentialist ethics of this century. Values have no transcendent basis but are all anthropocentric.

When we turn to social philosophy, again secularization is evident. Since moral ideals are related to desirable consequences, Sidney Hook treats them as hypotheses to be controlled by the sciences and their experimental inquiry. Democracy, for instance, is simply a hypothesis about how to organize human relationships for the ends we desire, not an extension of unchanging natural rights or moral laws.[24] Regarding marriage, again, the religious view that it is an institution ordained by God has been largely superseded by the contractual view that marriage is an entirely human arrangement, a social convention, one that we devised and can revise, and that only a legal contract holds a couple to it. As Paul Ramsey points out, this has profound significance regarding sex, abortion, adoption, sterilization, and so forth, for if a marriage is simply a conventional contract, and if the contract specifies nothing in these regards, then marriage has no ethical implications for them at all.[25]

22. Kai Nielsen, "Ethics Without Religion," in Kurtz, *Moral Problems*, p. 31. Cf. *The Jefferson Bible*, ethical materials Thomas Jefferson selected, leaving out all religious and supernaturalist elements in the New Testament record.
23. Elizabeth Anscombe, "Modern Moral Philosophy," *Philosophy* 33 (1958): 1–19.
24. Sidney Hook, "Naturalism and Democracy," in Krikorian, *Naturalism*, chap. 3.
25. See Paul Ramsey, *Ethics at the Edges of Life* (New Haven: Yale Univ. Press, 1978), pp. 9–18.

Humanism's presuppositions obviously have far-reaching consequences as the operating philosophy of a secular society with secularized values. In his classic work *The Secular City*, Harvey Cox gives a graphic account of how secularization occurred.[26] In a religious view, life is full of mystery; it speaks of something beyond itself, it is sacred, it both is what it is and bears witness to something (or Someone) else. Yet nature is now no longer an enchanted garden, but the arena for science and technology. Politics is no longer a sacred calling to the exercise of power entrusted by God, but a struggle between purely human powers for purely human ends. Our values no longer awe us with the echo of God's holiness, for we have made them for ourselves alone. This is secularism.

Contemporary humanism offers a secularized meaning and purpose to this troubled age. It will not be enough to recite philosophical criticisms of naturalism, nor of scientism, relativism, Romanticism, or Marxism. To be sure, we have drawn on some of that criticism. Yet we must above all see how Christian theism's insistence on the sanctity of creation, and of persons in particular, opens horizons for a Christian humanism with another basis for values, another conception of social institutions, and so on.

One prior task remains. To assess world views, and indeed to expound one in any depth, we must see what is involved in their formation and evaluation. Understanding the anatomy of world views will help us articulate Christian theism and envision a Christian humanism as reasonable and relevant options for today.

26. Harvey Cox, *The Secular City* (New York: Macmillan, 1966), chap. 1. Also F. L. Baumer, *Religion and the Rise of Scepticism* (New York: Harcourt Brace, 1960).

CHAPTER 3

THE ANATOMY OF
A WORLD VIEW

It is time to look more closely at the makeup of a world view. What about it unifies and guides both thought and action and defines the highest good? We must learn to distinguish this unifying perspective from the variables that give it a particular formulation at a certain juncture in history, or in a more specific philosophical milieu. Naturalistic humanism has taken many forms historically, and we have noted four current versions; but more basic and long-lasting claims may well be made for its unifying perspective (which we identified as a combination of naturalism and anthropocentrism) than for the particular distinctives of one version or another (scientism, existentialism, etc.). Naturalistic humanism, in other words, is a pluralistic tradition, and each of its varieties stands or falls with the unifying perspective they have in common.

Yet the appeal of naturalistic humanism is often the appeal of a particular version. Scientism is one way of articulating it, one that appeals to the scientifically educated Western mind. Romanticism is another appealing way of formulating it, existentialism is another, Marxism yet another; and each formulation appeals by virtue of its own distinctive characteristics. So we need to consider both the unifying perspective of an entire tradition and the variables shaping particular formulations.

THE UNIFYING PERSPECTIVE

The genesis of a world view is at the prephilosophical level. It begins, without either systematic planning or theoretical intentions, with the beliefs and attitudes and values on which people act. There are feelings about one's world, too, as well as beliefs and attitudes, and the values that different things in that world offer us. In this sense everyone has the beginnings of a world view, and from reflection on these unanalyzed and unsystematic beginnings a more carefully examined and systematically developed view takes shape.

One of the first to look closely at this process was the German philosopher Wilhelm Dilthey. He called the pretheoretical beginning a world picture (*Weltbild*), claiming that it arises from one's life world (*Lebenswelt*) and in time gives rise to a formulated world view (*Weltanschauung*). Since both we and our worlds have a great deal in common, the variety of possible world views is limited. Dilthey suggests that three basic types recur throughout history: where a scientific attitude rules, naturalism; where feelings and ideals predominate, objective idealism (as in Plato and Hegel); where personal freedom and a sense of obligation are to the fore, the idealism of freedom (as in Kant or the Stoics). These three correspond to the three human faculties that eighteenth-century psychology stressed—reason, emotion, and will—and so they express representative human reactions to the world. On the other hand, Herman Dooyeweerd, the Dutch Christian philosopher, looks for what unifies the inner life of a person, and so maintains that among all the possible pretheoretical sources of a world view the religious is central and provides the unifying core. So he recognizes basically two kinds of world view: that which stems from an obedient faith in the God of creation and of grace, and those which stem from apostate "ground-motives." His claim is that the unifying perspective within one's pretheoretical beliefs, attitudes, and values is an essentially religious one. Of course, it does not have to be religious in some overt or institutional sense; a religion substitute does the same thing, for in every case the issues of both life and thought come "out of the heart" (the unifying core) of a person.

Dooyeweerd's point is that the nature of a religion is to retie or reunite what would otherwise be fragmented thought or a fragmented life. When the Marxist claims that the socioeconomic performs this function, then the socioeconomic functions in a quasi-religious manner: he thinks and acts in all of his life from this naturalistic and anthropocentric perspective. Whether or not he agrees to call it his "religion," its function as a unifying perspective is the same as that of religious faith. The scientific humanist for his part unifies his life and thought around a parallel naturalistic confidence in science. Two of Randall's statements, quoted in the last chapter, reveal the quasi-religious nature of that commitment: "There is no 'realm' to which the methods for dealing with Nature cannot be extended"; and "The faith we need, the faith that promises salvation, is the faith in intelligence." And Wilfred Sellars: "Science is the measure of all things, of what is that it is, and of what is not that it is not."

A naturalistic world view appears to give the scientific or the socioeconomic an exaggerated role by making it quasi-religious in function. In a Christian world view, meantime, an actual religion plays its natural role as the unifying perspective, rather than being given an exaggerated place. But in either case what unifies and guides thought and action and defines the highest good is this religious or quasi-religious stance. All world views are thus "perspectival"; that is to say, they develop from the standpoint of such a unifying perspective.

I speak of "religion" at this stage rather than of beliefs, because a religion is more than a set of concepts or doctrines, more than theology. It also includes attitudes and values and hopes, and the activity of the "cultus" in celebrating its faith and implementing it; in fact, for the genuine believer religion involves all one's perceptions and aspirations and doings, one's entire "life world." The analogy in scientific humanism and Marxism is evident. In any "lived religion" that unifies the believer's life world, an overall perspective or "world picture" is present, the beginning of that more reflective conceptual scheme we call a "world view."

In theistic language, suggests Ian Ramsey, the word "God" serves as the "integrator word" that unifies the conceptual scheme, including one's view of science along with all thought and life. Theistic language about all these things can be mapped out in relation to God-talk. The theistic world view, as a conceptual scheme interpreting the widest range of experience, is unified by its theistic perspective.[1] A world view is thus the confession of a unifying

---

1. Ian Ramsey, ed., *Prospect for Metaphysics* (London: Allen and Unwin, 1961), chap. 10. Various philosophers have developed this general view of what unifies human thought. Dorothy Emmet talks of a "coordinating analogy" drawn from some form of experience and extended by analogy to everything else. (*The Nature of Metaphysical Thinking* [New York: Macmillan, 1945], chap. 1). Stephen Pepper talks of "root metaphors" and

perspective, and this confessional character is true of secular and religious views alike. By the same token, as we shall see shortly, the credibility of a world view may be seen to depend on the capacity of its unifying perspective to effectively unify all aspects of life and thought in a meaning-giving way.

WHAT THEOLOGY CONTRIBUTES

Theology studies the teachings of a particular religion. Christian theology expounds the biblical teachings that are basic to the Christian religion. What role has Christian theology, then, in the formulation of a Christian world view?

The first thing, obviously, is that Christian theology expounds on beliefs ingredient to the unifying perspective of a Christian world view and so contributes to the development of an initial *Weltbild* into a Christian *Weltanschauung*. The biblical concept of God is elaborated, the God revealed in Jesus Christ. The biblical account of God's relation to his creation is conceptualized, especially his relation to human persons as responsible agents and his role in history. The whole range of systematic theology is therefore potentially involved: the doctrines of creation and providence inform a Christian view of nature, the doctrines of general and special revelation inform a Christian view of knowledge, the doctrines of sin and grace as well as of the image of God in us inform a Christian view of persons, their freedom, and their moral and cultural responsibility; and the doctrine of the church informs our view of human relationships and of history. Moreover, a *systematic* theology that is effectively unified in itself by some pervasive theme (such as the God-creation relationship or the Incarnation) can contribute thereby to the unification of a world view, since all the topics a theology touches will be related to the unifying theme.

But theology does not always function this way, and professional theologians often evidence little interest in world views. This is because theology is also a technical discipline with methods and

finds four different ones underlying four general types of world view (*World Hypotheses* [Berkeley: Univ. of California Press, 1942]). J. V. L. Casserley suggests that the unifying perspective may be rooted not in a general type of human experience but in a particular historical event, such as God's act in Christ (*The Christian in Philosophy* [New York: Charles Scribner's, n.d.], pt. II, chap. 2).

tasks and subject matter of its own. We may therefore distinguish between "theologians' theology" and "world-viewish theology." The former is generally done by theologians for theologians: it addresses problems within theology using careful exegetical, hermeneutical, and critical techniques for theological purposes. Theologians' theology is often little read and little understood by anyone other than theologians, important as it may be. World-viewish theology, on the other hand, addresses theology to a world view and to particular topics within that world view. It asks, for instance, what the doctrine of creation says about meaning in life or about an objective basis for moral values. It asks what a theological understanding of human nature says to aesthetics, to theories of literary criticism, or to personality theory. It concerns itself with a theology of work and of the marketplace, a theology of play and leisure, a theology of art and of the senses, a theology of nature and of technology, a theology of social change and of social institutions, a theology of sex and of friendship, a theology of politics, of education, and so on. The second thing to note, therefore, is that theology can contribute world-viewish theology to the various areas of thought and life that a world view must encompass.

A third contribution surfaces when we recognize the diversity that has existed historically and exists today within Christian theology. If theology contributes to a Christian world view, then theological diversity contributes to diversity among formulations of a Christian world view. Historically speaking, Christianity is a pluralistic religion; theologically pluralistic and therefore world-viewishly pluralistic as well. An underlying core of biblical essentials and ecumenical creeds persists throughout (for instance, in the Apostles' Creed), identifying distinctively Christian theology and providing the unifying perspective to a Christian world view of whichever variety, but Christian theologies have been variously formulated—and so, too, have Christian world views.

I find this diversity helpful. Sometimes it is exaggerated, and sometimes it has become schismatic and overly contentious. Yet as finite human beings we tend to think one-sidedly, and even the Christian mind needs the criticism and balance provided by others who interpret biblical teachings differently or lay different emphases or systematize things differently. Criticism can keep us from unduly distorting things. Different emphases complement our own. Both can help us regard our own conclusions with appropriate modesty, and keep us from the kind of sectarianism that closes its mind to other formulations and emphases. Perhaps more importantly for our purposes, diversity can show the varied appeal of a Christian view of things and will prevent us putting all our eggs in one intellectually fragile basket. To vary the metaphor, theological options provide backup systems should undue problems develop with one particular formulation. After all, the formulation is man-made; only the biblical revelation itself carries unqualified divine authority.

The biblical writers themselves have different emphases, of course, so that we distinguish the prophetic vision of the Old Testament from the Johannine point of view, or Synoptic theology from Pauline, as mutually complementary ingredients of one biblical theology. The range of biblical concerns is vast, too: human perfidy and destiny, history and biography, joys and sufferings, governmental and economic problems, war and peace, moral issues and pagan ideas. The different concerns of different writers in different historical settings also give rise to diversity.

But the kind of theological pluralism I have in mind has arisen rather in postbiblical history, in the different Christian traditions discussed, for example, by H. Richard Niebuhr in his *Christ and Culture*—a world-viewish title if ever there was one, to be sure. Niebuhr details five "ideal types" of approaches to culture in Christian history, thereby providing a classic paradigm of theological pluralism.

(1) Christ against culture
(2) The Christ of culture
(3) Christ above culture
(4) Christ and culture in paradox
(5) Christ the transformer of culture

The first type represents a tradition of Christian opposition, not to culture *per se*, but to existing cultures (or philosophies, etc.). A Christian world view is seen as diametrically opposed to non-Christian world views and their cultural working. Tertullian, for instance, demanded, "What has Jerusalem to do with Athens?" The Christian's methods are not those of the culture—politics, art, philosophy, and so forth—but those of the prophet and preacher. The theological basis for this stance lies in the fallenness of man as evidenced in thought and life, along with the Christian witness to a different way of life. Consequently all areas of thought and action will be affected. Current examples might be found in the Amish life-style, or in the Christian "counterculture" of the "Jesus people."

Such a view is markedly different from the second type, labelled "the Christ of Culture," which identifies Christianity with existing cultural views and programs for action. This latter view character-ized the Gnostic movements of antiquity (to which Tertullian had reacted), the liberal theologies of the nineteenth century, and the tendency to identify Christianity with socialist or capitalist econom-ics, with liberal or conservative politics, or with revolutionary movements in the Third World. Thought and action in this tradi-tion present a very different view of life than in the first type, and underlying it is a more optimistic theology of man and of sin and a less radical view of the gospel.

If these two mark the extremes, Niebuhr's remaining three types identify mediating theological traditions. "Christ above culture" represents the Thomistic approach, which adds what revelation teaches to what reason alone can know, and adds the help of God's grace to that of which we are by nature alone capable. It is an attempt to value nature and the rational powers God has given us, yet it seems (to the first type, for instance) to underestimate both the radical perversion of creation by sin and the radical newness of "the new man in Christ" and the coming kingdom.

A fourth type, labelled "Paradox," represents Lutheran theology as well as some Anabaptists and others. Here the tension between nature and grace, the old man and the new, is openly admitted. Attention concentrates on living with the conflicting demands of citizenship in two kingdoms, without posing easy reconciliations. Among recent writers Jacques Ellul reflects this view, as do "Chris-tian realists" like Reinhold Niebuhr. On the one hand, Niebuhr sees that we are called to justice and love. But on the other hand, sin makes just laws and deeds of love ineffective in controlling evil. Realistically, we must use power as well—political, economic, and even military force. The resultant tendency is toward a pragmatic and situational ethic.

Augustinian and Reformed theology underlie the fifth type, "Christ the Transformer of Culture." Here the theological motif is "creation, law, sin, grace." Sin distorts God's law-governed cre-ation, but grace restores people to obeying God's law in their cre-ational tasks. Thus human culture, replete with art and science and work and leisure, is divinely ordained and subject to God's law. A

Christian world view therefore mandates cultural involvement with a view to changing things for the better.

Each of these five types has had at least some place in historic Christianity and together they illustrate its pluralism. The point here is twofold. First, a Christian world view will be formulated differently by representatives of different theologies. Second, one must avoid the kind of theological provincialism that fails to take stock of other emphases, even if he finds himself clearly in one tradition rather than another. In actuality, all five emphases have some biblical roots and are likely to appear to some degree in any balanced formulation, even though one type may predominate. I myself am closer to Reformed theology, but I hope the reader will also hear echoes of other traditions in what I say, echoes that are substantive, not hollow.

We have seen three contributions that theology makes to a Christian world view, but things other than theology are plainly involved as well. Nor is theology itself immune from other factors. The history of theology as well as the practice of theologians reveals philosophical influences on hermeneutics, on theological language, on concept-formation, and on theological methodology; in addition there are sociological and other historical influences. Theology is not exempt from what the sociology of knowledge reveals, nor are theologians exempt from personal subjectivity or historical dependence. Theology is not an autonomous discipline, independent of all other considerations. But the biblical core of Christian theology should nonetheless be more influential in the formation of a Christian world view than the content of any other single discipline.

WHAT PHILOSOPHY CONTRIBUTES

But what does philosophy contribute to an explicitly religious and specifically Christian world view? This is one facet of the wider intercourse between philosophy and theology. Theology, we suggested, studies the teachings of a particular religion about God and his relationship to humankind. Philosophy, at least as it is practiced nowadays, analyzes the logic of ideas and arguments in any field of experience or thought, religious or otherwise. Philosophy of religion looks at religious concepts and arguments, philosophical ethics at ethical concepts and arguments, philosophy of science at scientific ones, and so forth. These concepts and arguments fall into several distinguishable groups that make up the major branches of philosophy: 1) logic, methodology, and the claim to truth (epistemology), 2) the overall and varied nature of what is taken to be real (metaphysics), and 3) the values involved in such human endeavors as morality, art, and politics (axiology). Since these kinds of philosophical analysis relate to every area of life and thought, two consequences follow: philosophical issues are omnipresent, and overall philosophical positions of a synoptic and systematic nature arise. Some philosophical positions are unified by naturalistic beliefs, as we have seen. But some are unified by theistic beliefs, so that a major historical tradition of theistic philosophy exists and, within that, of Christian philosophy.[2]

Philosophy, in other words, has a different focus than theology, a focus on concepts and arguments basic to all areas of life and thought, including but not confined to religion and theology. It therefore contributes an understanding of foundational issues (epistemology, metaphysics, and axiology) that underlie science and history and art as well as theology, so that the integration of one's thought proceeds at a basic theoretical level that all disciplines have in common. Philosophy of religion, philosophy of science, philosophy of education, philosophy of art, philosophy of politics—all these meet in common philosophical foundations. Theology has similar philosophical connections, for it, too, is a theoretical discipline.

In practice, therefore, philosophy's integrative role is twofold. First, the *activity* of philosophical inquiry touches all the disciplines, as well as their interrelations. Second, the *history* of philosophical inquiry provides a repertoire of ideas and arguments about virtually every subject and virtually every major type of world view, naturalistic and otherwise. A serious discussion of world views therefore calls for an awareness of both philosophical issues and the philosophical heritage.

Yet philosophy, like theology, tends to be professionalized and technical and seems not always to contribute to world-view thinking. Some philosophers in fact have little interest in world views at all. We can therefore distinguish here between "philosophers' philosophy" and "world-viewish philosophy." The former is done

2. See this author's article, "Christian Philosophy," in *Encyclopedia Britannica*, 15th ed., 1974.

by philosophers for philosophers, and it addresses technical matters within philosophy using complex procedures for largely professional purposes. Philosophers' philosophy is often little understood by anyone other than philosophers, important and consequential though it be. World-viewish philosophy, on the other hand, brings the results of philosophers' philosophy to the formation and evaluation of world views and to particular topics within a world view. It asks, for example, what naturalism and theism imply about the meaning of life, and it formulates arguments that reinforce or criticize their views. Like world-viewish theology, it concerns itself with the philosophy of work and leisure, the philosophy of art and technology, the philosophy of social change and politics, and so on. World-viewish philosophy plainly can contribute to the formulation of a credible, contemporary Christian world view.

Implicit in what I have said about philosophy is the recognition of its pluralistic nature. Naturalistic philosophy is a pluralistic tradition. So is theism, and so is the history of Christian philosophy. A variety of philosophical approaches have been employed by Christian thinkers—Platonism and Thomism, of course, but also Renaissance and Enlightenment perspectives. Of special influence in America has been eighteenth-century Scottish Common Sense Realism, imported at Princeton but spreading from there among evangelicals and others. Also important is the personal idealism of Lotze and Bowne that was popularized at Boston by E. S. Brightman. Today these are minority positions: the methods and emphases of phenomenology and analytic philosophy are more evident in Christian thought. It follows, then, that the tradition of Christian world views, being influenced by different philosophies, will also be pluralistic.

The emphasis of this book is on the interplay of theology with philosophy in the formation of a Christian world view. But the philosopher is not exempt from other historical variables, nor is he any more immune from subjective factors than is the theologian. So our analysis of the anatomy of a world view takes yet another step.

WHAT SCIENCE CONTRIBUTES

After theology and philosophy, the natural and social sciences influence world views most. I say this with two qualifications. First, we are not talking about cultures largely untouched by the sciences as theoretical undertakings, where one would need to talk of less sophisticated ideas of nature and the world. Second, science contributes to a world view but does not itself contribute a world view. The theologian Rudolph Bultmann, however, advocates replacing biblical supernaturalism with a modern scientific world view, echoing the desire of the positivists of the 1920s in the Vienna Circle for a purely empirical "scientific world-conception." The popular mind, picking this up, often assumes that science has no limits; and scientific humanism builds on this notion.

Science, however, is an empirical and theoretical inquiry into natural processes and relationships. As such, its domain does not include the meaning and purpose of human existence nor the exposition of a unifying perspective on life. And it uses theoretical models limited to certain ranges of data, in conjunction with empirical and statistical methods that have no access to nonempirical possibilities and nonnatural processes and relationships. In this regard a "scientific world view" that admits only what scientific methods can handle is unduly restricting.

If with the positivists and many existentialists we regard science as purely empirical, then the most that science can offer is empirical generalizations of considerable generality. To extrapolate from *what is empirically observable* to *everything that is* involves a logical *non sequitur*. On the other hand, if with more recent philosophers of science we regard science as creative theorizing by the use of models or paradigms, then claims made for a scientific world view are claims for an overall model geared to natural processes and relationships. Again, a suppressed premise is at work, that everything in existence exhibits the same kind of relationships and processes and so can be subsumed under the same model. And this is the thesis of monism, in this case of philosophical naturalism. Such a scientific world view is therefore more "scien*tism*" than science; it is in reality a naturalistic philosophy.

World views have to do with values, with what *ought* to be, not just what *is*. Psychologists and sociologists describe the values people pursue, but theirs is more a look at what is or might be, not what *ought* to be ideally, independently of any particular consequences. In fact, the ultimate values of a world view determine what particular consequences we want, rather than vice versa, and ultimate values are not established by value-free empirical or statistical means.

In fact, scientists bring their values to their science: Maslow, for instance, brings the value of human fulfillment to his psychology. For this reason there is no completely value-free science.

What, then, does science rightly contribute to world views if not the values and all-embracing beliefs of a unifying perspective? The answer can be drawn from a look at intellectual history, where the history of science is interwoven with the history of everything else. The scientific concepts of a given period are reflected in the interests of artists, whether in space or weight or light; they appear in literature (compare Dante's *Inferno* with Pope's *Essay on Man*); they influence philosophy (compare Descartes and Whitehead), and they are reflected in political and even theological ideas.

An effective way of looking at this is suggested by Thomas Kuhn's emphasis on the changing paradigms produced by scientific revolutions.[3] We may distinguish four major paradigms or models in the history of science. The Pythagorean model, based on the view that nature has a mathematical order, was extended by Plato into a theory of universal forms and gave shape to the classical world view with its stress on rational contemplation, on harmonious unity as the mark of both justice and beauty, and on mystical union with the divine. Aristotelian science turned attention more to change in nature and human art, stressing final causes or ends. A teleological world view emerged, suggesting a hierarchical arrangement in both creation and society and a natural law ethic based on humanity's essential ends. Renaissance and Newtonian science, by contrast, abandoned final causes and explained things in terms of matter and motion only—the mechanistic model often likened to a "billiard ball universe." The notion of particles of matter combining by laws of motion found parallels in a psychology of atomistic sensations combined by laws of association, and a social philosophy of isolated individuals united by social contract. But nineteenth- and twentieth-century science has again been remodeled, this time by energistic physics, by Einstein's relativity theory, and by developmental biology, into the conception of a relational process of a more organic sort—like a force-field or a biosystem. Art no longer adheres to the form and uniformity of Newtonian space and time. The notion of community—even a community of nations—replaces hi-

3. See *The Structure of Scientific Revolutions* (Chicago: Univ. of Chicago Press, 1962). I am indebted for the elaboration of this to my physicist friend and colleague, Professor Joseph Spradley.

erarchical structures, and such themes as alienation and reconciliation have come to the fore.

A quick overview like this is sufficient to indicate how changing scientific concepts have consequences and analogies elsewhere. For our purposes it is also important to see that both the monistic and the theistic traditions have employed these various scientific models in the elaboration of world views. Within theism, for example, Augustine was a Platonist; Aquinas was an Aristotelian; Descartes, Locke, and Bishop Butler were mechanists; and a more organic model is evident in William Temple and Teilhard de Chardin. Within monism, on the other hand, we can contrast Plotinus or the Stoics with mechanists such as Spinoza and behaviorist B. F. Skinner, or again with process thinkers such as Hegel, Dewey, or Whitehead. The picture that emerges is of unifying perspectives developed systematically with the help of scientific models. Historical world-view traditions employ changing scientific models:

	M_1	M_2	M_3	M_4
W-V$_1$				
W-V$_2$				
W-V$_3$				

It would not be difficult to fill in this grid by locating in it philosophers, psychologists, political and economic theorists, artists, and even theologians. Mozart, for instance, is very much part of the Enlightenment (M_3), but contemporary music and abstract art (M_4) are not. The breakup of three-dimensional objects in art, contrary to some critics, need not mean a broken world but only a different concept of space. And the breakdown of any hierarchical order between the sexes may likewise reflect just a change in the conceptual model rather than the loss of a traditional world view. Examples will multiply as we proceed.

The distinction between world-view perspectives and scientific models will keep recurring in what we say, for it affects any topic we might take up. Scientific conceptions of nature affect our thinking about every natural process and human activity and are frequently extended by way of analogy to God. A careful evaluation of world views must then distinguish between criticisms of the way they are modeled and criticisms of their underlying perspective, and Christian thinking must be self-critical in regard to the models it employs. In due course we shall suggest that scientific models falsify when they are extended beyond their original domain of natural phenomena, and that a largely different model, a personalistic one, is needed for thinking about certain aspects of man as well as about God.

Thomas Kuhn's treatment of scientific revolutions merely makes room for this point. His main intent is to show that paradigm shifts do not occur for purely logical or empirical reasons. With a great deal of historical documentation he argues that sociological factors have been more decisive; that is, what the scientific establishment will accept or what the "official" journals will publish. Kuhn's critics have argued that he overstates his case, that objective controls do exist in revolutionary changes as well as in "normal science." But the point is made: from the standpoint of the history of science it appears that science is not as objective and empirical as we once supposed, and that subjective factors intrude. The British scientist Michael Polanyi points this out, too,[4] in terms of such personal influences on a scientist as his beliefs, interests, abilities, past experience, training, and so forth. Scientific findings are scientist-dependent. Not only is there no one authoritative "scientific world view" nor just one final scientific paradigm that explains everything, but science itself is a human enterprise dependent on the beliefs and attitudes and values—even on the world views—that scientists themselves bring to science rather than simply drawing them from their work. Science indeed influences world views, but world views also influence science.

OTHER INFLUENCES

Theology, philosophy, and science are not the only factors influencing the formulation of a world view. A particular problem that needs attention at a given time may well lead the formulation on in certain ways. Economic, political, and social conditions affect our perceptions of life, and in particular areas (like art or philosophy) new techniques make a difference. Certainly the availability of wealthy sponsors affected music history, the development of synthetic materials affected art, and the availability of U.S. govern-

4. Polanyi, *Personal Knowledge* (Chicago: Univ. of Chicago Press, 1958).

ment grants affects both science and the humanities as well as the current concept of a university and the scholarly task.

But all this poses a major problem. If these variables are at work, so that all sorts of subjective and relativizing influences are admitted and even a Christian world view has to be seen pluralistically, then are we committed to the kind of relativism in which nothing is true for everyone? Must subjectivism prevail?

THE PROBLEM OF SUBJECTIVISM

In ethics, subjectivism is the view that our moral judgments simply describe inner attitudes and feelings: the statement "stealing is wrong" is about our psychological states in relation to stealing, not about any objective state of affairs or objective criterion of right and wrong. C. S. Lewis criticizes this view in *The Abolition of Man*, illustrating his point with the subjectivist translation of "that is a sublime waterfall" into "I have sublime feelings about that waterfall."

Similarly, some people take a subjectivist approach to world views, as if to hold a world view is just to have certain feelings about things. And some adopt a subjectivist view of beliefs, so that believing something is simply to have a psychological state with reference to it rather than also to assert an objective truth about it.

The concept of a myth is used in similar fashion. While in one sense a myth is a symbolic story that states an important truth, in another sense it is a fiction of the imagination devoid of any objective truth at all. Even the term "ideology" is sometimes used this way; that is, of a fiction that affects both thought and conduct.

A world view embodies beliefs and values, and sometimes stories (a creation account, for instance) that symbolize truths beyond what they overtly describe, and so a kind of ideology appears. The subjectivist tells us that all this is purely subjective, without objective basis or truth. The usual argument is that because beliefs and values and world views differ from one person or culture to another they must be relative to (presumably a product of) those different cultures, histories, personalities, and other conditions. Pluralism argues for relativism, and relativism argues for subjectivism.

Some writers have gone so far as to offer psychoanalytic explanations. Freud is well known, of course, for claiming that belief in God is due to subconscious fixations on one's parents. J. O. Wisdom argued that the eighteenth-century philosopher George Berkeley denied the independent reality of matter because of a pathological aversion to dirt and excretion.[5] And in more general terms, Morris Lazerowitz proposed that a metaphysic is a case of wish-fulfillment: at the conscious level it involves the illusion of a theory about the world, but at the preconscious level it proposes to change the usage of language in order to counter subconscious fears or satisfy unconscious wishes.[6] Friedrich Nietzsche took this kind of view. Philosophy reveals the prejudices of philosophers more than it describes reality; logic flows from the biological need to stabilize a certain kind of life; positivism is the conceit of the intellectual who has freed himself from his masters; skepticism is a kind of nervous sickness.

Plainly, the subjectivist fallacy lies in supposing that beliefs and values are altogether subjective and not at all objective. An either/or mentality has taken charge, to which one could as well reply with Caesar's "et tu, Brute." The subjectivist theory, taken on its own terms, would be an entirely subjective affair. In order to make truth-claims for subjectivism, it must itself be an exception to its own rule. But then subjectivism as a general theory has contradicted itself and is false. This "self-referentiality argument" is hard for either the subjectivist or the relativist to avoid.

What will help here is a distinction that I introduced elsewhere[7] between epistemological and metaphysical subjectivity and objectivity. Epistemological subjectivity is the involvement of the person—his attitudes and values and so on—in his thinking and knowing. Epistemological objectivity would preclude any such involvement. The latter, I think, is patently false, the former unavoidable. On the other hand, metaphysical subjectivity means that an object has no existence outside of someone's mind and that nothing is true independently of whether or not we believe it. Metaphysical objectivity, in contrast, means that objects have independent existence and the truth is independent of whatever we may wish or think. In these terms epistemological subjectivity is quite compatible with metaphysical objectivity: that is to say, the per-

5. J. O. Wisdom, *The Unconscious Origins of Berkeley's Philosophy* (London: Hogarth Press, 1953).

6. Morris Lazerowitz, *The Structure of Metaphysics* (New York: Humanities Press, 1955), chap. 2.

7. Holmes, *All Truth is God's Truth* (Grand Rapids: Eerdmans, 1977), pp. 5–7.

sonal and cultural influences on our thinking logically do not prevent what we think being true. We must distinguish between the truth of a belief and how we come to think that way, or even to justify believing it to be true.

To acknowledge subjective feelings and to admit relative influences on our beliefs and values therefore need not imply a total relativism or total subjectivism. Moreover, within the plurality of world-view formulations (and conflicting beliefs and values) there are discernable *types* of view and *patterns* of argument; objective considerations are appealed to, and universally alike public facts are involved. Pluralism need not imply complete relativism, nor indeed does it imply subjectivism, but only that the incompleteness of evidence may logically allow different conclusions. Most thought is a mix of the objective and the subjective and of both universal and relative considerations, and reason's task has always been to disentangle them.

Phenomenological philosophy arose, in fact, over this very issue. Edmund Husserl was concerned about naturalistic explanations of human thought, whether "psychologistic" (explaining it all as a product of psychological processes) or "historicist" (explaining it as a product of historical processes). If those explanations are accepted, he argued, then science is altogether without a firm foundation in anything universal and can make no claim to universal truth. Consequently he proposed to describe what is *universal* in human thought and consciousness, when all particular objects and psychological and historical conditions are "bracketed." As one of Husserl's recent exponents puts it, the only cure for subjectivism is more discriminating and self-critical subjectivity, "which will show the very limits of subjectivity."[8] Objectivity exists amid all our subjectivity, and subjectivity in all our objectivity; we need, therefore, to identify the objective and universal and detach it from the purely relative.

I am not making a brief for phenomenology as such, although I do think it is on the right track in trying to disentangle the universal from the relative in our subjectivity. Whether or not we can argue (against cultural relativism) that the same values appear in all cultures, at least universal "value areas" are evident—areas such as life and health, sex and marriage, property and economic

8. Herbert Spiegelberg, "How Subjective is Phenomenology?" *Proc. of the American Catholic Philosophical Association* 33 (1959): 35.

needs, and so forth. Although we can hardly argue that precisely the same beliefs about nature appear universally or the same explanatory categories are universal (as Aristotle and Kant assumed), at least universal "category areas" are evident—some sort of causal or quasi-causal concept is needed, and quantitative concepts, and so forth. We can also appropriately speak of "universal basic beliefs"; belief in one's own existence, belief in a real world external to one's consciousness, belief in some ultimate reality that I cannot push around but must reckon with in the final analysis. These beliefs are very skeletal, and almost everyone would flesh them out in more particular ways, but there they stand nonetheless, unavoidable ingredients of human reflection. Moreover, whatever we think of the actual basis for logical laws, whether metaphysical or linguistic or whatever, at least the law of noncontradiction is a universal condition of intelligible thought. Aristotle's famous "negative proof" shows this by asking that one who denies the law practice his denial in speaking. Unintelligible utterances may be possible without it, like talk of a square circle, but unintelligible utterances hardly qualify as intelligible thought or speech. Where this law of logic is ignored, all logic and intelligibility are gone. These types of universality, at least these, are present in all world views, whatever the differences and whatever the subjective or relative factors involved. It is then to universal factors like these, prephilosophical factors rooted in the generic nature of human existence in a common universe, that appeal must be made in justifying the truth-claims people make.

It might well be objected that Kant transposed these universals into the human mind, reducing them to subjective principles of thought. A twofold response is immediately possible without getting into the technicalities of Kant's philosophy. First, we have already noted that epistemological subjectivity does not itself necessitate metaphysical subjectivity. It is at least possible that universal category areas and basic beliefs and laws of logic apply to what is independent of our thinking. Second, the universal value areas we have mentioned apply to human "action spheres" of a universal sort, so that overt activity in the world around us is involved and not just a subjective theoretical framework. If thought is in fact related to action, then the "pure reason" Kant criticized becomes a philosophical fiction. "Practical reason," related to overt action, admits metaphysical postulates of its own. The question then concerns the truth of what is proposed.

THE QUESTION OF TRUTH

Pluralism logically implies neither subjectivism nor relativism. Neither the plurality of different world-view perspectives nor the different elaborations given any one perspective imply that world views are entirely relative. Truth-claims can still be made, and ways must be found for evaluating the claim that a certain world view is objectively true.

We have distinguished between the unifying perspective of a world view and the particular elaboration it receives under the influence of other factors. The elaborated form is rarely a set of logical deductions from the underlying perspective, but more often a creatively proposed theory adduced to flesh out our understanding. We must therefore distinguish between claiming that the unifying perspective is true and claiming that every part of a specific elaboration is true. A stronger truth-claim may be made for the perspective than for its detailed elaboration. Thus, as a theist I find it more important that biblical theism (my unifying perspective) be true than the particular formulations offered in this volume be true. I am much more open to the possibility that some of what I shall say in Chapters Seven or Eleven is partly mistaken than to the possibility that Christian theism in any and every form is wrong. Particular formulations are changeable and negotiable when a basic biblical theism is not. Indeed, on some matters we may do well to realize that a variety of particular formulations is possible, without jumping to just one conclusion.

Yet of course I do think that what I propose is both true and important, or else I would want neither to say it nor to put my name to it; so it becomes important to see how truth-claims should be evaluated. Briefly, three alternative strategies present themselves, which I label fideism, foundationalism, and coherentism.

Fideism, first of all, stakes its truth-claims directly and uncritically on what is believed. No further evidence or argument is needed. The Marxist may accept Marxist views uncritically because he is personally convinced of their reliability no matter what. The Christian likewise might accept Christian beliefs uncritically, being personally convinced of their reliability no matter what. He does not weigh his views against someone else's, nor does he examine their self-consistency and range of application. Perhaps he accepts them on someone else's authority, without assessing the competence of that authority. The key to fideism, in any case, is uncritical acceptance.

In effect, fideism is a refusal to take seriously the plurality of alternatives, the problem of subjectivism, and the question of truth: it refuses to weigh conflicting claims. And as a result it is difficult to keep it from mere credulity. One must somehow evaluate competing authorities or conflicting views if one's beliefs are to stand up under scrutiny. And one must be prepared to examine his or her own assumptions.

Foundationalism, the second strategy, lies pretty well at the opposite pole. In recent philosophy the term refers to the procedure of deducing all one's beliefs from basic premises that are themselves both beyond possible doubt (indubitable) and beyond any need for correction (incorrigible). This, of course, was Descartes' procedure in his *Meditations*, where he suspended judgment on everything until he could identify an indubitable and incorrigible starting point: *cogito*, I think. Then he proceeded to infer the existence and nature of the soul, of God, and of the material world—the entire scope of his philosophy. Spinoza followed the same procedure and organized his *Ethics* like a geometry textbook, complete with axioms, corollaries, theorems, and proofs. Foundationalism became the standard method of Enlightenment rationalism. It is also employed in modified forms by such recent empiricists as A. J. Ayer, Bertrand Russell, and Roderick Chisholm.

Some Christian thinkers choose this kind of strategy, and the tradition of natural theology with its strictly logical proofs for the existence of God is a case in point. But when it comes to an overall world view, difficulties arise. The strategy is best suited to proving particular propositions, but a world view is more than a set of propositional beliefs. If a world view is not a deductive system, it cannot be established one logical step at a time as the foundationalist wants. But if it is a deductive system, then enough indubitable and incorrigible first premises must be available to imply logically both its unifying perspective and its entire detailed formulation. And that seems to be asking for more explicit and indubitable foundations than we actually have. Others may want to try the foundationalist strategy, but I am not convinced it can work, and I have elsewhere argued at length that not only Cartesian-style philosophy but contemporary styles as well fail to be as presuppositionless as they claim. Philosophy is always to some extent "perspectival."[9]

Coherentism, the third strategy, is the route I prefer: a belief is justified by virtue of its coherence within the entire body of what one knows and believes. My underlying justification of this strategy, apart from the problems I see in the other two alternatives, lies in what we may call *the unity of truth*, which is to say that truth *in toto* is itself an interrelated and coherent whole. My reasons for this claim are three. First, the law of noncontradiction in logic, itself a universal principle, insists on the logical consistency of whatever we claim as true. At least no incompatibility can be allowed. Second, we noted in Chapter One that the quest for understanding itself seeks unity amid diversity, the one amid the many: the unity of truth expresses that ideal. Third, the theist believes that an omniscient God sees everything in relationship to his own creative power and purposes, thus as an interrelated whole. But this interrelated unity of things implies the unity of truth to which the overall coherence of what we believe will bear witness.

Within this coherent unity, particular beliefs should be mutually supportive, but not necessarily by way of strictly logical implication. Consider, as a starting point, the way in which any theory is responsible both to the range of data it addresses and to whatever other theories one holds. Wolterstorff, as we noted before, refers to the other theories as "control beliefs," and to data as "data beliefs," and he suggests that to be acceptable a particular theory must "comport" with both. His point in calling both "beliefs" is that neither theories nor data are incorrigible or indubitable as the foundationalist supposes. Rather, these various beliefs are mutually supportive.

In the case of a particular scientific theory, this simplified rubric may perhaps suffice. But a world view is a very complicated kind of theory intended to guide and unify thought and action, so that "coherence" becomes more complicated as well. Yet we can make good use of the universal points of reference discussed above in

9. See *Christian Philosophy in the Twentieth Century* (Nutley, NJ: Craig Press, 1969). Other writers have argued the theory-dependency of concepts, and the person-relative nature of proof. See G. Mavrodes, *Belief in God* (New York: Random House, 1970); Stephen Toulmin, *Foresight and Understanding* (London: Hutchinson Univ. Library, 1961). The problems with foundationalism are summarized by N. Wolterstorff in *Reason Within the Bounds of Religion* (Grand Rapids: Eerdmans, 1976), pp. 24–58.

trying to ensure a coherence that maintains contact with "meta-physical objectivity." *Universal laws of logic* make it possible to draw logical implications so as to see if a set of beliefs leads to self-contradiction. A world view must be both internally consistent and consistent with whatever more general beliefs it accepts. *Universal value areas* identify the range and variety of human concerns that a world view must address. The supreme good it affirms must give value to the "goods" in universal value areas and must bring all these values into a coherent unity. This, it will be remembered, is intended in the very nature of a world view. *Universal action spheres* are given guidance by a world view, which must therefore speak to both ends and means of human action, giving meaning both to each action sphere and to human life as a whole. *Universal categories of thought* need the explicit formulation and interrelation a world view gives if they are to function as explanatory principles. Yet in inter-relating categories, a world view must not blur their differences by reducing, for example, the causes of historical events to the purely physical or purely psychological. Coherence integrates without re-ductionism. *Universal basic beliefs*, too skeletal in themselves to give much guidance to thought or life, gain content from the general outlook of a world view and are fleshed out within the particular historical formulations that view takes. Coherence is not evident at the skeletal level, but it is provided by a world view. Yet different views offer different unifying foci, and various degrees of overall coherence result.

These considerations apply by virtue of the inclusive nature of a world view, with the range of beliefs and values it seeks to draw into a coherent whole. The intent is to explain the whole range of human experience by reference to what is most ultimately real. By identifying what is universal, then, in human experience, we can evaluate alternatives in terms not only of their consistency but also of the completeness with which they integrate things into a unified and meaning-giving whole.

Inasmuch as this approach depends on the nature of world views, it is in principle "meta-perspectival," independent of any one view, and applies to the evaluation of theistic and naturalist views alike, which will differ in these regards by degree. Moreover, this approach addresses not only logical and theoretical concerns, but also human values and actions and the overall meaning of life. It seeks what is most "think-with-able" and "live-with-able," a world view that has most intellectual adequacy and most human relevance. World views, it must be remembered, arise at the prephilosophical level, in the whole-personal context of human existence and reflection. A Christian world view's claim to truth, then, will be justifiable in these wholistic terms. [10]

10. This approach is further developed in chap. 7 of this author's *All Truth is God's Truth*. See also the discussion of universal beliefs at the conclusion of Chapter Nine below.

PART TWO
CONTOURS OF A WORLD VIEW

CHAPTER 4

GOD AND CREATION: THEOLOGICAL

Among the very skeletal universal basic beliefs to which reference has been made, the recognition of some ultimate reality is the most fundamental. More specifically, what is the nature of this reality with which we have to reckon? Is it matter, laws of nature, uncaring and impersonal forces? Is it some evolving cosmic consciousness of which we are insignificant parts? Is it a personal God on whose wise and beneficent will the existence and destiny of everything depends? These questions are the watershed for different world views.

"I believe in God the Father Almighty, Maker of Heaven and Earth," affirms the Apostles' Creed, repeated by believers through the centuries. At its very outset, the creed recognizes a distinction and a relationship between God and his creation. On that distinction rests our hope. In that relationship God acts. And so the creed goes on to speak of Christ's Incarnation, the Holy Spirit, the church, and our eternal destiny, for the God-creation distinction and relationship sets the stage for the whole drama of human history and hopes. It is the overall context of Christian belief and the basis of all ultimate meaning. The creed confesses a living God; no detached spectator on the world and its fate, God is the leading actor. All powerful, he retains and exercises the initiative. This is the most basic theme in a Christian world view.[1]

1. Of particular interest on this subject, in addition to the items specifically referred to below, are J. Langdon Gilkey, *Maker of Heaven and Earth* (New York: Doubleday, 1959); James Houston, *I Believe in the Creator* (Grand Rapids: Eerdmans, 1980); and L. Berkhof, *Systematic Theology*, 4th ed. (Grand Rapids: Eerdmans, 1949) pp. 126–140.

A DISTINCTIVE PERSPECTIVE

Since everything else is an amplification of this theme, it therefore differentiates, when more fully developed, Christian from non-Christian views of life and the Christian faith from non-Christian religions.

I speak of both the *distinction* and the *relationship* between God and the creation, for both are important. In Chapter One, for instance, we differentiated Christian theism from monistic and dualistic views. Monism loses the *distinction* between God and creation, either absorbing the creation into God (as with neo-Platonism, pantheism, and some Eastern religions) or else losing God in the creation (as with materialism, philosophical naturalism, and secular humanism). On the other hand, dualism confuses the *relationship* by affirming the coeternality of God and matter, or spirit and matter, and so denies that God is an almighty maker of all, who acts with full freedom in his creation. The God-creation theme thus differentiates Christian theism from other world views and is crucial to thinking Christianly about anything at all.

I shall substantiate this claim as we go along. Eighteenth-century deism, for instance, affirmed the distinction between God and creation but fell far short of a Christian exposition of their relationship: the living God who acts in self-revelation and in redemption was missing from deist thought. Nineteenth-century Romanticism reacted to the opposite extreme, blurring the distinction between God and nature, and exalting nature's vitality to the ultimate meaning-giving role that God alone can have in a Christian view of things. Contemporary forms of naturalistic humanism, as we saw in Chapter Two, are monistic. By losing the God-creation distinction and reducing everything to nature, they become anthropocentric rather than theocentric: their hope resides in man. As John Courtney Murray sums up the matter, monism translates the question of God's relation to his creation into a choice: God *or* creation. To choose God without a distinct creation is to opt for pantheism. To choose the creation without God is to choose naturalism.[2]

But a biblical view asserts that man is not alone in the cosmos,

---

2. John Courtney Murray, S.J., *The Problem of God, Yesterday and Today* (New Haven: Yale Univ. Press, 1964), p. 95.

for the Almighty is still maker of heaven and earth. To the pantheist it replies that God transcends the cosmos rather than being bound to its necessities and limitations. To the dualist it replies that God is supremely in charge, rather than forever wrestling with the Other. The Almighty is the living, personal God who acts.

> If God, the creator, *is*, then the gloomy idea of fate and fatality which lies like a spell over the ancient as well as the modern world, loses its basis. It is not a fate, an impersonal, abstract determining power, not a law, not a something which is above everything that is and happens, but He, the creator spirit, the creator person.[3]

The Old Testament reveals this contrast between biblical theism and other world views in the way it addresses other religions. The living God of creation is constantly contrasted with other deities. Other religions saw the gods as part of creation, akin to natural phenomena or nature's inhabitants. Mesopotamian gods were identified with celestial bodies, the moon-god and sun-god especially, or with the behavior of the birds of the sky or even with the deep waters supposedly "under the earth."[4] Yet the Genesis creation story, for all its parallels with Babylonian accounts, declares the heavenly bodies and the waters and the fowls of the air and every living thing to be created by God, and in no sense divine. Other religions might worship them, but the biblical religion knows only one God and can serve none other. The psalmist adds that the heavens and the earth declare the glory of the living God, bearing witness to the goodness and power his saving acts also display.

The plagues of Egypt at the time of the Exodus were a direct affront to the gods of that land. The Egyptians had their sun-god; they addressed a hymn to the Nile and held as sacred the creatures that lived in and around it; even frogs and locusts had religious significance; and cattle somehow related to the goddess of love and were revered in effigy.[5] Yet these objects bore the brunt of the affliction: the light was turned to darkness; the river ran like blood; frogs and locusts became devastating pests; the cattle died. To rein-

3. Emil Brunner, *Christianity and Civilization* (London: Nisbet, 1948), p. 18.
4. For more detail see Helmer Ringgren, *Religions of the Ancient Near East* (Philadelphia: Westminster Press, 1977).
5. See Henry Frankfort, *Ancient Egyptian Religion* (New York: Columbia Univ. Press, 1948).

force his point, when the Israelites gathered soon afterward at Sinai, God declared that *he* had delivered them from Egypt, then forbade gods other than he and outlawed worshiping images of anything in the heavens or the earth or the water. He is maker of heaven and earth, sovereign Lord of history, the living God.

The "living God" of creation is contrasted throughout the Old Testament with the unresponsive and dead gods of the heathen. Joshua assured Israel of the living God's presence during their entry into Canaan (Josh. 3:10). Goliath defied the armies of the living God who acted to vindicate himself through David (1 Sam. 17:26). In confronting the priests of Baal on Mount Carmel, Elijah chided them that perhaps their god was asleep. Nothing they did could awaken any response. But when Jehovah acted, the people saw that he is the one living God, the Almighty (1 Kgs. 18:17–39). The psalmist thirsted and cried out for the living God (42:2; 84:2), and even the Persian King Darius called Jehovah "the living God, and stedfast for ever" (Dan. 6:26 KJV). This contrast is what differentiates the biblical faith from other religions.

By the same token, Christianity differs from other theistic religions like Judaism and Islam in the fuller account it gives of the God-creation relation. In this regard, the Old Testament is incomplete and anticipates the New, where God acts by incarnating himself in his creation, something fully consonant with theistic possibilities. What Jesus is and does and makes possible is seen as God's active relationship to his creation: his life and death and resurrection; his teaching and that of the apostles; his church and its role in the world; his active presence through the Holy Spirit; his kingdom among us yet still to come. Christ fulfills the Jewish and anticipates the Islamic hope in a God who is active. Moreover, the bare theism of philosophical theology is given rich content, and the "stuttering deism" that thinks God might act just occasionally in a world he made is put to shame. The full scope of the Christian religion is not only self-consistent but also makes theism more complete and more internally coherent than other theistic faiths appear to be; such scope, inner coherence, and self-consistency are marks of truth we identified in Chapter Three.

Yet by the same token, not all that other religions claim is completely false. We live together with our common needs and common humanity in a common universe—God's creation, whether we recognize it as such or not. All human beings have access to this "general revelation," for God has not left himself without witness. Some religions perceive its significance more than others. Some misconstrue, distort, and reject it more than others and add entirely mistaken elements. But the creation and its witness to the Creator is a necessary if insufficient factor in understanding the religions of the world.[6] Paul's preaching built on it, with the added assertion that the witness of nature holds all people accountable to God (Acts 14:15–17; 17:22–31; Rom. 1:15–32).

The Judeo-Christian tradition benefits as well from biblical revelation, and Christianity from its fullness. The content of the New Testament, when all is said, is ultimately responsible for Christianity's richer understanding of God's relationship to us in Jesus Christ. As Karl Barth argues in his classic treatment of creation, faith in Jesus Christ is a life lived in the presence of the Creator, in recognition of his right over us and of his benevolence to us in Christ.[7]

A Christian world view indeed has similarities to non-Christian views, and the Christian religion to non-Christian religions. But the distinctiveness of both the world view and the religion lies most fundamentally in a distinctively Christian understanding of the God-creation distinction and relationship, and at that we now look more closely.

THE COMPONENTS

A Christian world view draws on Christian doctrine for its unifying perspective. The *doctrine* of creation concerns the meaning and implications of the fact that God is the almighty maker of all. Indeed, the Bible is less concerned about *how* God did it than about *who* and *why*: its focus is on theology rather than biology or geology or chronology. Thus the Genesis creation account introduces God's relationship to the world and everything in it, providing the context within which human existence should be understood and life should be lived. Man's meaning is to be found not in himself or in his

6. On this subject see Hendrik Kraemer, *The Christian Message in a Non-Christian World* (New York: Harper and Bros., 1947), and *Religion and the Christian Faith* (Philadelphia: Westminster Press, 1957). Also, E. C. Dewich, *The Christian Attitude to Other Religions* (Cambridge: Cambridge Univ. Press, 1953).

7. Karl Barth, *Church Dogmatics* (Edinburgh: T. & T. Clark, 1958), III,1, p. 32. See further his whole treatment of Christian ethics in III,3.

natural environment but in relationship to the Maker, for God is the source not only of all being but also of value, hope, and purpose. This is the emphasis throughout the Bible.

(1) To get at the components of this doctrine, let us revert first to a term we used in Chapter One to differentiate theism from monism and dualism. *Ex nihilo* (out of nothing) creation is not itself a biblical phrase, unless Hebrews 11:3 hints at it: "what is seen was made out of things which do not appear." But it captures the biblical insistence that God alone is the source of all that is, "alone" apart from any eternal matter or other being. He is therefore not at all dependent on other things; he is free to do as he will, contrary to pantheistic and dualistic claims. The creation is entirely dependent on God, for there is nothing other than him and what he has made. The dependence is asymmetrical, a one-way street: God does not need his creation; he was not forced to make it, nor does he have to create at all.

Here we see what God's trancendence means. First, he is numerically distinct from his creation, being in no sense part of it, nor it part of him. Second, he is qualitatively different from it, eternal and self-existent rather than created and dependent. Third, because the creation depends utterly on him, he remains sovereignly in charge.

(2) Accordingly, a second component is the *continued creative activity* of God, for he is the living God, active in his creation. He did not stop being creative when he rested on the seventh day, but remained actively involved. He continually imparts existence to his creatures, for they were not made to be henceforth self-sustaining. The biblical writers speak of him sustaining also the orderly operation of what he made, of his providential care, of the history of redemption, of his present and coming kingdom—all of this is included in his creative activity, both the old creation and the new. He is "God with us" in all our circumstances, immanent in his works.

When Moses asked God's name he was told "I am who I am" (Exod. 3:14). Various attempts have been made to interpret what was meant by this. Is it a play on the verb "to be" (*hāyāh*) in relation to the name Yahweh (Jehovah)? Is it, then, as Etienne Gilson claims, the metaphysical assertion that God is the very essence of being, a radically different notion than the Greeks ever conceived?[8] Or is it, as John Courtney Murray prefers, a promise that God forever continues to be, and so to be here with us, the Almighty?[9] Whichever was intended—and I find Murray quite persuasive— Moses plainly saw in it the promise of God's continued creativity.

The theme pervades Scripture. Isaiah offers magnificent words of encouragement to Judah:

> Who has measured the waters in the hollow of his hand
>   and marked off the heavens with a span,
>   enclosed the dust of the earth in a measure
>   and weighed the mountains in scales
>   and the hills in a balance?
> Who has directed the Spirit of the Lord,
>   or as his counselor has instructed him?
>
> The Lord is the everlasting God,
>   the Creator of the ends of the earth.
> He does not faint or grow weary,
>   his understanding is unsearchable.
> He gives power to the faint . . . . (Isa. 40:12–13, 28–29)

And Job, too, was reminded of the continued involvement of the Creator and of our "asymmetrical dependence" on the living God, the Lord of creation (Job 38–41).

(3) God creates *freely* and *with purpose*. On the one hand, he is entirely unconstrained, for apart from himself nothing else could even be. Nor does he have any inner compulsion necessitating creation, for he is quite self-sufficient, has no needs, and requires none other for his own satisfaction. He therefore freely chooses *whether* to create or not, as well as *what* to create. But God is not capricious. His choice is purposive, not random. In creating at all, and in continuing to act in his creation, his good ends are unchangingly the same. His gracious purposes are at work throughout history, manifesting his goodness and glory to and through his creatures.

Here the New Testament understanding of creation goes beyond the Old Testament to something fuller. The Creator is the Christ

8. Etienne Gilson, *God and Philosophy* (Bloomington, IN: Indiana Univ. Press, 1941), chap. 2.

9. Murray, *Problem of God*, chap. 1. See also Claude Tresmontant, *Christian Metaphysics* (London: Sheed and Ward, 1965).

himself, and all things were created by him and for him; he holds everything together (Col. 1:16–17). So the creation is inseparable from the kingdom of Christ wherein lies its purpose. And the divine transcendence becomes evident in a purpose that transcends all our little ends and passing days.

The world should not therefore be thought of just mechanistically, in terms of impersonal causal mechanisms, even of mechanisms created by God, for a living and loving God remains active in it. In contrast to the Greek view of time as a recurrent succession of cycles without overarching purpose or ultimate goal, history is an end-pursuing activity of God, the arena of his gracious purposes. The doctrine of creation is the standpoint for a very different view of history and of time.

This is, then, a teleological universe, one designed and guided for the achievement of intended ends. It is not the impersonal teleology of immanent forces limited to processes already given to us in the world as it is, such as some of the Greeks and nineteenth-century evolutionary thinkers asserted. Rather, it is a personal teleology, a transcendent Creator's active pursuit of good ends for his own creation. The means he uses in providence and grace are many: he is the living God.

(4) A fourth component is summed up in the Latin phrase *ad extra*. God creates "to the outside" of himself: he gives something a reality of its own and grants it the exercise of delegated powers. As Barth says, "he does not grudge it its own reality, nature and freedom."[10] But creaturely reality, dependent, contingent, and finite, is different from divine reality. Creaturely freedom, dependent and limited as it is, differs from divine freedom. No finite being can be absolutely free, for by definition the finite is limited and dependent on others. Yet our freedom can nonetheless be real.

God's delegation of powers implies that he works through means that he has made: physical, psychological, economic, and political—for all these are delegated powers. In his general providence God works within their limited possibilities. In special acts of providence he achieves what otherwise would not occur, and miracles transcend the limitations of creaturely processes. Yet none of this is capricious, for in all God does there is purpose.

10. Karl Barth, *Dogmatics in Outline* (London: SCM Press, 1949), p. 54.

(5) Because God delegates powers to his creation, it is consequently *ordered, structured, and law-governed* for good ends. The Old Testament writers acknowledged the orderedness of nature:

> Day to day pours forth speech,
> and night to night declares knowledge. (Ps. 19:2)

> For everything there is a season,
> and a time for every matter under heaven:
> a time to be born, and a time to die;
> a time to plant, and a time to pluck up what is planted;
> a time to kill, and a time to heal;
> a time to break down, and a time to build up;
> a time to weep, and a time to laugh;
> a time to mourn, and a time to dance;
> a time to cast away stones,
> and a time to gather stones together;
> a time to embrace, and a time to refrain from
>   embracing . . . .   (Eccles. 3:1–5)

They find that order in creation makes knowledge possible, even wisdom, because it makes things intelligible and we can learn how to act. Knowledge reveals our interdependence within an overall order (including the ecosystem and biosphere) of which we are a part. The wisdom that guides daily life comes from observing creation's order and taking heed.

That kind of wisdom respects the way things are made. Some might regard them as products of chance, to be adapted and exploited as we wish. But the biblical attitude respects nature's order as God's beneficent doing and heeds it well. The fear of the Lord is thus the beginning of wisdom (Ps. 111:10). This attitude was lacking in those Paul describes in Romans 1, who served the creature rather than the Creator and exchanged the truth of God for a lie.

We live in God's world under the rule of God's law. The concept of natural law, in ethics as well as in science, underscores the fact that both nature and society are subject to the Lord of creation. Some theologians develop this theme by delineating different creation orders (economic, political, familial, etc.), which cannot be reduced one to another but must be respected in their integrity as given. Herman Dooyeweerd speaks of various law spheres, themselves accessible to scientific inquiry, all of which ultimately agree in pointing to the Creator. While their religious and world-viewish significance may be lost on the unbelieving mind, the essential laws in each sphere are equally binding on all.[11]

The concept of law is, of course, biblically based, although some see its extension from ethics and politics to all of nature as a product more of Stoic philosophy than of distinctively biblical themes. Others therefore prefer to speak of a logos structure in creation, picking up on the theme of John's prologue and of Paul's Colossian epistle on the Christ of creation:

> In the beginning was the Word, and the Word was with God, and the Word was God. He was in the beginning with God; all things were made through him, and without him was not anything made that was made. In him was life, and the life was the light of men. (John 1:1–4)

> . . . in him all things were created, in heaven and on earth, visible and invisible, whether thrones or dominions or principalities or authorities—all things were created through him and for him. He is before all things, and in him all things hold together. (Col. 1:16–17)

The Old Testament antecedent of logos is the "word" of God that commanded things into existence (Gen. 1) and becomes God's law to his creatures. But the logos concept has the advantage of tying the doctrine of creation more closely to the person of Christ and his coming kingdom, which as we noted is the distinctively New Testament theme about creation. The idea of a logos structure also draws on earlier Greek concepts: Heraclitus, for instance, proposed that an impersonal logos principle gives rational order to a world of constant change; the Stoics conceived of a cosmic logos ruling through seminal "logoi" in every living thing; Philo regarded the cosmic logos as an emanation from God and so a subordinate deity himself. John may have had this kind of usage in mind in introducing the term "logos," but he is careful, as is Paul in the Colossian epistle, to ascribe personhood and full deity to Christ while speaking of him as the life-giving and living Logos who enlightens the minds and lives of men.[12]

The church fathers built firmly on this logos concept, and it

11. See H. Dooyeweerd, *Roots of Western Culture* (Toronto: Wedge Publishing Foundation, 1979), chap. 2.
12. On this topic, see Carl F. H. Henry, *God, Revelation and Authority* (Waco: Word Books, 1979), vol. III, chaps. 10–15.

became a significant part of their developing theology. In the Arian controversy about the nature of Christ, for example, the full deity of the Logos was challenged by those who wanted to speak of him as of a different nature (*heterousios*) than or a similar nature (*homoiousios*) to the Father. But in the final outcome, the Nicene Council affirmed the same nature (*homoousios*), for otherwise the whole God-creation relationship is confused by an intermediary being, and the Son is not fully the living God acting incarnately for our redemption.

Yet the logos of creation does not as such distinguish separate orders of creation. That idea is rather an inference from "orderliness" to distinguishable "orders." As Emil Brunner points out, the fundamental idea is that there are constants in every aspect of nature which have been created by God, and to know something about them is to know something about the will of God.[13]

(6) God's *purposes* in his work of creation are the basis for all value. This is introduced by the value judgment in Genesis 1—"it was good," five times—and the summary evaluation, "it was very good." "Good" indicates that it was just what God purposed, that creation in every part matched his beneficent purposes and had value accordingly. God said "Yes!" to what he made.[14] This stands in marked contrast to Plato's depreciation of the physical, or to the world-denying aspects of some Eastern and Western mysticism.

In a similar vein, the psalmist repeatedly sings the wonders of nature in praise of its maker: a land that flows with milk and honey is undoubtedly "good." Here is objective basis for aesthetic and economic and other values. But the way God intended things to be also serves as a moral indicator. Jesus points out that "from the beginning" divorce was not intended (Matt. 19:8), and Paul denounces homosexual behavior as "unnatural" (Rom. 1:24-27), while still asserting that "everything created by God is good" (1 Tim. 4:4), including food and sex. He explicitly rejects asceticism, while in the same context he affirms the doctrine of creation (Col. 2:20-23). If God's creation has value, then the enjoyment of its benefits can celebrate God's goodness. All of life, in fact, becomes just such a celebration—provided one recognizes the one who made it so heartily good.

13. Emil Brunner, *The Christian Doctrine of Creation and Redemption* (Philadelphia: Westminster Press, 1952), pp. 24-26.
14. Barth, *Church Dogmatics*, III,1, p. 330.

For this reason the early church rejected the Docetists' claim that Jesus only appeared to have a physical body, for physical things are not evil but good. God is not tainted by a real incarnation, for evil is not inherent in the creation as such.

Here the whole problem of evil intrudes. Did God create this present world and call it good? To answer affirmatively is to be blindly optimistic and ignore the perversion of both nature and man. To answer negatively (as the ancient Gnostics did) is to undercut the entire doctrine of creation that is the core of a Christian world view.

But evil is not God's doing, nor were God's creatures originally made evil. Rather, evil has occurred in a creation that was good. This in bare outline is the basic Christian affirmation. It is customary to distinguish natural from moral evil, the former resulting from natural processes like the tornado and the infections that afflicted Job, the latter including man's own perversity and misbehavior. Natural processes sometimes prevent the realization of good possibilities. They are limiting factors, related to our finiteness and dependency, depriving us of something of value. If, then, God created natural processes freely and with purpose, the question concerns his purpose in it all. But the very question assumes that natural evil is not purposeless, nor dysteleological, and that God has good purpose nonetheless. Aquinas asserted that God permits evil for a greater good, and the history of Christian thought includes a soul-making theodicy to the effect that God intends by means of suffering to build faith and character into our lives.[15] Such was, after all, the case with Job and with a variety of people in the New Testament, like the man born blind (John 9) and Paul's "thorn in the flesh" (2 Cor. 12:7–10).

Moral evil, on the other hand, is our own doing. The biblical emphasis on human responsibility gave rise to the "free will" theodicy, most notably in St. Augustine. At times it is extended to natural evil as well, tracing adversities to human wrongdoing or demonic agency. In either case free agents are responsible.[16] What

15. John Hick traces this tradition in *Evil and the God of Love* (New York: Harper and Row, 1966), but he extends it to moral evil as well as natural. Cf. Aquinas' *Summa Theologica*, I.48–49.

16. See Augustine, *On Free Choice of the Will*. Also Alvin Plantinga, *God, Freedom and Evil* (New York: Harper and Row, 1974; repr. ed. Grand Rapids: Eerdmans, 1977); Hugh Sylvester, *Arguing With God* (Downers Grove: Inter-Varsity Press, 1971); and C. S. Lewis, *The Problem of Pain* (London: Geoffrey Bles, 1940; New York: Macmillan, 1962).

purpose has God in allowing this? Again we are reminded of his benevolence and grace.

First, there is common grace, God's goodness to all people in extending so widely the gifts of his creation and in restraining evil as extensively as he does. But there is also his special grace dramatically revealed in Jesus Christ. The Incarnation is a vivid reaffirmation of a living God's continued activity, of his purpose in creating, and of how he values his creatures. Moreover, Christ's exposure to the evils, natural and moral, that beset humankind was real, and he became the victim of man's inhumanity to man and ingratitude to God. Yet his cross signifies God's grace, and his resurrection proclaims God's triumph over the evil in sin and death. As a *bodily* resurrection, it reaffirms the value of the physical world of which he made us part and became part himself. In the face of the most radical evils, the Christian therefore still affirms the goodness of the creation because he affirms the goodness of God in Christ.

This is an affirmation of hope, not the claim that ours is now the best of all possible worlds. It is the affirmation of a transcendent teleology in which God's good ends will prevail and his kingdom will come. The Christian approach to evil is thus theocentric, not anthropocentric, for the values that evil threatens have a theistic basis. Our highest good, our true well-being, is to serve God's good ends, not the other way around. Understandably, then, we cannot always see how evil benefits us and our little ends, for it may not do so directly and may not at all. This is not an anthropocentric universe. Job's problem remains. Yet it still has purpose, and God in all his goodness is still sovereign. This is what the death and resurrection of Christ proclaim, and that is why the believer can still put his heart into life's tasks.

(7) The final component in a Christian doctrine of creation therefore concerns creational tasks or *mandates* (Gen. 1:26–28). A world view, we have said, mandates certain responsibilities. That God has delegated powers to his creatures implies that we are responsible for assignments that are implicit in the very nature of things. That this is a law-governed creation requires our adherence to that law. That its orderliness is intelligible mandates us to try to understand and to act in relation to what we know. That the creation is good requires us to value it, too.

We shall look in Part Three at what follows for human science, for economic tasks, for beneficent and wise uses of technology, and for human creativity. In all these areas we are servants, not masters; servants who discover order in God's creation and good possibilities in what he has made. These tasks, which serve and bear witness to the Creator, are attended by the handicaps of our finiteness and are twisted by our perversity. Evil and error show themselves in science and art and society: all that man is and does, all of human culture cries out for the grace of God. The whole creation awaits the kingdom yet to come, while yet it praises the Maker.

Within this context the Christian thinks and lives. There can be no legitimate division of life into the secular and sacred, no separation of fact from value, no divorcing of human purposes from God's. Anthropocentrism gives way to a thoroughly theocentric approach to everything. And this, as we shall see, has far-reaching ramifications for ethics and society, for work and technology, and for art and even play. What makes the world and history what they are is not impersonal nature nor arbitrary fate nor human device but rather the creative activity of God.

CHAPTER 5

GOD AND CREATION: PHILOSOPHICAL

In examining the anatomy of world views, we found that while theology expounds the essential beliefs ingredient to a Christian's unifying perspective, philosophy contributes to a particular formulation by addressing metaphysical issues (among other things) that underlie every area of inquiry. The history of philosophy therefore provides a repertoire of ideas that have been formative for world views. In this chapter we shall look at metaphysical concepts that have been brought to bear on the doctrine of creation.

Philosophy itself has been influenced by successive scientific models for understanding nature, and the initial metaphysical formulations we shall look at are modeled on four different scientific views. The problems they pose seem to stem from trying to conceive of everything in the same way as we think of natural processes. The analogy does not always work, and a reductionist tendency often results in which God and man are made in the image of nature. Consequently, I shall suggest that a more personalistic model is needed in formulating a philosophically adequate Christian world view.

SCIENTIFIC MODELS FOR CREATION

(1) One philosophical version that still influences our thinking is *Platonic*. Plato's view of nature was derived largely from Pythagoras' theory that a mathematical order rules throughout the cosmos, producing a harmonious and well-proportioned system where otherwise

71

change and decay would prevail. For Plato matter was uncreated and chaotic, and particular things were formed under the influence of eternal archetypes that (like geometrical patterns or mathematical relations) give the world some semblance of order. The only thing that keeps particulars from disintegrating is their participation in these unchanging forms, which are the only source of goodness and beauty.

Implicit in this account is a dichotomy between eternal, unchanging forms on the one hand, and temporal, changing particulars on the other. Man's soul is eternal, his body temporal. Things of time are markedly inferior, and history is characterized by recurrent cycles that achieve nothing of eternal worth. The eternal alone is good, for it is without beginning or end, without change: it is timeless.

The Greek gods were neither timeless nor perfect. They were quasi-natural beings, subject to whim and change, hence inferior to eternal forms. Insofar as Plato approached the idea of a Supreme and Perfect Being, it was the supreme form, the Form of the Good, that gave order and unity to things. But it did not create out of nothing, nor was it continuously involved in providential activity, nor could it declare creation good and mandate creational tasks. It was the ideal of ultimate perfection and harmonious unity, impersonal, unresponsive, remote, powerless; it was not an object of religious devotion at all, only an object of intellectual contemplation for the rational elite. The "Demiurge" of Plato's *Timaeus* was the effective cause of this world, molding preexistent matter in accordance with eternal form. Matter and form, then, are uncreated ingredients in Plato's ultimate dualism.

But Christianity changed this picture. Some of the church fathers, admiring the emphasis on an eternal soul and an unchanging good, ascribed Plato's wisdom to the eternal logos, the source of all such light. Augustine best adapted Plato for Christian thought. Retaining the time-eternity and body-soul dualisms, and distinguishing the unchanging good of forms from changing particulars, he identified the Form of the Good with God, the One source of all being and goodness. The eternal forms became the eternal counsels of God, his ideas implemented in creation. The divine fiat that called things out of nothing, commanding them to be, Augustine claimed, was the divine word, the logos. By giving forms to shapeless matter—for the earth was "without form and void" (Gen. 1:2)—God created an ordered world of change, and time began.

For all his use of the Platonic model, Augustine was clear-sighted about most of the components of the doctrine of creation: God created *ex nihilo*, for even formless matter was divinely made and is dependent on him; God created freely, in contrast to the necessary emanations of neo-Platonism, and he gave to nature its own order and powers; God made all things good, so that evil is an aberration rather than an essential part of finite existence or an eternal adversary to the good in some dualistic scheme. But Augustine's Platonism created problems. It justified his ascetic tendencies and turned the contemplative life in a mystical direction, for by depreciating the temporal and the changing he had depreciated the creation itself. Since timelessness is better than time and immutability than change, freedom from natural appetites and freedom from change are the ideal. Augustine was particularly close to the neo-Platonism of his day, which superimposed a hierarchical order on things, a great chain of being, complicating Plato's relatively simple ranking of time and eternity. The hierarchical concept affected medieval thinking about good and evil and about the structure of nature and society, whether political, ecclesiastical, or domestic. And it persists in our thinking today.

The heritage of Platonism in Christian thought is a mixed blessing. On the one hand it provides a metaphysic for explaining the order of creation and gives an objective basis to value; on the other hand it introduces an unchanging order, a fixed hierarchy that downplays the gift of being as such. On the one hand it values the eternal, but on the other hand it depreciates the temporal. It confuses evil with change and good with immutability. It stresses contemplation of unchanging truth and the knowledge of God, but not the scintillating variety of earthly experiences. Thus it can detract from daily tasks of stewardly service and the physical enjoyments of life.

(2) By the thirteenth century Plato's distinguished student, *Aristotle*, had been rediscovered, and Christians, like Aquinas, found his a better model than Plato's. The concept of unchanging forms remained, along with the hierarchy of being, but change was no longer seen as chaotic and without good purpose. The hymn line, "Change and decay in all around I see," is Platonic, implying that the two are synonymous. But this was not so for Aristotle and

Aquinas. Rather, change is ordered for good ends: Aristotle's was a more fully teleological metaphysic. Thus every being and every process of change has not only a material cause (the stuff of which it is made), an efficient cause that produces it, and a formal cause that accounts for its structure but also a final cause or good end to which it tends. Creation was likewise for Aquinas, for an analogy exists between all levels of being—natural, human, and divine. God is both the efficient cause whose power creates, the formal cause whose wise counsels order things, and the final cause for whose sake all things exist. Creation is for good ends; it was an act of goodness and of God's love. He chose to create freely and for good. But there was no preexistent matter, no material cause of creation, for creation is out of nothing.

Here, then, is a more positive view that sees the gift of finite and changing being as good. No longer should temporal existence be depreciated. All being is sacred, blessed by God, participating in his purposes, participating in his love. Where the Thomistic view prevails, positive consequences have followed for art and science, along with a lessening of the ascetic and mystical tendencies of the Platonic train. Literature and art have flourished, and some have argued that confidence in the purposive order of nature encouraged scientific inquiry and the rise of modern science.

Yet even with this advance the Greek models still appeared to create problems, which the medievals debated. If in the hierarchy of things particulars are ruled by archetypal forms of universal types, how do we explain individuality and how can individuals be free? And if God created in accordance with universal forms, was his really a free creative act? Is God subordinate to the forms, as in the case of Plato's Demiurge? Or does the analogy between God and other levels of being break down, so that a different model might be needed?

In the fourteenth century, William of Occam rejected the reality of universals, Platonic and Aristotelian alike. Largely out of respect for the sovereignty of God, he explained creation and its order simply as what God willed to be, and the good as what God decrees. But the Greek models address questions that will not go away. Is this a teleological universe, or not? Is nature's orderliness imposed on it from outside, by God's power, or is it somehow inherent in the essential nature of things he made? Are God's good ends revealed in universal aspects of the creation, or are fact and value intrinsically unrelated? Renaissance views of nature pointed to a mechanistic universe ordered by forces imposed on matter, a world of value-free facts, and Christian thought explored that route at length, but Platonic and Aristotelian strains persisted and later surfaced in new shapes.

(3) *Renaissance science* produced what is often called the "billiard ball universe." Without eternal forms or any inner teleology, it settled for causal mechanisms: natural forces move particles of matter, creating new and changing configurations. Most fully developed by Isaac Newton and, in its philosophical implications, by such thinkers as Descartes, Thomas Hobbes, and John Locke, it saw God's act of creation as a supernatural force that caused things to exist that had no prior being, and that started the operation of forces maintaining the natural order. Arguments for the existence of God therefore pointed to a first cause in the vast causal chain (the so-called cosmological proof), and to a cause for the order of nature (the teleological argument). But three emphases went unaccounted for in this model: the purposiveness of God's creation, his continued creative beneficence, and the relation of fact to value. As a result, the God of Christianity seems distanced from the God of mechanistic philosophy.

That God as first cause is not a sufficient account of the biblical Creator became evident in deism, the religious view of such eighteenth-century intellectuals as Voltaire, Thomas Paine, Jefferson, and Franklin. While they acknowledged "the laws of nature and nature's God," they stopped short of accepting his continued creativity in special revelation, in miracles, or in saving grace. Their God was not incarnated as the Christ of the Colossian epistle, the logos-redeemer of all creation. However helpful it may be, then, to think of God as the cause of all, that is neither enough, nor is it distinctively Christian. Others of their contemporaries went further, doubting or rejecting the idea of a first cause altogether, so that a surge of materialism and skepticism arose. The causal proof for God did not seem logically compelling, and for them no vital religious demands required it.

The mechanistic model was extended by some writers into psychology, biology, and what we now call the social sciences. Raising questions about freedom of the will and the nature of human action, they maintained that values are basically desires, physically produced and without normative weight, and that politics and economics have to do not with moral principles but with the rule of laws over constituent elements. The way was opened to deterministic accounts of history. These applications will interest us later.

But some philosophers dissented. One dissenter was George Berkeley, the Irish bishop known to beginning philosophy students for denying the reality of matter; in fact, he denied the independent reality of all the ingredients of the Newtonian model—matter, force, absolute space, and absolute time—arguing that all of them are unempirical abstractions. Our experiences of physical things are caused directly by God rather than by mechanical forces, so that God is continually involved with his creatures' lives. And the German philosopher Leibniz traced matter and motion back to units of force, each with its own good end, generated continually by God. Both he and Berkeley were concerned to provide a more adequate Christian alternative to the mechanistic views of the day. God is more than a first cause, and his relationship to creation is more than a rule of natural forces initiated long ago.

(4) *Nineteenth-century scientific conceptions* provided yet another model for thinking about God and his creation. Dissatisfaction with the mechanistic view of a nature that is lifeless and alien to humankind, and dissatisfaction with the lifeless god of deism that went along with that view became evident in Romanticism. Meanwhile a new awareness of process and change arose, both with the rise of history as a discipline and in developmental biology. At the micro-level modern genetics was beginning and at the macro-level evolutionary theories gained widespread attention. Physics was shortly to provide new understanding of the interrelatedness of things, first in electromagnetic field theory and then in relativity physics. The result was a picture of organismlike growth and unity in nature.

A parallel conception of God and creation rapidly developed, an immanentistic and evolutionary theology. Immanentism reacted against the remoteness of an overly transcendent God with a monistic metaphysic that made God immanent in nature and the human spirit. The first major exponent was Schleiermacher, for whom God is revealed in one's inner experience of dependence on nature as a whole. Analogies can readily be found in the romanticist sense of oneness with Nature (capitalized as if divine), and in American transcendentalists—such as Emerson with his "Oversoul." God is not a transcendent Creator who brought worlds into being out of nothing; in fact, *ex nihilo* creation is explicitly denied. Rather, God is the all-embracing creative spirit manifested in human consciousness and culture.

This so-called World Spirit, like nature itself, is evolving to full self-expression in the course of history. For Hegel, Absolute Spirit is most fully manifested in the flowering of human culture: art, religion, and philosophy. Since this is a metaphysical monism rather than traditional theism, Christian theology can no longer be taken literally but becomes a symbolic way of talking about the creativity of the Absolute. Revelation is present in humankind's highest thoughts. The Incarnation signifies that the logos is in us. Christianity, while further advanced than other religions, is neither qualitatively different nor exclusive in its truth.

From this, one more step leads to recent process theology, a step suggested by A. N. Whitehead's powerful metaphysic based explicitly on the new science but made theologically more explicit by Charles Hartshorne, John Cobb, and others. Here, too, monism prevails in panentheistic form: everything exists *in* God, a constituent in his experience, rather than external to him and created *ex nihilo*. The God-creation relation is therefore symmetrical rather than asymmetrical: the creator is with his creatures, sharing their experiences and their destiny, and he himself changes in certain regards—a far cry from the remote god of deism. But God is only a final cause, luring nature to higher ends, not an efficient cause, a God who acts.[1]

The process model is attractive to some Christians for several reasons. First, it sees the God-creation relation in a continuous historical teleology, rather than as an isolated first beginning of things. Second, it admits that every finite thing is changing and contingent: no fixed forms confuse the scene or depreciate change. Third, it overcomes the radical time-eternity dualism that Plato bequeathed to theology, and so it brings God closer to our experience. Finally, it has made peace with modern science.

But from the perspective of biblical theology problems persist. The process theologian calls God creator in that he provides the goal that draws out nature's creativity and allures it for his ends.

1. Another version of process theology, developed by Teilhard de Chardin, speaks of the progressive divination of the creation. The destiny of the whole creation is a kind of evolving incarnation, for it is gradually taken into the Being of God and redeemed. Parallels occur in Eastern Orthodoxy.

But nature is still immanent in the process-God, part of his experience, not an *ex nihilo* and *ad extra* creation. He does not transcend it, nor does he perform mighty acts in history. The acts of God recited in Scripture are but symbols of his immanence in our creative powers, so that any real difference between nature and grace, or general and special revelation, is forfeited. No uniquely divine Incarnation occurs. Again, if both we and nature are part of God's experience, then the further difference between good and evil blurs, and hope depends on natural historical change rather than on the saving acts of God. A totally different world view, more monistic than theistic, results. Kierkegaard's complaint about the immanence theology of his day applies here: the apostle is reduced to a genius, revelation becomes originality, and the essential qualitative difference between God and man has disappeared. God and man, like king and servant, have become equals. [2]

Both the immanentism of process theology and the claim that God himself undergoes change are due, at least in the Whiteheadian tradition, to an underlying ontology. For Whitehead, all reality is analogous to a complex experience made up of interwoven and successive events. God is the all-encompassing experience, not a transcendent and unchanging being, nor an active agent. To say that God's experience changes with the world-process is therefore to say that God himself changes. Since God's experience is all-inclusive, it draws everything that occurs, good and evil alike, into a harmonious whole. But he is not an unchanging substantial being with changing and satisfying experiences, for being *is* experience. He is therefore not a transcendent, free, independent God of biblical theism, nor is he a supernatural agent who acts in a world he created *ex nihilo* and *ad extra*. Process theology is closer to a monistic view, with consequent difficulties in distinguishing good from evil and nature from humankind, as well as in distinguishing God from his creation. In fact, Whitehead speaks of creativity independently of God.

What of the evolutionary concept, on which a lot of process thought depends? A great amount of debate here has been chasing red herrings. The fixity of species is not a biblical but an Aristotelian doctrine that leads us away from the real issues, for an ordered

2. Soren Kierkegaard, "The Difference Between a Genius and an Apostle," published in *The Present Age* (New York: Harper & Row, Harper Torchbooks, 1962).

creation may or may not require fixed species. Nor is the origin of biological life a biblical issue, except in that God is ultimately Creator of all, Creator of every kind of thing. "Life" in the biological sense may well be a function of highly complex chemical processes, rather than something over and above them.[3] Nor is the antiquity of the earth an issue. None of these are biblical concerns. The biblical focus from which we must not be diverted is rather on God as transcendent maker of all, on the goodness of his handiwork, on the uniqueness of humankind, and all this with a view to relating humankind to the Creator in whose image we stand.

This is not to say that the evolutionary account is problem-free. The incompleteness of the fossil record, the intermittent nature of evolutionary change, and the uncertain connection between differences in genes and differences in anatomy and behavior—such factors allow the possibility of other modes of change than a gradual process of natural selection. And evolution leaves the question of ultimate origins unanswered. Major tensions arise, moreover, when evolutionary explanations are universalized. In the first place, when everything, man and God included, are made entirely subject to evolutionary origin and development, then their transcendence of nature—their uniqueness, their independence of action, their freedom—is lost. This is what tends to happen in process and immanentist theologies. In the second place, when everything is explained *entirely* in terms of the physical, then evolutionary theory has become evolutionism, a metaphysical theory, a naturalistic version of monism with all of monism's problems. And this is what happens in naturalistic humanism. The tension is between theism and imperialistic, scientistic reductionism. It is "scientism," not science, that confuses science with metaphysics and universalizes a theory of limited scope.

Whether the human race was divinely created by evolutionary means is another matter, for the doctrine of creation entails God's use of the powers he delegated to nature. Some Christian writers accordingly accept an emergent evolutionary account of human

3. Still an option for some, however, is vitalism, the view that life is a force or energy distinct from the elements of purely material things. This view, traceable to Aristotle, was popularized by Henri Bergson in the early twentieth century and is represented today by Hans Jonas in *The Phenomenon of Life* (New York: Harper and Row, 1966). Sometimes it is associated with panpsychism the view that all of nature is in some sense alive, a view espoused by Charles Hartshorne.

origins in which God creatively guides the process. Others hold (as I do) that some kind of special creative act of God is indicated in the Genesis account and is implied by human uniqueness, while acknowledging that our relation to nature exposes us to subsequent microevolutionary influences. The issue here is partly hermeneutical (how Genesis should be interpreted) and partly metaphysical (whether God's image in man can be adequately explained in evolutionary terms). It is not a choice between explicit biblical statements and a scientific theory but a question about theological and philosophical theories that relate the two.

Fundamental to the debate, then, is the God-creation distinction. Evolutionary philosophies stress developmental possibilities inherent in nature itself, often within a purely naturalistic framework, as if nature, man, morality, and society are one unbroken continuum. Process theologies major in God's relationship to nature and his presence within human history and experience, as if the continuum runs from God through the human spirit into material things, and all are gradations of one and the same Being. God's transcendence is missing, both his qualitative otherness and the numerical distinctness by virtue of which he is free to act in his creation in ways that immanent processes alone could not produce. An immanent teleology is their stress, not a transcendent God who acts. But for Christian theism the created world is not a finite and passing appearance of some more inclusive reality; it is real in itself, even if dependent on God.

We have seen four ways of conceptualizing the God-creation relationship:

	Point of Origin	Concept of Nature	God the Creator
(1)	Plato	transcendent forms, time-eternity dualism	gives form to matter
(2)	Aristotle	inner teleology	gives being and purpose
(3)	Renaissance	causal mechanisms	causes what is
(4)	Nineteenth Century	process and organic unity	is Being itself

The problems pose a methodological question: if God (and human beings to a lesser extent) is qualitatively different from nature, how far can models drawn from natural science help? Are we not asking for problems by conceiving of God in the image of nature?

To get at this methodological question, consider whether God, on "nature" models, can still be conceived of as a fully personal being. Monistic philosophies have most difficulty here, and naturalism most of all, if nature is unthinking, unloving, unchoosing in all it does. For God the Creator thinks, loves, and chooses. How, then, can understanding nature help us to understand persons, especially a personal God who, unlike us, is not part of the natural world at all? He is far more discontinuous from nature than we, and transcends it in ways that we do not. Idealistic forms of monism have trouble too, for personhood implies a capacity for deliberate action, which in turn implies an agent who transcends the situation in which he acts. Yet the idealistic monism that underlies much of immanentist theology denies God that transcendence. Hegel's Absolute does not love or choose or act, but habitually and relentlessly manifests its own self-concept in outward ways. Hartshorne ascribes personality to God, but only the muted personality of an all-embracing, sympathetic consciousness without any power to act in ways that transcend the ordinary processes of nature and history. And Paul Tillich, whose theology also is shaped by the German immanentist tradition, takes the notion of a personal God to mean not that God is a personal being who acts but only that he is the ground of our personhood—the ground of our courage to be persons at all. A more fully personalistic model is needed.

PERSONALISTIC MODELS FOR CREATION

The concept of a person received new attention as a result of Immanuel Kant's clear-cut distinction between natural processes determined by causal mechanisms and free moral agents acting out of respect for duty. The distinguishing thing about persons was no longer rationality in the sense of theoretical or contemplative thought but rather the freedom to act under one's own direction. This emphasis has been developed in various ways, providing nonscientific models for thinking about God, nonscientific at least in terms of natural science, although personality theory and the "sciences of man" may well contribute.

(1) One model comes from American *personal idealism* and in

particular from B. P. Bowne, E. S. Brightman, and Peter Bertocci.[4] Creation *ex nihilo*, Bertocci argues, is essential not only in distinguishing theism from dualism and monism, but also in explaining the orderly world in which we live and the freedom humans experience. For how could dualism give ordered unity and how could monism find room for individual freedom within an inwardly determined whole? But how should we conceive of God and his creative act? Bertocci's model, adapted in measure from the personality theory of Gordon Allport, is that the person is "a knowing-willing-caring unity in continuity." God is a "unity in continuity" in that he is unchanging in the structural unity and essential form of his person, unchanging therefore in the loving purpose that guides his creative activity, but he experiences changing awarenesses and satisfactions as the finite persons he creates exercise their delegated powers. God, like other persons, is conceived of as being temporal while having continued self-identity; but unlike other temporal beings he is everlasting.

This "temporalistic" view parts company with Plato's time-eternity dualism, but it also differs from process theology in ascribing to God the richer personal qualities of knowing, willing, and loving, as well as the kind of unchanging identity and transcendence of his creatures that theism needs. However, problems arise with the metaphysical idealism that is involved. As Brightman sees it, while created persons plainly have separate identity from God, so that God's transcendence is preserved in that regard, this is not the case with nature. The natural world is not a reality in itself distinct from God, but is rather the creation of a changing yet continuous experience within God that he yet shares with created persons. It is our direct experience, and God's, of God's own self-created experiences, not of a world external to God and us, and qualitatively different. Divine transcendence and *ex nihilo* creation are therefore compromised, and nature's delegated powers can no longer be a factor in explaining natural evil. Further, what God experiences so depends on what we do in the natural world that God is limited in his power to achieve the experience he purposes for himself and us without our cooperation as his cocreators.

4. Peter Bertocci, *The Person God Is* (New York: Humanities Press, 1970), especially chaps. I and XI; E. S. Brightmen, *Person and Reality* (Ronald Press, 1958) and *A Philosophy of Religion* (Englewood Cliffs: Prentice-Hall, 1940).

Bertocci still stresses the teleology involved. His case for theism involves an enlarged teleological argument that appeals not only to our own experience of nature's orderliness but also to the rich moral, aesthetic, social, and religious experience that life affords: the reality behind it all must value these things, and must be a Person himself. Religious experience, moreover, is a creative struggle amid the insecurities that evil brings, an enriching struggle that contributes to making people and lives more valuable. In this "soul-making theodicy" an overall teleology prevails, for evil does not frustrate God's purposes but is ingredient to their achievement.[5]

The problem is not with these teleological claims as such, but with two features underlying them. First, it is unduly optimistic to assume that all the extreme forms of evil we know, while indigenous to things, will in the natural course of events be eliminated. Bertocci allows for no willful human fall into sin and no culminating intervention by omnipotent deity, as Christian orthodoxy does in treating the problem of evil. So the goodness of the original creation is called into question, along with the transcendent power of God. God and man struggle together to create a world for themselves that eventually will be good. This optimism is remarkably akin to that of the evolutionary theology from which it is historically descended.

Second, the underlying thesis that nature exists only as the creative experience of God and other persons is highly implausible. It is the kind of phenomenalism that George Berkeley first proposed, and that became widespread among some forms of nineteenth-century idealism. But the *prima facie* evidence is stacked against it. In the first place, a realistic epistemology more readily fits our ordinary experience of nature. Material things and causal processes give every appearance of existing independently and of functioning "under their own steam"; and the experience of our own "embodiment," as various phenomenological philosophers have argued, acquaints us directly with the causal efficacy of the world. In the second place, a more realistic epistemology is appropriate in natural science. Admittedly, scientific knowledge interprets its data and remains somewhat provisional, but the repeatability and predictability of scientific findings and the vast superstructures of scientific technology amass a *prima facie* case for the reality of physical things. In the third

5. See *Religion as Creative Insecurity* (Westport CT: Greenwood Press. 1958), and *Introduction to the Philosophy of Religion* (Englewood Cliffs: Prentice-Hall, 1951).

place, a realistic view of nature is the most natural reading of the doctrine of creation. The down-to-earth acceptance of physical things that the Old Testament writers manifest, along with God's delegation of powers to an *ad extra* creation, most readily points in a realist direction. In terms of logical consistency, metaphysical idealism may indeed be possible, but at the cost of almost squeezing human experience into unrecognizable shape. If it is so implausible, moreover, the claim also is implausible that evil has no basis outside the experience of God, and that God is therefore limited in his power. Some other metaphysic is needed.

(2) Personalistic models as distinct from "nature models" appear in other contexts, too. Existentialists, like Kierkegaard and Sartre, focus on *freedom as the distinctive* of persons. Sartre does so by denying the ultimacy of any universals, any natural order, any structure of laws, any meaning or purpose. There is neither an immanent nor a transcendent teleology, for existence is prior to any fixed essence at all. Sartre saw that Christian philosophers rightly linked the notion that things have essential nature in an ordered world with the idea that they are the products of a rational creator.[6] So he denies the existence of God. If God is dead then anything is possible, and our freedom is therefore absolute. For Sartre, this is dreadful. He is indeed a humanist, for he believes that values are of our own making; but no ultimate hope results.

Kierkegaard, on the other hand, is a theist who recognizes limitations to the freedom creatures can enjoy. Freedom to choose and act out of what I am inwardly, the freedom to be a subject who initiates his action rather than being just an object acted upon—this kind of freedom is essential to faith and love. Inwardly, in the heart, a person believes; inwardly he loves. Martin Buber accordingly describes the difference between an interpersonal "I-Thou" relationship and an impersonal "I-It." The I-Thou is marked by faith and love, by empathy, rapport, mutual understanding, and communication that deeply affect the persons involved. An I-It relationship is objective and detached, perhaps using the other as a means to one's own ends.

Christian theologians have picked up on these proposals and applied them to God. Some, like Barth, speak of God as a subject

---

6. On this point, see E. L. Mascall, *The Importance of Being Human* (New York: Columbia Univ. Press, 1958), pp. 22f.

free to act as he will toward his creation. Others, like Emil Brunner, suggest that God reveals himself to us in I-Thou fashion rather than revealing objective I-It truth. On the other hand, are personal relationships even possible without some knowledge of what the other person is like? We reveal things about ourselves both by what we say and by what we do, and knowledge about a person can make or break a relationship. Various degrees of objectivity are present all the time, and so revelation can be both personal and objectively informative at once.

Yet the existentialist has recovered an important theme by stressing the concept of a personal God who freely acts in relationship to his creatures. For example, Soren Kierkegaard's *Concluding Unscientific Postscript* masterfully traces the limitations of objective knowledge, whether philosophical or historical, in one's becoming a Christian, and shows how a full and inwardly passionate faith is elicited by the dramatic action of the personal God incarnated in Jesus Christ. Theologians Thomas Torrance and Gordon Kauffman have employed an analogous model, drawing on the Scottish philosopher John Macmurray, who develops from Kant his concept of persons as active agents.[7] For all these writers, the model of free personal action helps explicate the God-creation relationship.

(3) Another personalistic model comes from recent *analytic philosophy*, where a distinction has been drawn, based on what ordinary language reveals of human experience, between events and actions.[8] An event is produced by causes and therefore occurs in the natural course of things. An action is performed by an agent for reasons of his own and with inner intentions. An action might be prevented by moral persuasion, but not an event. The one is personal and free, but not the other.

The living God of Christian theism is an agent who acts. Creation was not a natural event with natural causes, nor were the

7. See John Macmurray, *The Self as Agent* (London: Faber & Faber, 1957); T. F. Torrance, *Theological Science* (New York: Oxford Univ. Press, 1969); G. Kauffman, *God the Problem* (Cambridge: Harvard Univ. Press, 1972). Also cf. Helmut Thielicke, *The Evangelical Faith*, vol. I (Grand Rapids: Eerdmans, 1974), and Robert Blaikie, *Secular Christianity and The God Who Acts* (Grand Rapids: Eerdmans, 1970).

8. For example, L. W. Beck, *The Actor and the Spectator* (New Haven: Yale Univ. Press, 1975), and G. E. M. Anscombe, *Intention* (London: Blackwell, 1957). The distinction goes back to Aristotle's *Nicomachean Ethics*.

Incarnation, the prophetic word, or Christ's founding of his church. These were intentional acts of God, for reasons of his own. Miracles are spoken of in the New Testament as signs and wonders, signs of God's activity that make us wonder at his power and purpose. They require the notion of persons, not the analogy to a natural process.

The model works, moreover, without a time-eternity disjunction. God's transcendence and sovereignty are preserved without a Platonic timeless eternity devoid of change, successive experiences, or duration. How a timeless God could purpose, act, and then delight at the outcome would remain unknown. Rather, on the personal action model, his sovereignty is preserved by his mighty acts: the Creator-Logos acts in providence, in revelation and Incarnation, in saving grace, in his church, and in final triumph. The concept of an agent who acts clears the ground for such affirmations.

Eternity need not mean timelessness but simply everlasting duration, in God's case without creaturely limitations but with perfect memory and anticipation, with an unbroken flow of consciousness devoid of frustrated purpose or of change of mind and intention. As the "Supreme Agent," God transcends all others and remains forever the sovereign Creator of all.

The picture that results, then, is not of one great chain of being in which all beings, God included, differ only by degree and so are qualitatively alike. God's transcendence means not only that he is numerically distinct from his creation but also that he is qualitatively different. Of all his creatures, we are told, humans bear the clearest resemblance to their maker; yet God is far more than any image we bear.

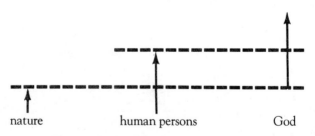

As the above diagram suggests, in some regards we are qualitatively like the natural world, yet in other regards quite different. We are persons, free agents, able to transcend in some ways the causal processes that otherwise rule. In this regard we image God.

But God has no roots in nature at all, so there the analogy between him and human beings ceases. He is absolutely free. He is infinite in wisdom, goodness, love, and power, the catechism states, and we are finite in these qualities. But God is qualitatively far more than all of this, for he is *sui generis*, unique, the only God there is, and he is self-existent.

The process categories of the nineteenth-century model, therefore, seem remarkably applicable to man as part of nature but pose problems when it comes to humans as persons and to God. Is God in process at all? The Bible suggests what the agent model implies: successive acts which he anticipates, acts he subsequently performs, whose results he calls good. But God himself, who he is in his nature and character, does not change. This is not the symmetrical relationship of process theology in which both God and the world are changed:

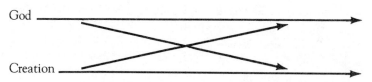

Nor is it the unmoved and unmoving God of Platonic dualism or Enlightenment deism:

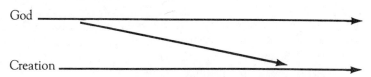

It is, rather, an asymmetrical relationship in which God both cares for the lilies and sparrows, and rejoices when sinners repent:

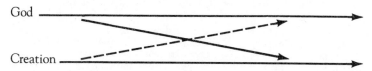

Thus a Christian view of the God-creation relationship can avoid the pitfalls against which recent religious thought has over-reacted, and can learn from what both process and existential thinkers have tried to reinsert. The One who acts is indeed a living God who is with us, the source of hope in every sphere of life.

PHILOSOPHICAL THEOLOGY

First, it is clear by now that we should distinguish at least three qualitatively different kinds of being: nature, man, and God. Limited analogies exist between nature and man (as we shall see further in the next chapters), and a different analogy exists between man and God, but no overall qualitative similarity runs through them all beyond the fact that they all *are*.[9] Monistic metaphysics, which makes everything qualitatively alike, distorts the picture either of nature (as does idealism) or of man (as does naturalism) or of God (as does anything less than a theism with creation *ex nihilo*). Monisms have a reductionist effect, leveling differences too real to deny.

Second, thinking about nature as the ordered creation of God may well be feasible with any of the scientific models that have so far dominated Western thought. Indeed, Christian theists have worked with each, and made notable attempts to handle the implicit problems. In terms of nature itself as seen by modern science, the process model is persuasive, although it is important to insist on an ordered and law-governed process. A theory of universals must therefore come into play. Nature itself allows a vast array of possibilities, only some of which are ever actualized, universal possibilities rather than simply particular events. But nature disallows other possibilities: granted the laws that govern the world, some things are inconsistent with those laws. In this sense, ours is one ordered world out of many that are possible, with distinguishable classes of things and definable uniformities, a world of intricately interwoven events. This reverses the Platonic picture in which universal forms were more real than the world of particulars, so that universals can now be conceived of as possibilities, and the particulars that actualize some of those possibilities as the world that is real.[10]

9. ie., the distinctiveness of these three kinds of being does not preclude the fact that they are all *beings*. Scholastic metaphysics allows an analogy between all beings in terms of their transcendental qualities, i.e., qualities that transcend all difference of kind, and Duns Scotus affirmed the univocity of being. Yet of God it must still be said that he is the only self-existent one.

10. Whitehead's metaphysical categories, it seems to me, may well be applicable to nature, despite their insufficiency in regard to human persons and their marked inadequacy in regard to the Judeo-Christian God. He treats universals as eternal possibilities. So, too, does N. Wolterstorff in *On Universals* (Chicago: Univ. of Chicago Press, 1970). And Alvin Plan-

Third, human persons are free agents who actualize possibilities in both themselves and their world, which nature as such would not produce. This raises old questions about the relation of mind to body, about freedom and determinism, and about the relation of human values to the possibilities we perceive. These questions we shall take up in later chapters.

Fourth, the personalistic model for thinking about God's relationship to his creation is consonant with what we have called a transcendent teleology. That is to say, the end-achieving character of things is due not just to the ordinary processes of nature and history, but also to the providential and redemptive activity of a transcendent personal deity. Evil is both allowed for good purpose and is made by God's mighty acts to serve those ends. In the final analysis, history and the entire world-process, for all the evils that arise, are not dysteleological but teleological.

Finally, what does this suggest about natural theology's classic arguments for the existence of God? Each of the philosophical formulations at which we have looked has its forms of argumentation, and invariably the arguments have their critics. Characteristic of the Platonic variety is the ontological argument that Anselm developed, which begins with the innate idea of a most perfect being, and argues that such a being necessarily exists. A perfect being is analogous to Plato's Form of the Good, which is also the most real being in the entire hierarchy of beings. It is Anselm's Platonism which therefore makes his argument work, but it is also the Platonic depreciation of nature which leads him to an argument that ignores natural objects together. On the other hand, Aquinas' proofs began with Aristotelian concepts about nature and change, and he argued certain attributes of God by analogy from similar attributes in the whole hierarchy of things. The mechanists emphasized causal arguments and claimed that this ordered universe requires an intelligent cause. And the nineteenth- and twentieth-century immanentists found evidence in religious experience, moral con-

tinga has developed a "possible worlds" ontology in relation to theism in *The Nature of Necessity* (Oxford: Oxford Univ. Press, 1974). Of related interest is Nelson Pike, *God and Timelessness* (London: Routledge & Kegan Paul, 1970), and Wolterstorff's "God Everlasting," in *God and the Good*, ed. L. Smedes and C. Orlebeke (Grand Rapids: Eerdmans, 1975), pp. 181–203.

sciousness, aesthetic experience, or existential concern to argue to an all-encompassing Ground of Being.

What strikes me in the light of this rehearsal is that both the God-concepts involved and the arguments offered are system-dependent. That is, they take the forms they do under the influence of a philosophical scheme; they trade on a philosophically developed model. God is the *ens perfectissimum*, the Form of the Good, the most perfect being. He is both a necessary being and an unmoved mover. He is the first cause in the whole series of natural causes. He is the immanent Ground of Being. The biblical account of God the Creator leaves this God of the philosophers far behind. Where in natural theology is the God of Abraham, Isaac, and Jacob who became incarnate for man's redemption? At its very best, natural theology remains incomplete, hungry for the self-revelation of a living God who acts. Its God is not distinctively Christian.

Discussion of theistic arguments usually focuses on their logic. What do they prove? What is their worth? The problem is twofold. First, are the premises sufficient to imply the conclusion and sufficiently neutral not to beg the question? Are they known to be certainly true so as to produce certainty about the conclusion? Second, is the argument itself logically valid? Does the conclusion validly follow? The answers are by no means clear. Hume and Kant challenged the underlying epistemologies and questioned both the premises and the validity of the arguments. But supposing that the arguments are logically inconclusive, what then is their worth?

Their very system-dependency turns out, to my mind, to be their strength, for thereby the central role of the God-concept in each of their philosophical systems is exhibited. Each scheme is incomplete without the Creator-God. But he is no last addendum, for the God-concept unifies and interrelates everything else and provides overall coherence. That kind of coherence, we recall, attests to truth.

The coherence of a Christian world view seems more complete and compelling with a personalistic formulation than on the nature-models of earlier thought. The Platonist indeed needed a most perfect being to complete and unify his system, the Thomist a necessary being and prime mover, the mechanist a first efficient cause, and the idealist an immanent Ground of Being. God, so conceived, satisfies the philosophical need to complete and unify one's understanding. But can any and every philosophical conception of God serve as the supreme good a world view calls for, unifying human values and purposes and giving ultimate meaning to life? Where in their schemes is the living God we need? Yet it is precisely this need which the personal agent model meets, extending beyond the theoretical demands of abstract thought to the more existential demands of life and hope.[11] Any argument for God as agent will of course be system-dependent, too. George Mavrodes suggests that arguments are person-relative in not being uniformly persuasive.[12] This is plainly so with an agent-God argument: it will be most effective for those who, seeking the supreme good, see that only a God who acts gives life unity, wholeness, and hope. This subjective precondition affects the argument's worth. As Jesus himself said: "If any man is willing to do . . . he will know."

---

11. Unusual in this regard is Richard Swinburne who, in *The Existence of God* (New York: Oxford Univ. Press, 1979), develops a cumulative inductive argument for the existence of a personal agent God modeled not on scientific-type causal explanations but on explanation by reference to a person's intentions. He appeals both to the inner coherence of theistic belief and to the superiority of theistic to nontheistic explanations. See also *The Coherence of Theism* (New York: Oxford Univ. Press, 1977).

12. George Mavrodes, *Belief in God* (New York: Random House, 1970), chaps. 1 and 2.

CHAPTER 6

PERSONS IN CONTEMPORARY PERSPECTIVE

The first and overarching theme of a Christian world view is the God-creation distinction and relationship: we think about everything within that framework and live in every sphere of life in relation to the God who acts. The second major theme has to do with human persons, what we distinctively are and what meaning human existence has. The fact that it is second to the overall God-creation theme immediately distinguishes Christianity from naturalistic humanism, where human beings come first and everything else follows, and where both God and man are engulfed by impersonal processes and events. But we need to pursue the contrast further than that if we are to see what a Christian view of persons really offers us today. This chapter therefore looks at two key aspects of naturalistic humanism's thinking on the subject, human freedom and human failure, examining some historical models it has adopted in order to see what, from a Christian perspective, is missing. The following chapter will then develop a Christian view more fully.

HUMAN FREEDOM

To the modern mind, freedom is an enigma, even a sadistic lie. We find ourselves in the grip of forces beyond our control, biological and historical forces that seemingly make us what we are, then sweep us along and engulf us in their impersonal path. Genetics, depth psychology, behavioral conditioning, and socioeconomic conditions can be neither avoided in life nor ignored in thought.

Like powerless observers bound to the screen of life, we watch the relentless rise and fall of political leaders, the irresistible surge of social forces, the exploding emotions of the repressed and under-privileged, and inevitable reactions from the left and from the right. In the face of all this, are we free? In what sense? To what degree? To what end? Or is freedom, along with all the hopes we tie to it, an illusion?

(1) *The rationalist model.* Naturalistic humanism, we have noted, takes a number of forms, some of which draw from the Greeks an emphasis on reason's liberating power. In the Aristotelian model, humans are distinguished from other species as *rational* animals, and so we alone in nature can be free. I say "can be," because the potential for rationality is not always actualized, and unless it is actualized freedom is not possible.

Aristotle in effect defines freedom as deliberation plus deci-sion:[1] by nature we seek good ends, but we deliberate about possible means to those ends, then choose whichever means are most prac-ticable. That we choose the means we employ implies that actions can be voluntary and that we can voluntarily develop habits: virtue and vice are within our power. But this depends on our rationality, and three kinds of people are insufficiently rational to be free: young children, women, and some men who by their nature should be slaves. All these must be ruled by others rather than being treated as free.

Undoubtedly ignorance is a cruel master, and some degree of understanding is essential to freedom in any meaningful sense: oth-erwise we function by caprice or chance and are carried along by emotions or whim or past conditioning. While Aristotle's identifi-cation of who is sufficiently rational is blatantly aristocratic and chauvinistic, two more basic assumptions quickly surface. In the first place, he thinks that people naturally seek the good. They may of course be mistaken as to what ends in fact are best, but this is a matter of ignorance, which reason might correct. If the good is always what they really desire, however, no place is left for moral perversity and radical evil, as Kant called it, which ignores the right in its desire for other ends. People in fact often ignore moral ques-tions because of their self-interest, and even become enslaved to their passions and habituated away from what they recognize to be

1. *Nicomachean Ethics*, III. 1–5.

good. Aristotle might say this is contrary to nature, a moral weakness or an abnormal condition, but freedom from moral perversity does not come just by rational deliberation over means. Deliberation can be a mask, self-deceptive, and decisions can be self-serving, when emotions are tied to bad ends, not good.

In the second place, then, Aristotle further assumes that reason can overrule irrational desires and emotions. He does not unmask the self-deceptions of reason, to which a Christian understanding of human depravity alerts us, and which Hegel later described. Nor is he sufficiently realistic about the moral struggle we all experience between what we know and what we want regardless. He recognizes a difference between moral weakness and moral strength, and the need to cultivate the latter; but he assigns that task to reason, thinking it can overrule emotional distractions. The conflict is simply one of reason versus emotion: we are rationally ruled animals, so reason can always win. It is this conception of persons, and the too easy optimism that goes with it, that Christian theology and human experience alike question; as Augustine pointed out, we are ruled more strongly by what we most love than by what we know.

The rule of reason in relation to human freedom was upheld by the Stoics, it reappeared in Enlightenment political and ethical theories, and today it feeds the hopes of scientific humanism for the human race and its future. But a further problem arises with a contemporary naturalistic metaphysic. Aristotle believed that reason can rule because it is the distinctive function of the human soul, which is itself qualitatively different from body and bodily functions. The Stoics believed that reason rules because it rules the entire cosmos. Enlightenment thinkers believed it on a similar basis: the laws of nature and nature's God reflect God's reason and are reflected in our own reason, which is the distinctive function of the human soul, not just of the body. But naturalism allows us no such luxury as a soul. Rather, we are entirely a part and product of the physical world, with no immaterial part to us and no ingredient essentially different from what other physical things have. Yet if reason is not an independently powerful force, able itself to initiate action and control behavior, but is instead a function of brain processes that we cannot fully control, then can reason ever be a sufficient cause of freedom?

The rationalistic model for understanding freedom, despite its long and influential role in Western thought, does not seem a sufficient explanation. True, in reasoning we do objectify situations, somewhat freeing ourselves from unreflective and unconscious involvements. True, reasoning can persuade and guide. It appears necessary to human freedom, but is it sufficient? And what influences rule reason? It can hardly be wholly independent and autonomous, in the light of what is known about the sociology of knowledge, the cultural conditioning of thought, and other historical and personal influences on our thinking. And the causal mechanisms of behavioral science pose additional problems, both for the rule of reason in particular and for freedom in general.

(2) *The mechanistic model.* Casual explanations of human behavior, including verbal and cognitive behaviors, have become the stock-in-trade of behavioral science. Strictly speaking, it is recognized that we only describe regularly observable sequences of events rather than actual causal connections between successive events. But regularity still suggests causal necessity, and some naturalists conclude that human behaviors are strictly determined in a mechanical fashion rather than being freely adopted and freely developed. By implication at least, this is the position of B. F. Skinner and the radical behaviorists.

Mechanistic determinism is not new. In antiquity, materialists, like Democritus, held that view, as did the seventeenth-century British thinker Thomas Hobbes and the Frenchman d'Holbach with his so-called "hard determinism." While contemporary behaviorism is much more subtle and complex than such antecedents and appeals to far more impressive empirical evidence, the conceptual model involved is essentially the same: cause-effect mechanisms rule human thought, values, and behavior.

Freedom is thus thrown into question. Some in effect deny it any actuality at all: note Skinner's title, *Beyond Freedom and Dignity.* Those who do find it a place may regard freedom as indeterminism, and a free decision or action as one wholly uncaused. Appeals have been made, for example, to the Heisenberg principle of indeterminacy, suggesting that the problem in predicting both the direction and the velocity of submolecular particles is due to actual indeterminacy, rather than to casual interferences we cannot altogether control. Again, modern physics is sometimes said to allow for human freedom during quantum leaps. These considerations may indeed indicate that the case for mechanistic determinism at the micro-level is incomplete, but it is plainly insufficient as an account of freedom. Human choices and actions operate at the macro-level, affecting bodies and ordinary events where physical indeterminacy and quantum leaps are not in evidence. But more than that, freedom is not simply *in*determinism, a lack of any causal connectedness, and unconscious cause-effect mechanisms are not the only influences at work. It is a kind of self-determination, in which personal factors of a nonmechanical sort are at work, too: the influence of other persons we respect and love, interpersonal dynamics, ideals that attract, ends we adopt, and the like. Within any materialistic view, the term "cause" has to stretch beyond the mechanical to embrace all of these.

One alternative, I suggest, is to think of freedom on a more personalistic and teleological model in which the purposes and values we deliberately embrace play the crucial part. Teleology means that a process or activity is end-oriented rather than just antecedent-oriented, so that intentions and ideals also shape what we do. Human action starts with the freedom to consider pursuing some project, and then the nature of that project defines what is actually possible in the light of the limitations that various causal mechanisms impose. Thus causes operate too, creating both the situations in which freedom acts and the possibility and limits of action. Physical circumstance, genetic inheritance, and so forth are causally given; they define the limits of what is possible, and perhaps incline us more in one direction than another. But at times the values we see in another direction become attractive and alluring, and that direction takes precedence over what would eventuate if we did nothing at all. We then break away from the prior process and rise above the "otherwise" course of events in pursuit of our ends. In retrospect, we say that we could have done otherwise than we did, that we had the power of contrary choice. What decides things here is often the values we have interiorized for ourselves and have made our own in the projects we pursue. In some cases it takes a major effort of will to counter habits and, as C. A. Campbell points out, to resist the temptations of our own nature.[2] This is not a teleology,

2. C. A. Campbell, *In Defense of Free Will* (London: Allen and Unwin, 1967), chaps. 1–3. See also A. I. Melden, *Free Action* (London: Routledge & Kegan Paul, 1961); Richard Taylor, *Action and Purpose* (Englewood Cliffs: Prentice-Hall, 1966); and Gerald Dworkin, ed. *Determinism, Free Will and Moral Responsibility* (Englewood Cliffs: Prentice-Hall, 1970).

then, that is altogether immanent in nature; it is a teleology that is free at times to transcend immanent processes.

This is often true of the way we influence one another. In an I-Thou relationship that makes the other person an end-in-herself, of value for her own sake and considered in all one does, the other person is not manipulated or forced in mechanical fashion. Rather, she is liberated from both outer constraints and inner restraints, to think and act freely for herself. The relationship offers values she freely embraces. On this model, freedom is the capacity to transcend what causal mechanisms alone would produce, the capacity to act for the sake of ends with inner self-determination. This "libertarian" alternative is neither complete indeterminism, nor is it a matter of causal necessity.

The mechanist's problem is that he sees the person as a natural object in relation to nature alone, rather than as a person in relation to persons. Such a monistic outlook reduces persons to something less than persons, and in the process either makes freedom hardly possible at all, or else leaves it an undefined something that operates in the gaps between causes.

(3) *The romanticist model.* For some, this is an appealing alternative to those lifeless mechanisms and to the rationalist model. Freedom is not a gap in the deterministic chain, a gap that allows whatever may be to be, nor is it a product of reason alone. Rather, freedom is native to the human spirit, to the vitality of an inner creative force that runs throughout all nature. While some earlier Romanticists, Coleridge for example, were philosophical idealists who traced this vitality to an all-encompassing Spirit, others were naturalists who traced both natural and human creativity to the vitality of nature itself. Biological vitalism, the view that life is a force distinct from inert matter or mechanical causes, was its typical basis, and human freedom is its most highly developed manifestation. Freedom, then, is a biologically based spontaneity that surprises us with novel ideas and actions.

Again, however, I question whether spontaneous novelty or a creative drive are all that human freedom is, different only in degree from unpredictable events in nature, whether novel species or novel animal behaviors. Biological vitalism, moreover, was a hypothesis introduced to explain life functions before the rise of modern genetics and biochemistry. Today's naturalist is more likely to reject vitalism and to ascribe life's novelties to complex chemical processes rather than to a distinct life force. For many modern scientists, life is not a separate force at all, but a function of certain organic compounds. Human freedom, then, if a product of biological energies, is not qualitatively different from other physical effects except in the complexity of its causes.

Freedom, for the Romanticist, amounts to the exercise of creative energy. But as a biological phenomenon, it can no more be deliberately directed and ordered than can other psychological drives. It is spontaneous and impulsive, often in defiance of reason and form, seeking novelty for novelty's sake compulsively in what it does. Freud traced it to sexual energies, Nietzsche glorified it as a will to power that cannot be restrained. Reinhold Niebuhr understandably chides Romanticism for giving rein to the demonic: when vitality usurps all form and rules untamed, the result can be even worse than when form usurps vitality, as in the rationalist's case.[3] Freedom, he claims, requires both form and vitality in balance; responsible freedom gives order and direction to human choice and the pursuit of one's ends. But responsibility is hard to define if freedom reduces to biological drives.

(4) *The dialectical model.* Both existential humanists and Marxist humanists develop a dialectical picture of freedom. It goes back to Hegel, for whom every process in both nature and thought moves through conflicting opposites into an emergent synthesis. Hegel himself saw freedom emerging in this way, in the evolution of man and the development of family and state.

Jean-Paul Sartre also sees all of life and its every relationship in dialectical terms, what is already in itself (*l'en-soi*), confronting the one who struggles to become what he will (*le pour-soi*). Freedom consists in negating the world as it is, in mastering that "other," in shaping even my passions by my deeds, and becoming authentically my own. The Marxist, meantime, sees history evolving through the clash of opposing socioeconomic forces to liberate the working class in an eventually classless society. Conflict and confrontation are the path to freedom: confrontation accordingly became the tactic of the radicals of the 1960s, as it is in Marxist geopolitics still.

Again, problems arise. Sartre is ultimately pessimistic because freedom is absolute, transcending every kind of structure and limi-

3. Reinhold Niebuhr, *The Nature and Destiny of Man* (London: Nisbet, 1941), chap. 2.

tation, a dreadful responsibility; and in the final analysis it too will be negated by the brute reality of a death that makes me just an object for others. Freedom is ephemeral, almost a sadistic joke. No happy synthesis awaits us in the end. But Marxists expect a synthesis to come in the collectivity of human labor, wherein alienation will supposedly be overcome and liberation from repression will be lasting and real. In *An Essay on Liberation*, Herbert Marcuse confronts the entrenched establishment of both East and West, denying the productivity principle on which its repression is built, and waiting to see what kind of society will eventuate. Yet as a result, his freedom is empty of content and devoid of positive direction: how then can it give hope and define what it is to be human?

More fundamental than this poor optimism is the problem with dialectic itself, which seems imposed on nature and human existence as an arbitrary and enslaving grid. Hegel, as an idealist, based it on the dialectical thought-processes of the Absolute, but the naturalist has no inclusive Absolute, no such metaphysical ground. He depends rather on the observable processes of nature for his dialectical laws, yet as an empirical generalization the dialectic seems incomplete and artificial, an overstatement by far, and any specific synthesis is impossible to predict. Freedom from alienation and repression of one sort or another may at times and in some degree emerge, although the neo-Marxist Adam Schaff admits it will not do so completely[4] There may not come a wholly conflictless state of affairs. What then is the overarching and integrating end for humankind, and what good can we call supreme? Liberation as the end of alienation is a negative theme. What positive ends should we pursue, and what unifying focus should life have? The human person is his own supreme good, and so the best possible conditions for human happiness should be the goal. And yet neither this happiness nor human freedom receive positive content in the Marxist description.

The naturalist's models for thinking about freedom all have the same problem: any distinctive, positive meaning to humanness eludes us when we see it only in relation to nature. In the image of nature alone, the uniqueness of personhood and the meaning of freedom fade, for then we are not unique after all and do not transcend this

4. Adam Schaff, *Marxism and the Individual* (New York: McGraw-Hill, 1970), chap. 4.

world of which we are a part. A more personalistic understanding is called for, one that conceives of persons more positively rather than reducing us to something else.

This was the very conclusion we reached earlier in thinking about models for creation: a distinctively personalistic model is needed. Regarding freedom, it has been attempted since Kant by existential thinkers, like Soren Kierkegaard, and by idealists, like Peter Bertocci.[5] In Christian perspective the key is that persons are made not in the image of nature but in the image of a personal God: both the person and his freedom must be seen first in relation to God, and only secondarily in relation to nature. That will be the starting point for a more Christian view proposed in the next chapter. Biblically, human freedom is neither absolute nor illusory, but is dependent on God and on the particular form the relationship to God takes. Freedom starts there, and so do its limitations and failures.

HUMAN FAILURE

The same conceptual models have shaped naturalistic accounts of human failure as shaped human freedom.

(1) *The rationalistic model* talks of moral weakness. Aristotle, for instance, locates it in the tendency of emotion to distract reason from its task, a tendency that moral education can overcome by shaping rational habits. Education addresses not only the cognitive but also the affective life, however, and the arts serve to purge the emotions of fear and pity, which would otherwise upset reason's rule. Moral strength can only be acquired by ensuring the rule of reason in its struggle with the emotions.

This analysis of the human problem is characteristic of the rationalist tradition in humanism. Stoicism followed the same line in describing the tension between reason and passion that humans experience. Nature's order is what it is regardless of how we feel; it is rationally ordered without reference to our desires. Rather than fighting what is and yearning for what is not, then, or writhing with pain or fear, it is only rational to accept the way things are and to discipline oneself accordingly. Evil arises when passion rules, but virtue with the rule of reason.

5. See for instance Kierkegaard's *The Sickness Unto Death* (New York: Doubleday, Anchor Books, 1954), pp. 146–75, and Bertocci's *The Person God Is* (New York: Humanities Press, 1970), pt. 2.

The Christian church itself was tempted by this rationalism early in the fifth century. Pelagius claimed that moral failure and sin generally, to use the theological term, are due not to any inherited evil, but to the weakness of the will under the emotional influence of bad human examples. Such moral weakness can be offset by understanding the teachings of Scripture and by good human examples, especially that of Jesus. Knowing the right strengthens the will to choose the good. In characteristic Greek fashion, the rule of reason triumphs when it is informed by truth, while ignorance and irrational passion breed moral failure.

We see at once how anthropocentric such a view is, and how it confines one to human and natural resources. It fits the naturalistic and anthropocentric presuppositions of secular humanism but contrasts starkly with a theistic view. Human failure, from the latter standpoint, is due to more than a natural weakness of will in the tension between reason and passion. Human finiteness indeed makes us vulnerable, because we are dependent on other people and things, vulnerable as well to emotional distraction and obsession. Yet our dependency is not on people and things only, but more basically on God, and it is distraction from that relationship which upsets the rest, not just distraction from rational concentration. Our ultimate hope lies then, not in our own rational self-discipline but in the gracious activity of the Creator. Human reason is indeed fallible; but, along with the emotional life, it is also affected by sin. In the final analysis, moral failure cannot be traced to a conflict of reason and emotion, the one good and the other evil, but involves a more basic moral perversion that stems from rejecting a more basic dependency on God.

The rationalistic model, moreover, traces human failure to a flaw in the very nature of things as they forever are. A subtle dualism underlies the supposed tension between reason and emotion, a dualism of order and chaos, of good and evil, that is at the very heart of reality. What hope is there for man or beast in such a world? This dualism echoes Plato's dualism of mind and matter, soul and body, that vested hope in mind or soul because it transcended matter and was eternal. Yet naturalistic humanism denies the reality of an immaterial soul and any nature-transcending thing; and even from a theistic standpoint the soul could not be eternal but is created, dependent, and of limited power. So what basis is there for confidence in reason's power to rule?

The response is often pragmatic, not theoretical; the rule of reason depends on reason's ability to anticipate the consequences of what we do, and so to guide our actions. This may well be true in cases where we know enough, and where we are willing to act on what we know, but in many areas we know far less than we need: in recombinant DNA, for example, or in economic forecasting and control, or merely in predicting individual human behavior. In some cases, moreover, we simply are not willing to act on what we know, and the weight of knowledge does not make us change our values: in environmental matters, in the needless waste of irreplaceable resources, and in the amassing of nuclear weaponry. What we know may well conflict with what we want, but the human perversity involved runs deeper than a temporary weakness of will. Kant spoke of radical evil; others call it demonic; G. K. Chesterton asserted that original sin is the one Christian doctrine that can really be proved.[6] The rationalistic view of human failure appears too superficial and simple in this regard. Yet it is also too pessimistic, for by tracing evil to the very nature of reality it has pulled out the rug of hope from under its own feet.

(2) *The mechanistic model* ascribes human failure to psychological and environmental influences so that the individual cannot be held responsible for how he acts. Where the rationalist tells us to educate the wrongdoer, the mechanist tells us to recondition him. Characteristic of this approach are recent attempts to replace punishment with therapy. B. F. Skinner, for example, rejects any notion of guilt or responsibility. Drawing on studies of animal behavior, he claims that punishment only represses behaviors that will later erupt, for it removes what offenders desire and adds things they have aversion to. But those desires and aversions will remain. Instead, we can reinforce the behaviors we want by providing the stimuli people desire and removing those they react against.[7] In Britain, Barbara Wootton abandons the legal notion of *mens rea*, which means an offender was in his right mind, a voluntary agent, responsible and guilty. The language of responsibility, reproof, and shame has no value. Wootton prefers to treat criminals like patients, to practice penology like medicine, and to organize a penal insti-

6. *Orthodoxy* (1908; New York: Doubleday, Image Books, 1959), p. 15.
7. Skinner, *Science and Human Behavior* (New York: Macmillan, 1953).

tution like a hospital. Criminality is a mental or social disease requiring treatment, not blame.[8]

Thomas Szasz, on the other hand, himself a naturalist and a humanist, attacks this "myth of mental illness" as an all-inclusive rubric that could justify incarcerating individualists and social critics, and subjecting them to behavior modification techniques aimed at eliminating nonconformity.[9] When the line between criminality and other kinds of deviance is removed and moral responsibility is denied, then what happens to freedom and what kind of brave new world results? What would have happened to Vietnam protestors in a society of hawks, to a Martin Luther King in a segregationist world, to an Amos or John the Baptist, or even to Jesus? The denial of individual responsibility for moral failure opens the door to monstrous repression, to preventing reform, and to silencing the prophets.

Undoubtedly a penal system should be interested in reforming offenders or at least deterring repeats; but it should more fundamentally be a way of holding offenders personally responsible for their actions. Without this, attempts at reform can only address social conditions and patterns of behavior and perhaps work at genetic modification. The utility of "therapy" will be sadly limited if persons remain free to act out of what they are and what they choose for themselves.

C. S Lewis rightly condemns the "humanitarian theory" about therapy as dehumanizing, because it treats an offender as less than a person responsible for his deeds. Others have spoken of "the right to be punished," for that right is a corollary of the right to be treated as a person rather than used as means to others' ends.[10] Forced therapy for social rehabilitation violates individual rights, destroys personal freedom, and tells the offender he is not really to blame. It pours everyone into the same mold of existing mores in an already twisted society. The naturalistic humanist again fails to do justice to being human, this time by first making man in the image of

8. Wootton, *Crime and The Criminal Law* (London: Stevens and Sons, 1963), esp. pp. 32–57. See also Karl Menninger, *The Crime of Punishment* (New York: Viking Press, 1968), and his *Whatever Became of Sin?* (New York: Hawthorn Books, 1973).

9. Szasz, *The Myth of Mental Illness* (New York: Harper and Row, 1961).

10. C. S. Lewis, "The Humanitarian Theory of Punishment," in *God in The Dock* (Grand Rapids: Eerdmans, 1970). Also Herbert Morris, "Persons and Punishment," *The Monist* 52 (1968): 475–501.

nature and then remaking him into the twisted image of society itself.

(3) *The romanticist model*, reacting against the mechanistic extreme, focuses on the free and creative spirit as a manifestation of nature's vitality. Since nature bursts out with novelty in promiscuous ways, human vitality cannot be restrained by appeals to reason or the imposition of society's laws and standards. Failure is due to aborted vitality, to stagnancy, to unimaginative and uncreative ways, whereas the free spirit "lets it all hang out." Creativity for creativity's sake tends to be applauded, a kind of aestheticism in which the unconventional and novel is valued for itself.

Underlying this view, we have seen, is the kind of evolutionary theory in which novelty is essential and creativity is the highest value. The old order ever gives place to the new. Failure, then, is remaining static, insisting on the structures and values of the past. But change and creativity can be both beneficent and demonic. The problem is that no unchanging moral norms for either success or failure are possible when creativity takes priority, nor are fixed values to guide life's path and human progress. Progress of some kind becomes inevitable, yet progress that reduces simply to change loses meaning. Change and creativity for their own sake too readily bring chaos. The logic of this was evident in the life of the poet Oscar Wilde, and in the thought of the philosopher Nietzsche with his will to power asserted over all else. It allows the demonic possibilities of a Hitler and leads to a hell on earth, a Nazi holocaust with creative power berserk. The benign pragmatist, however, will discipline creativity with reason and order, for he finds that failure in practice arises from more than inertia and success from more than creativity.

Creativity, of course, is a necessary condition for many kinds of things, but it is not sufficient. Alone, it can lead to good or evil, to failure or success. Creativity must be exercised responsibly, but the Romanticist whose highest value is to be creative and free has no higher values to which to hold his freedom responsible. The naturalist in particular is in this quandary: if nature is all there is and man is part of nature, if creative freedom is nature's highest end, then no higher obligation exists than to be creative and free, and all else should serve that end. Such is the nature of a highest end, and Nietzsche was consistent about it. For the Christian theist, however, since nature is not all there is, higher values have basis and our creativity is accordingly held responsible, first to God, and then to persons he made and values.

(4) *The dialectical model* of Marxist and existentialist humanism interprets human failure differently again. For the Marxist, failure is reactionary and counterrevolutionary behavior: it is being on the wrong side in the dialectic process. As such, it is a crime against the people rather than against any lasting moral law, for the morals of a society result from its place in the class struggle that has shaped it. No reference is possible to other than the material conditions of life, for man is still made in the image of nature.

In the dialectic of existentialism, too, failure is being on the wrong side of the dialectic in progress. For Sartre, the dialectic is between myself and the world that I must negate and make my own. But to fail to act freely, to lapse back and simply accept what life throws my way, is to fall prey to bad faith (*mauvais foi*). It is inauthenticity, for I fail to be the free self I might be. Yet in the final analysis, authenticity and inauthenticity make no real difference, for the world will negate me in the end and I will be part of the other, my freedom extinguished in the relentless dialectic that sweeps us all away. Other people cannot help, for they are what they are themselves (*l'en soi*), part of the world that negates. Being in the image of nature thus deprives human failure of lasting significance, because success and failure both come to the same end.

Not all humanistic existentialists seem that pessimistic. But even Albert Camus gives little further meaning to human failure and hope. In *The Plague*, for instance, people find themselves by fighting the pestilence ravaging Oran. The criminal, the wastrel, the physician—this is their finest hour. But once that dialectical opposition ends they go to pieces, and suicide, dereliction and empty routine rule instead. Because no better synthesis results, their authenticity fails.

The reason for ultimate failure in both Sartre and Camus, of course, is that the dialectic of thesis and antithesis leads nowhere, not to a synthesis, not to a good end. Realistically they see that while an idealist like Hegel could move the process to a triumphant end through the freedom of his Absolute Spirit, the naturalist cannot. God is dead and anything is now possible. There is no guarantee that the dialectic of opposites can fulfill our dreams. Conflict exists, without further promise: life's little successes are transitory, as are its failures. For when we exist only in relation to nature, then nature triumphs finally and extinguishes our flickering hopes.

> . . .All our yesterdays have lighted fools
> The way to dusty death. Out, out, brief candle!
> Life's but a walking shadow, a poor player
> That struts and frets his hour upon the stage,
> And then is heard no more. It is a tale
> Told by an idiot, full of sound and fury,
> Signifying nothing.[11]

Failure is both cosmic and inevitable. There is no highest end, no good that will reign. For Camus and Sartre, that is the truth of the matter.

The problem common to these forms of humanism should now be plain. Persons seen as naturalists see them, in relation to nature alone, often find little if any meaning in either freedom or failure. To be truly responsible requires that we be more than a part and product of nature. In the next chapter we shall see the difference it makes when persons are considered in relation to God. A personalistic model for freedom develops, and God holds us responsible for our dealings with others, not least with him, and with nature as well.

11. Shakespeare, *Macbeth*, V.v. 22–28.

CHAPTER 7

PERSONS IN CHRISTIAN PERSPECTIVE

The contrast between naturalistic and Christian views of the person focuses on two essentials: whether our unique freedom is to be understood most basically in relation to nature or to God, and how we can be held responsible for our failures. This chapter will enlarge on these two points from a Christian perspective, presenting a way of speaking about human persons that is both biblical and pertinent to the humanities and behavioral science.

We must bear in mind that the Bible speaks about humankind both in explicit assertions and in its history and its realistic portrayal of individuals. Moreover, it presents Jesus Christ as the Ideal Man, Son of Man as well as Son of God, both fully human and fully divine. In him we see what the Creator intended us to be like. Humankind was made in God's image, but, among all the daughters and sons of Adam, only Jesus Christ fully embodies the image of the living God. A Christian view of the human person should therefore be explicitly Christocentric.

First we shall look at persons as relational beings, then as responsible beings, and finally at the effect of sin and grace on both relationships and responsibilities. It is a three-layered approach, the second layer being an overlay on the first, and the third an overlay on the other two.

PERSONS ARE RELATIONAL BEINGS

Human beings exist within a vast and complex system of interrelationships. No individual, nor all of us together, can exist in isolation, for both individually and collectively we originate and draw sustenance from outside ourselves. Physically, psychologically, and in every way, we depend on the whole scheme of things in which we participate. No man is a self-contained island, nor can I alone ever master my own fate or captain my own soul.

In a day informed by the sciences and with an increasing awareness of ecology and environmental matters, this is a truism. The secular humanist readily admits its truth, and moderates his optimism accordingly. But the theist did not have to wait for recent knowledge and recent shortages to convince him of human dependency and finiteness, for it is explicit biblically, even supposing it has not always been plain in everyday experience. Creatureliness means dependency, so we are relational beings. Theism goes further in this regard than naturalism can. I am dependent not only on nature and on other persons but also on God, directly so as his creature, and indirectly so because the world of things and people on which I depend is created, too. Unavoidably I exist in relationship to God, to nature, and to other persons, as well as to myself.

(1) Most basically we exist *in relation to God* the Creator. From him we draw our very existence, our livelihood, our abilities and resources, every good quality of our existence, our purpose, meaning, and hope—all this the doctrine of creation implies. In him we live and move and have our being, and to him we remain accountable. It is the overarching theme of the Bible, and it is central in both Christian theology and a Christian world view. We exist before God in all we are and do. Whether we recognize it or not, if God is Creator of all, then we are always and in everything dependent on him.

But this relationship includes more than dependency, for human beings are made in the image of God. Persons in God's image have their focus and meaning outside themselves, their uniqueness consists in a theocentric existence, and they therefore cannot be viewed in naturalistic fashion. The Bible does not point to one unique part or aspect of the person as God's image, but takes a more wholistic view. As entire beings combining spiritual and physical existence in personal and historical activity, humans reflect the God who is personal and who also acts historically. One writer, following an ancient usage whereby the king was an image of the gods, their representative on earth, suggests that God's image in us means that we represent him who is spiritually present but physically unseen.

We symbolize his presence in the way we combine the spiritual with the physical in this earthly life.[1]

The New Testament points in a similar direction, for there it is the Son of Man who is the image of the invisible God. He is the eternal spirit incarnated and active physically, fully God and fully man, reaffirming thereby not only the value of creation in general but also that of human persons in particular. The value of being human is thus ultimately in bearing God's image in this world, an astounding calling indeed.[2]

Some theologians have been more specific. Origen and Clement of Alexandria took the image to be humanity's distinguishing characteristic, and in Greek fashion called it reason. Thomas Aquinas and many of the Scholastics agreed, distinguishing it from Adam's likeness to God, which they identified as an original righteousness that sin destroyed. The Reformers, on the other hand, viewed original righteousness as part of the image, all of which is now terribly marred by sin. So the Westminster Shorter Catechism says "God created man male and female, after his own image, in knowledge, righteousness and holiness, with dominion over the creatures." Luther, however, confined the image to human power over other creatures. More recently Karl Barth has maintained that God's image is in the male and female relationship itself (Gen. 1:27).

Whichever way one goes in these specifics, however, a human being's relationship to God, seen both in dependency on God and in bearing God's image in this world, makes us all at heart religious beings. Our highest end, our all-inclusive supreme good, is to glorify God and enjoy him forever. As Dooyeweerd has emphasized, this religious heart of the matter lies at the root of both human action and theoretical thought: out of the heart are all the issues of life. As dependent, we must seek God in all we are and do. As responsible image-bearers, we represent the Creator in all of it, too.

---

1. D. J. A. Clines, "The Image of God in Man," *Tyndale Bulletin* 19 (1968): 53–103. He goes on to suggest that in contrast to other ancient usages all human beings, not just the king or some special envoy, represent God on earth. On the general subject of the image of God, see G. C. Berkouwer, *Man: the Image of God* (Grand Rapids: Eerdmans, 1962). On other topics in biblical anthropology, see Werner Kümmel, *Man in the New Testament*, rev. ed. (London: Epworth Press, 1963); H. Wolff, *Anthropology of the Old Testament* (Philadelphia: Fortress Press, 1974); and G. Carey, *I Believe in Man* (Grand Rapids: Eerdmans, 1980).

2. E.g., Gen. 9:6; James 3:9; Eph. 4:24; Col. 3:10; Heb. 1:1–3.

This makes religion far more basic and inclusive than it sometimes appears. Civil religion is a fringe benefit that blesses the political status quo without either grounding or challenging it. Mystical religion can remove us from involvement in this world. Much popular religion is a romanticized experience of peace with ourselves, and too much piety is compartmentalized from "secular" life. But if in the very essence of our humanity and its every expression we depend on God and represent him, too, then no compartmentalization of life is possible, and religion is far more foundational than any veneer or heartwarming experience. Human persons are by nature God-seekers created to worship and serve the living God with their whole being. This is first and basic in what it means to be a human person.

(2) We therefore do not exist in relation to God apart from but rather within our other relationships. We exist before God *in relation to nature*, for we are made of the dust of the earth, our origin and potentialities rooted in the physical, and our present duties there. Genetic identity, established at conception, is physical. The nourishment necessary, if not sufficient, for bodily and emotional and mental development is physical. The work of our hands and mind take and deploy the physical. Arts and crafts give it pleasing and enriching form. Science and technology explore and employ it. Even our eternal destiny involves a resurrected body. Implicit in this relation to nature, we find a mandate for physical and behavioral science, for work and play and art.

We are both dependent on nature and responsible for it, and some have taken the image of God to refer specifically to this responsibility (Gen. 1:26–30). Adam's sin, like ours, disrupted nature's balance (Gen. 3:17–19). Yet Isaiah's hope for redemption includes nature's restoration; and Jesus reminds us of God's concern even for lilies and sparrows. C. F. D. Moule accordingly speaks of "a Biblical ecology" in which we play a part.[3]

We can be both dependent on nature and responsible, for while we are physical beings, in us spirit is present and active, too. This is evident in biblical terminology, which lacks the Greek dichotomy we often superimpose on it. "Soul" (OT *nephesh*, NT *psychē*) is used of a living being, not of an immaterial, eternal entity imprisoned

---

3. C. F. D. Moule, *Man and Nature in the New Testament* (Philadelphia: Fortress Press, 1964).

in a body, despite the fact that we have a destiny beyond death. "Spirit" (OT *rûach*, NT *pneuma*) conveys the idea of life-giving breath, God-given, but it also comes to refer to the religious life of a person and to the living God himself, the unseen but life-giving Spirit. The human spirit also is active, life-directing, not at all reducible to physical energy. Both soul and spirit, however, refer primarily to phenomena in human life as a whole. Biblical language is prephilosophical, without the metaphysical distinctions that Greek philosophy introduced.

Sometimes "spirit" contrasts with "flesh" (*sarx*). The latter term is used in two different senses: it may simply refer to the physical body, or it may speak of the person as a sinner. Corporeality is not sin, and our tie to nature is not the cause of evil: if it were, the purpose of human existence in terms of spiritual activity within the physical would be denied. Human responsibility would dwindle, asceticism would result, and a disembodied state would be our only salvation.

A Christian understanding allows no such *other*-worldliness, whether Manichean or Platonic. Manichean dualism took matter to be eternal and our bodies to be the cause of evil. Plato thought matter by itself to be chaotic, a handicap to ordered existence, rational understanding, and moral virtue. But at the creation God called our participation in nature "good." The Old Testament writers rejoice in physical beauty and are awed by its grandeur. They delight in food, drink, sight, sound, sexuality. In Christ, moreover, God incarnated himself in the physical, and the Ideal Man dearly enjoyed the world of nature and readily took his place in it. He even became a craftsman, an artist.

But a Christian view also cannot harbor *this*-worldliness, because it would reduce humankind to a mere part and product of nature, and deny humanity's spiritual nature. Naturalism is disallowed because, while we are indeed a part and product of this world, we are not just that, and our being cannot be wholly explained by causal laws alone. To be sure, we can be studied biologically and behaviorally, as objects of scientific inquiry, but there is more to us than natural objects. We are subjects, too, with an inwardness that transcends the world around us in relationship not only to God but to other persons as well.

The contrast with the naturalisms of the last chapter is plain. In the Christian view, persons are subject to the physical influences to which naturalism points, but they are more than that alone allows. Human hopes, values, and ideas, our frustrations, our freedom, and our foolishness—subjects of much literature and art—say something important too. We formulate theories and criticize them; we even come up with mistaken views and judge them to be right or wrong. In pursuit of values, we rise above the predictable. If naturalism has problems accounting for all this, it is because of the claim that freedom and hope and worth and rationality all depend on our place in nature alone.

At the other extreme, when our relationship to nature is ignored, people are taken to be more free and more fully responsible than in fact they are. When environmental limitations are not seriously regarded, the victim and the criminal are told they can do and be anything they choose. But even the American frontier individualist faced the stark facts of barren deserts, impassable mountains, and psychological limitations. We are not completely free. Genetic conditions afford the ground and establish parameters for what we become. Environment provides both possibilities and limitations. In these regards, biological and behavioral science do illumine the humane scene.

(3) In a natural world devoid of *other persons*, a man or woman would be alone, with no fitting life-helper; but "it is not good for man to be alone," said the Creator. This again underscores the uniqueness of humankind: the person is qualitatively different to such an extent that he has none but his own kind to identify with. More than herd instinct is involved, for what persons need is friends, both to give and to receive love. A person is no Robinson Crusoe, alone on an island with his goats and his God. The kind of individualism Defoe's Enlightenment philosophy portrays, which sees human relationships as something added to what a rational being already is by nature, is alien to the essential nature of persons and unknown in Scripture. I am what I am, I gain self-awareness and identity, I discover my own inwardness in relationship and not in isolation. A woman bore me, parents named and nurtured me, family and friends filled my early years with experiences that shaped me, teachers and employers played their part, and for many years now my own wife and family and associates have contributed to what I have become. I exist, necessarily, in relation to other persons.

No one is completely independent, but complete and unilateral dependence is not the picture, either. Rather, interdependence prevails. The male-female relationship, biblically and experientially, is the paradigm case. God made each to complement the other, interdependent individuals in a fully personal relationship with each other. Marriage expresses a kind of biological, psychological, economic, moral, and religious unity that is possible only between persons.

Existential thinkers have seen the difference that a personal quality to relationships can make. If I relate to my wife as to an object, I to it, then I dominate her and use and repress her, and remain closed to what she could be to herself. But if we relate to each other as persons, subject to subject with trust and openness and mutuality, then communication develops, as does friendship. This is egalitarian, equal persons equally respected and equally responsible. It evokes love, not the *eros* that desires for oneself, often selfishly, but the *agapē* that gives of oneself in serving the other. Such relationships to other persons are the matrix where freedom and responsibility come alive. I become my brother's keeper, and he becomes mine.

Relations with other persons, like relationships to God and to nature, reveal both dependence and responsibility. The life of Jesus, the Ideal Man, also reveals biological dependency, for he, too, was conceived and nurtured by a woman. Like any child, he depended for years, physically and economically, on others. He chose disciples to share his life and work; he called them friends. In his dying he depended on others for a sop and a grave. In his living and dying alike, then, the dependence was plain. But he also accepted responsibility for family and friends, for the sick, sad, hungry, and guilt-ridden. Where marriage was formerly the paradigm for relationships between persons, the life and death of Jesus now became the prime example of love.

Pure religion and undefiled, said James, is like that. By the time James wrote, the church had become a visible image on earth, born and nurtured by God's love, composed of interdependent people serving one another responsibly in love. And we shall see later that this informs the Christian ethic.

Much of this interpersonal emphasis is evident in other than Christian thought. This is to be expected if interpersonal dependency is indeed rooted in human nature; although the Christian is likely to ascribe to divine providence its resurgence in a world struggling with dehumanization. It is also to be expected in view of the historical influence of the Judeo-Christian heritage. The equal worth of all human persons, implicit in the image of God doctrine, was unknown in Plato and Aristotle, and the self-giving, *agapē* love that Jesus taught and exemplified is entirely lacking in Plato's discussions of love and Aristotle's extended account of friendship.

The modern mind acknowledges this historical influence of Christian values. The crucial issue is whether it can continue to sustain them either intellectually on naturalistic presuppositions, or in practice. For even the Christian ethic is likely to be ineffective without the operation of divine grace.

(4) How, then, is the individual to be viewed, and what is a person's *relationship to herself*? Recent years have produced a surge of narcissism,[4] obsessed with individual well-being and fulfillment as if this were the supreme good for all of one's life; and the rugged individualism fabled in American lore is preached as the only alternative to totalitarian and collectivist extremes, and sometimes even labelled "Christian."

There are two extremes: on the one hand, the repression of individuality and freedom in oppressive systems of politics or economics and even in the family; on the other hand, the exaltation of freedom as savior and lord in narcissism and other individualistic extremes. Of course, individuals are important and so are the individual rights we have learned to cherish. But the value of a person stems from the image of God, from being God's creature capable of knowing God, not primarily from our individual differences; we are told that each snowflake is unique, too, but we don't value snowflakes like people. It is the person created in God's image that has worth; and a person divinely endowed with the capacity for self-direction should be free to exercise that gift. But, contrary to Sartre, human freedom is not itself absolute and unqualified; contrary to Mill, it is not to be limited by society only when one person harms another; contrary to Locke, social institutions do not rest ultimately on individuals contracting together, but on our native interdependency and (as the marriage ceremony puts it) on God's ordinance.

The limited nature of our freedom and the limited value of individuality are evident in our relational existence. I am a creature of God, subject to God's laws and purposes. I depend on nature,

4. See Christopher Lasch, *The Culture of Narcissism* (New York: W. W. Norton, 1978), pp. 69f.

which supplied my genetic materials and much of my environment. Other persons and the society of which I am a part shape me, too. Together, all of these relationships provide possibilities and parameters for what as an individual I can become. To that extent I am a product of relationships; my freedom is limited; I cannot do or be whatever I might want.

Yet I am not a product of these relationships alone. I am what I am, the individual I am, by virtue of the possibilities I have actualized out of many that existed. It depends on how by the grace of God I have put it all together, interiorizing experiences, accepting, rejecting, sifting, reshaping. Human individuality is real, because God's image in man makes it possible for spirit to shape a life, and so I am in measure under God my own doing.

The key to individuality, in biblical terminology, is the "heart." This is not the seat of emotion as in common English parlance, but rather the integrating core of a person's life and character. Out of the heart are the issues of life; as a man thinks in his heart so he is, and with the heart he believes or not. While the terms "soul" and "spirit" are extended biblically at times to animals, though with somewhat different associations, the term "heart" is so used only once to my knowledge, and then in a markedly different sense. The human individual has self-conscious inwardness, with intentions, attitudes, and values of his own, and as such he has distinctive possibilities and responsibility, too. He stands back, he thinks and chooses, he examines his own life, and then he examines that self-examination. By reflecting on his life he transcends it, and by evaluating that reflection he transcends it again. He transcends in thought and purpose what he already is, and in acting on that purpose he becomes different. By virtue of this inner freedom of the human spirit, God has given us the possibility of shaping our individuality as well as our societies. Individuality is then to be appreciated. I can accept my individual possibilities and limitations as God's good gift, or I can resent what is given and either try to be what I cannot or should not, or else listlessly drift.

Naturalistic world views, however, lack this standpoint, and according to Reinhold Niebuhr, they destroy individuality.[5] Any monism, where everything is of one sort and subject to one kind of

5. Reinhold Niebuhr, *The Nature and Destiny of Man* (1941; New York: Scribner's, 1964), chap. III.

causal process, struggles to make room for individuality. But without the vitality of the human spirit with its self-transcendence and freedom, physical processes alone cannot give rise to freedom and meaningful individuality. For Marx, therefore, the individual is subordinated to the socioeconomic conditions of history. For Nietzsche, even the difference between strong and weak wills is biologically grounded. The result for naturalism is that individuals too easily become objects, replaceable, and not valued for themselves. Sexual partners become interchangeable commodities without distinctively individual worth. In extreme individualism and collectivism alike, workers (and customers, too) become replaceable parts in an economic machine, rather than remaining human individuals of worth in themselves and valued as such by others. A Christian view of persons, mediating between extremes, leads to an ethic of love that is far different from this.

Another aspect of the person's relationship to self concerns temporality. I am the individual I am through past, present, and future. Identity continues, though its character changes. As Shakespeare said, one man in his time plays many parts; yet to be human embraces them all—their foibles, anxieties, triumphs, and failures—and I must live with all this in relating to myself. To accept this self may not be easy: guilt cannot always be repressed; self-worth inflates and the self can suffer.

The realization of "being unto death," in Heidegger's words, adds to life's anxieties. It grows with advancing years and is underscored by an annoying litany in biblical genealogies: he lived so many years, "and he died." This realization affects my present, and how I interiorize it contributes to making me the individual I am. Death shapes life, and my view of death shapes my view of myself. Here the contrast with naturalistic humanism could not be greater. Is this life terminal or not? And what does that say of my value?

A Christian view of persons deals realistically with each aspect of temporality. It knows no escapist solutions, but it encourages acceptance of youth, old age, and even dying, not a fatalistic acceptance but one filled with hope and purpose because of God's providence and grace. Christ's relationships with people reveal the value he placed on them at all stages in life. His own life and death reveal purpose, too. He died young. But he extended to others the purpose and hope he knew in living and in dying. He knew that what matters most in being human is not temporary but everlasting.

116

Nothing can separate us from the love of God, nothing time can ever bring, for that relationship endures. Moreover, the Christian anticipates the resurrection of the dead with its continued relationship to the physical, and the eternal kingdom with its relationships to other persons. Personal identity in these relationships will last, and I can accept myself and live this present life with joy and responsibility as a result.

PERSONS ARE RESPONSIBLE BEINGS

If the relational character of the human person is one dominant theme that confronts us in Scripture, a second and equally dominant theme is that God holds us responsible. This fact of being obligated and answerable to God is overwhelmingly clear, and distinguishes humans from other earthlings. We are responsible for imaging God's activity in the physical world. Our vocation is summed up in the creation mandate to be responsible for filling the earth and exercising dominion. We are here by divine appointment.

The scope of human responsibility includes the entire range of relationships we have just considered. We are obligated and answerable first and foremost and in everything to God, responsible for a relationship to him that is marked by creaturely worship and loving obedience, responsible therefore for how we think about God as well as how we act. We are responsible to him in our relationship to nature, for respecting our physical being and the natural resources with which we are entrusted, for using and conserving them wisely for economic and aesthetic and other ends, not with self-indulgent exploitation or abuse but with a grateful enjoyment that celebrates and responds to God's goodness. Responsible art and science, a responsible economy and technology, responsible bodily care and physical enjoyment—all this is implied. We are responsible, too, for other persons: I am always my brother's keeper. Social morality arises from respect for others, because their worth and dignity depends on their being God's creatures in God's image, too. But respect for persons extends equally to myself as to others: I am responsible for how I treat myself and how I handle my present and future possibilities. Self-respect and personal development are matters of Christian stewardship.

To be responsible in any of these regards implies that I can do something that will make the relationship different. Freedom and responsibility are inseparable, for as creatures of God we are never completely autonomous or independent, never absolutely or unqualifiably free. We exist always in relation to God, with God-given freedom and with responsibility to him.

Responsibility is unique to persons. Persons act intentionally, with purpose and thought. Natural events are not intentional and self-conscious, but are caused. Persons can often act otherwise than they do, but things have no choice in the matter. Events simply occur, but actions are performed. Not everything a person "does" is an action in this sense, deliberate and with reasons, for man is a biological and emotional being, too, outwardly as well as inwardly oriented, a creature of habit responding to stimuli as well as a creature of choice initiating actions. Yet act we do, rather than remaining spectators or going with the tide of events. How we act makes a difference, and in a world of relationships we are properly responsible to people other than ourselves alone.[6]

Responsible action requires conscious thought and moral decision. As a responsible agent, a person is then both a reflective and a valuing being. The old label "rational being," at least as sometimes understood, is too narrow. To many, it connotes the Greek or Enlightenment rule of reason that we declined to endorse before, and the incessant demand for logically certain knowledge. But "reflection" includes various sorts of mental activity with reference to myself, my relationships, and my responsibilities. It may include belief as well as knowledge, passionate involvement as well as detached inquiry, practical concerns as well as theoretical contemplation. Creative imagination is present, too, in the artist, the planner, the thinker who explores possibilities he has sensed but not known. Weighing of ends and means, the choice of words and materials, pondering problems, evaluating options, perceiving, intending, arguing, interpreting, reminiscing, questioning the meaning of life—all of this and more I include in reflection. The human person is in this broad sense a reflective being.

Yet it is not reflective capacity alone, any more than it was the old-style "reason" alone, that makes the person a responsible agent.

6. For recent philosophical discussions of these distinctions, see Lewis Beck, *The Actor and the Spectator* (New Haven: Yale Univ. Press, 1975); Richard Taylor, *Action and Purpose* (Englewood Cliffs: Prentice-Hall, 1966); Jerome Shaffer, *Philosophy of Mind* (Englewood Cliffs: Prentice-Hall, 1968), chap. 5.

For we reflect not only on things that happened once or happen now when we decide on a responsible action but we reflect also on what we want to happen in the future, on why we want it, and what we value most. We are valuing beings, too.

To value is to prize, to idealize a goal or end. What we value therefore guides what we do. How we value it affects the intensity and determination with which we do it. How responsibly we act depends significantly on our values. The Bible speaks of this when it speaks of what and how we ought to love, for to value is to love. We are not to love ourselves more highly than we ought, not to love the things of this world in certain ways, not to love the praise of men, but to love God, to love justice, to seek first the kingdom of God and his righteousness.

We love a vast array of things and all sorts of possibilities, sometimes less and sometimes more of them than we should. Some are more valued than others and some less, and it is possible to be lured in a variety of conflicting directions by conflicting values. What we need to give life order, unity, and overall direction is a unifying end that we value most of all and regard as the very highest. For if values shape actions, then one's highest value or supreme good will shape the other values themselves and doubly shape the actions. Free and responsible action requires not just values but the right values, rightly ordered to enhance the highest good.

If as responsible beings we are responsible for our actions, then as reflective beings we are responsible for our thoughts and imaginations, and as valuing beings we are responsible for our values. This goes against the humanistic tendency to blame behavior and values on social or genetic factors, yet the tenth commandment speaks to the sin of covetousness that combines thoughts with mistaken values into wrong desires and intentions. Jesus held the person guilty who committed adultery or murder "in his heart," and Paul clearly and repeatedly advised his readers where to set their affections. We are held responsible for loving both what and as we ought.

What we have just said about persons as free and responsible agents raises metaphysical questions that lurk barely below the surface of this whole discussion about human beings. What in our makeup is different from other creatures? What makes possible the kind and degree of freedom we seem to possess, as well as other distinctively personal properties? What in us survives death? Is there indeed a free and immaterial soul as has often been supposed?

A variety of philosophical alternatives has been used in articulating a Christian point of view on these matters. A Platonic sort of position influential in the early church was that the soul is an immaterial entity, physically indestructible and therefore immortal. But physical indestructibility merely shows the possibility of surviving bodily destruction, not complete indestructibility for whatever cause; every created thing, the soul included, remains contingent on God's creative power and is therefore destructible still. Descartes' view, which has held attention now for several centuries, is that body and soul are two separate entities with different properties, each causing events to occur in the other, but the soul is endowed with free will. His problem was twofold: to explain how two so qualitatively different things could interact, and to account for the essential unity of a personality. The preferable view here was the Aristotelian, that soul and body are organically united, each being essential now to the proper functioning and development of the other, while the soul actualizes in this life the capacity both for rational deliberation and free decision. Some have preferred idealist solutions, such as the gradualist proposal that everything in existence is a manifestation of underlying spiritual reality, of which the human soul emerges as the fullest actualization we know in this world. Some even suggest a naturalistic view of the human person (though not of God) and think our distinctively human functions are entirely supported by highly complex physical processes, yet allow for a future life simply by virtue of a resurrected body.

The biblical components for an acceptable view of persons are relatively simple, if we remember that the scriptural notions of "soul" and "spirit" are not metaphysical concepts but more descriptive of functions. Our creaturely dependence on God for every aspect of our existence is the first. The uniqueness of persons in God's image is also crucial, along with the fact that we are ourselves agents whom God holds responsible for character and choices, thoughts and actions. Human beings, too, are capable of a kind of community that is unique in creation. As far as a future life is concerned, relatively little is said in Scripture about disembodied existence (between death and resurrection) beyond Paul's statement that absence from the body means being in the presence of God. The larger emphases and fuller statements refer to a fully orbed life following the resurrection of the dead. In this, an essential unity of personality, functionally at least, is clear.

Within these parameters are various alternatives. Some options may appear better suited than others if we think, for example, that Platonic and naturalistic solutions squeeze the biblical components out of their most natural shape. Some may appear more adaptable to our knowledge of cybernetics or the like. My own preference is for a body-soul dualism in close organic unity, so that we function in many if not all regards as wholistic beings rather than having separate body functions and soul functions. But this preference must stop short of claiming that no other kind of view will do. We simply do not know enough to make so strong a claim.

RELATIONSHIPS AND RESPONSIBILITIES ARE RADICALLY AFFECTED BY BOTH SIN AND GRACE

Psychologist Karl Menninger tells of a stern-faced, plainly dressed man on a street corner in the Chicago Loop, pointing an accusing finger at people and intoning one word: "Guilty!" Embarrassed, wondering how he ever knew, his victims hastily passed him by. Menninger was introducing the subject of his book *Whatever Happened to Sin?* which underscores the lack of a sense of responsibility in society, and claims that socially unacceptable behavior is a symptom of social or emotional conflicts, or the result of bad social conditioning, as if nobody is really to blame. President Carter once stunned and amused government employees by chiding those who were "living in sin." In a day of shifting mores, "sin" was supposedly too old-fashioned to name in such a way. Even Menninger was arguing for no more than that society should accept responsibility for doing something to offset its bad influence on individuals.

Undoubtedly society is much to blame, and changing mores do leave moral confusion. But this cannot detract, if there is any individual freedom, from individual responsibility for one's own values, intentions, thoughts, and deeds. The scientific humanist, tied to evolutionary concepts, tends rather to stress the effects of social and psychological problems that arise in a rapidly changing world still marked by conflict. The Romanticist tends to exonerate nature, human nature in general as well as one's own, and to criticize the institutions of our culture. The existentialist for his part finds an underlying cause in the dehumanization and emptiness of existence, and the Marxist points to class conflicts and counterrevolutionary conduct. Naturalists who see a human person as wholly a part and product of nature thus do not hold an inner subject individually responsible, but have to turn instead to other influences which they claim make a person what he or she is.

In church circles, too, the starkness of sin is quite often attenuated, and individual and societal failings are blamed on a new morality, or just on "the times"—calling them environmental conditions, as if "environment" sufficiently explains our sin. The emphasis often turns to finding fulfillment and "happiness in Jesus," as if complete fulfillment and unqualified happiness is achievable by sinful or even finite people in a limited span of time in a bent and twisted world. The church is not a community of fulfilled, perfectly adjusted people living harmoniously together, but rather another kind of new society: a community of confessed sinners forgiving one another as Christ has forgiven them; a community of hope and love.

Humanity's biggest and most basic problem is not the environment, nor is it dependency relationships, nor finiteness, nor being unfulfilled. Our biggest and most basic problem is what the Bible calls sin. Denials of sin are related to denials of a theistic world view, and superficial views of sin relate to a superficiality there. One kind of misdirection comes from the Greek legacy about reason and emotion. If we are rightly ruled by reason, then the sin that replaces reason's rule is really the influence of emotions stirred by bodily needs. Asceticism then becomes salvation. Or if we are rightly ruled by reason then reason must be guided aright, and sin is due to the guidance of bad examples. Good examples become our salvation. Again, if we are ruled by reason, then it is wrong thinking that produces sins in word and deed, and sin consists only of these particulars. The Pelagian heresy in the early church thought along these lines.

The biblical view differs from these because it sees the human person as far more (not less) than a rational being, with more depth and unity and individuality to his personal being and to his sin. It is legalism that talks of sin just in terms of particulars. We must look further than that.

In the first place sin, like the sinner, must be viewed within the God-creation distinction and relation. At the heart of a person is a creature's relation to God, and the heart of sin is a refusal of creatureliness. Paul, in Romans 1, relates sin to loving the creature rather than the Creator; and as we read in Genesis, the tempter first offered to Adam the prospect of being as God. Among recent theologians, Reinhold Niebuhr has turned attention to this heart of sin as the refusal to take a creaturely position, to accept our dependency and finiteness, to recognize that the center of our existence is outside ourselves, in God the Creator. Sin makes creatures the center of our being, so that a person does not worship and serve the Creator but serves herself or other finite things instead. Pride and power are her concern, the pride and power of race or sex or profession. Niebuhr suggests that sin refuses even to settle for the union of nature and spirit that makes us distinctively in God's image. Either sin exalts the physical and turns to naturalism, or it exalts the human spirit, turning optimistically to rationalistic and idealist extremes. In either case human ends replace the divine purpose, self-satisfaction displaces pleasing God, and personal fulfillment overrides the love that sacrifices as it serves. The result of life off-center is loss of virtue, meaning, inner liberty, and hope.

In the second place, then, sin cannot be confined to some segment of life but extends throughout its relationships. Our relation to God is at its heart, if sin is revolt against God. But alienated from God, we exploit nature for ill-conceived ends with imprudent means, and suffer the effects on ourselves. The Genesis story of man's fall significantly talks of thorns and thistles that turn work into toil, and of expulsion from the garden. The Romanticist forgets this alienation from nature, yet nature's forces are not altogether benign, nor is man's domination of nature. Consider the havoc we wreak all about us!

Our relations to other persons suffer from alienation as well. We alienate our fellow human beings, thereby tearing the fabric of society and polluting the refinements of culture. We suffer from self-indulgence and from the overindulgence of others, for people are all askew. Even my relationship to myself is affected, for if my identity lies in relationships that are now distorted or destroyed, then my identity suffers, too. My self-image is deflated by isolation, or else it inflates to compensate. I mistake life's meaning in trying to relate to nature and people apart from God. My efforts fail and I find it hard to forgive myself; or I lose touch with who I am at heart. All of life suffers.

Sin, thirdly, is a pervasive condition of the inner life as well as the outer. Contrary to Pelagian and legalistic conceptions and to the naturalistic view, it extends beyond the particulars of thought and deed to the inner core of our being. The heart, in biblical terminology, is deceitful and desperately wicked. The phenomenon of self-deception, of role-playing and wearing masks, is well known to psychologists, sociologists, and philosophers. We mask not only particular things about us, but also the evil in our hearts, perhaps by deeds that outwardly are beyond reproach. But responsible beings are responsible also for the intents of the heart, for the possibilities they imagine and the values they love but would never confess. God, we are told, desires truth in the inward parts.

This pervasiveness of sin deprives us of the ability always to think and do and intend and speak aright. It infects every area of life. It traps us in horrible moral dilemmas in which no altogether good option is possible. Life becomes a tangled mess, riddled with helplessness and guilt.

Pervasive as it is inwardly, sin is equally pervasive outwardly. It can no more be confined to individuals than to particulars; it is not just the condition of individuals, but the pervasive condition of society as well. Since relationships between people give rise to the institutions of society, relationships pervaded by sin produce institutions pervaded by sin. David's adultery with Bathsheba is a case in point. He corrupted the institutions of marriage and government, multiplied abuses of political power, and trapped servants and soldiers by implicating them, until only the word of God could awaken his conscience. But nothing could correct the social corruption and personal harm that had been done forever.

Since an institution assumes a life of its own apart from the private functions of individuals, its structures and purposes are affected by sin, along with its day-to-day operations. Sin is a social reality, not just a private affair. The Old Testament therefore recognizes corporate as well as individual responsibility. A family, a tribe, a nation can be accountable, their corporate sin judged.[7]

This account of human sin, it should be remembered, presupposes the doctrine of creation. A law-governed creation has a moral order that is independent of human wish and historical variation. The sin that perverts relationships is a violation of that law, inwardly in the human heart, outwardly in word and deed, and societally

7. See Russell Shedd, *Man in Community* (London: Epworth Press, 1958); Stephen Mott, "Biblical Faith and the Reality of Social Evil," *Christian Scholars Review* 9 (1980): 225–60.

too, for God's law also extends to institutions that arise. In refusing the creaturely position, sin is lawlessness.

Two comments are needed here. First, the idea of an objective moral order often (but not in all cases) goes against the humanist vein. Some forms of naturalism allow no objective basis for morality, but relativize it to changes in time and place, sometimes even making it wholly subjective. In Chapter Ten, therefore, we shall explore further the claim to a theistic basis for values that underlies the concepts of sin and moral responsibility.

Second, sin's broad extent does not mean that no good deeds are done. The Creator remains the living God, active in the world in spite of sin, and pursuing good purposes still. Christians speak of common grace, the goodness of God that causes the deeds of wrathful men to praise him, so that human relationships, society, and culture are in measure beneficent yet. Governments and workers, artists and teachers, parents and friends, sinful as they be, may continue to serve God's purposes whether they acknowledge it or not. Creational tasks continue.

This is not the place to elaborate the Christian doctrine of salvation, but a view of human persons would be incomplete without some comment about God's grace. Christians hold that God forgives sinners and that the new life in Christ is as pervasive as, and more powerful than, sin. This is quite coherent with what we have seen, for the basic point is that the living God acts creatively in dealing with our sin. The moral law sin violates is God's law in all its parts, so it is ultimately his prerogative to forgive. And if sin extends to every human relationship, grace can, too. Reconciliation to God is followed by reconciliation to other persons in a life of love. Barriers come down—racial barriers (neither Jew nor Greek), sexual prejudice (neither male nor female), socioeconomic aloofness (neither slave nor freeman)—for all are united in Christ. The new life in Christ, like sin, has societal dimensions in the kingdom he preached and brought. The work of grace, like that of sin, begins inwardly in the human heart and its relationship to God, but extends outwardly into every other relationship and responsibility as well.

A Christian conception of liberty now emerges. It is not the liberty of the individualist who accepts no responsibility to others except to respect their equal rights. John Stuart Mill's libertarianism, with its basic principle that liberty can be restricted only to avoid harm to others, falls short of the kingdom of God. The rule of self-interest, from a Christian point of view, is bondage. Christian liberty is freedom from that, a freedom to obey the law of God from the heart and to serve others sacrificially in love. It is liberty limited by what creatureliness implies of interdependency and interrelatedness, and captivated by God's purposes. It renews the person, restores relationships, and gives a present taste of what the kingdom of God was at creation intended to be, and what it will yet become.

CHAPTER 8

TRUTH AND KNOWLEDGE: THEOLOGICAL

Persons are reflecting and valuing beings. To pursue the implications of this more fully, we shall look here and in the next chapter at truth and knowledge, and in the following chapter at the basis of values. In both these areas, the overarching theme of God and creation affects how we think and act. Christian theism is a creational world view: this chapter draws out its epistemic consequences, while the following one examines some epistemological problems that naturalistic humanism seems not to resolve.

The prevalent naturalistic humanisms of our day show plainly that one's view of truth and knowledge is part and parcel of an overall world view. We drew attention in Chapter Two, for example, to the scientific humanist's exclusive adoption of scientific methods in checking out human beliefs, in providing knowledge, and in handling life's problems. This exclusivism narrows the range of acceptable discussion and leads in a naturalistic direction. Moreover, in those cases where naturalism has no unchanging locus for truth in this changing world, relativism and subjectivism arise. So the Marxist, for example, makes truth relative to the class struggle, and naturalistic sociologies of knowledge make it depend on the historical conditions in a particular time and place. Can knowledge not transcend the relative? Is there no unchanging truth?

To this historical relativism, romanticist and existential humanists add a concern for human subjectivity. Disillusioned with the one-dimensional world of scientific rationalism, and hungry for something more fully human and alive, they turn to another strain that runs through human culture. Persons are taken to be primarily affective beings, ruled by irrational drives rather than by reason. And so truth and knowledge and theoretical inquiry in particular are devalued, and anti-intellectualism appears.

These symptoms should concern us, whether the overconfidence of a dogmatic rationalism or the despair of a subjectivist relativism, for in neither case is the God-creation distinction and relationship taken into the epistemological account. The God-creation distinction speaks of a transcendent and all-wise knower, whose thoughts are far greater than ours. No self-acknowledged creature can reasonably expect to be like God in knowledge: epistemic *humility* results. The God-creation relationship, moreover, means that God acts in our knowing: he is the self-revealing God who gives us hope of knowing, epistemic *hope*. Humility and hope thus combine in a creational view to avoid both the dogmatism of the rationalist and the pessimism of the relativist.

The epistemological implications of the doctrine of creation can readily be drawn from the ingredients of that doctrine, as outlined in Chapter Four.

	CREATION	EPISTEMOLOGICAL CONSEQUENCES
(a)	transcendent God, creating *ex nihilo*	– a locus of unchanging truth
(b)	living God, creatively active	– "God with us" in our knowing – the possibility of revelation
(c)	purposeful creation	– the knowledge we need in responding to God's purposes is accessible
(d)	delegated powers	– our cognitive powers are God-given
(e)	an ordered creation	– knowledge and wisdom are possible – reason itself is law-governed
(f)	creation has value	– human knowledge has value – error is due to either natural lack or moral perversity
(g)	creational tasks	– a mandate to seek and act on the understanding that is possible

Now we must try to bring these consequences into an organized account of truth and knowledge.[1]

_____

1. For a fuller treatment of some of these themes, the reader may wish to consult some of my previous work toward a Christian epistemology: *Christian Philosophy in the Twentieth Century* (Grand Rapids: Craig Press,

A TRANSCENDENT LOCUS FOR TRUTH

Theism gives us a point of reference in thinking about truth. That point of reference is neither human knowledge in general nor science in particular, nor anything in creation. It is the transcendent, unchanging, and omniscient God. He knows everything about every conceivable topic regarding himself, his creation, and things that are possible but that he never created. He knows it all perfectly, everything past and present, and every future possibility. He knows everything in every one of our disciplines, every possibility for creative art, creative thought, and human technology. He understands it all thoroughly, all the interrelationships, and how everything serves his purposes. God's own knowledge, all-inclusive, perfect, and unchanging, is the ultimate locus for truth. To say something is true, then, properly includes the claim that God knows it to be the case.

Truth therefore is not relative to changing times but is unchanging. It is not subjective, projected by our feelings or thoughts, but is objective to all of us creatures. Our purported knowledge may vary from time to time and place to place and be distorted by subjective factors, for we "see through a glass darkly," but God's knowledge is never distorted, and neither is there any change to truth as God knows it to be.

Paul pointed this out in his Colossian epistle. Confused by the Gnostic rationalists' claim to a corner on truth, the church needed his reminder that in the Creator-Christ are all the treasures of wisdom and knowledge (Col. 2:13). That and not human wisdom is the ultimate point of reference in thinking about truth and evaluating knowledge claims. The God-creation distinction implies that all truth is God's truth, like everything else is his.

This further suggests that truth is not a self-existent, independent thing like Plato's Form of the Good. It is a property rather than a thing, a property ultimately of God's wisdom and knowledge and only derivatively of ours.

1969); *Faith Seeks Understanding* (Grand Rapids: Eerdmans, 1971); *All Truth Is God's Truth* (Grand Rapids: Eerdmans, 1977). Along parallel lines see Jerry Gill, *The Possibility of Religious Knowledge* (Grand Rapids: Eerdmans, 1971); and E. J. Carnell, *Christian Commitment* (New York: Macmillan, 1957), pt. 1.

A THEISTIC BASIS FOR KNOWLEDGE

Creation *ex-nihilo* means that God transcends all that he has made: independent of the limitations and problems of finiteness, he is the ultimate hope for his creatures. Our quests for knowledge, on the other hand, are limited and problem-laden, for we are finite and never fully transcend the changing conditions on which we depend. Some degree of ambiguity, ignorance, or uncertainty always seems to remain. How can we be assured that our cognitive powers are reliable, that the world does not deceive, that some malign demon is not playing games with us as Descartes hypothesized? The God who transcends all creaturely limitations and fears is the source of epistemological assurance and hope.

He who has perfect knowledge in every regard is with us in our knowing, a continually active and self-revealing God. Whereas the Greeks saw themselves wrestling secrets from nature and prying into the mysteries of jealous gods, the Christians by contrast see humans invited to inquire by one who purposely made nature orderly and gave men and women the intelligence to discover its laws. There is good purpose in our desire and power to know, and so there is hope of success. All we can know and shall ever know is thanks to God and still depends on him.

This theistic basis for knowledge stands in contrast to the anthropocentricism of the humanist whose only hope for knowledge depends on what humans alone can achieve. The scientific humanist may pride himself on the self-sufficiency of autonomous reason, but the Christian's hope is built on God's reliability. God is both the locus of truth and the one who makes knowledge possible. Confidence about human reason is confidence in God.

This notion of "reliability" is central to the biblical concept of truth. The Old Testament word for truth (*emeth*) is used primarily of moral qualities like loyalty, veracity, and faithfulness in keeping one's word. People can be be faithful, but God himself is the wholly reliable one who can be trusted completely. He is true. The same notion is conveyed in the New Testament. We read of faithful men and faithful (reliable) sayings, and of a true (or reliable) vine. Words can be both trustworthy and true (Rev. 21:5; 22:6), for a true statement is one that honestly tells us how things really are. A true belief about something is one that is assured. To know the truth is to have reliable knowledge that should be followed. Said the Pharisees to Jesus, "we know that you are true, and teach the way of God truthfully. . . . Tell us, then, what you think" (Matt. 22:16–17). Even in their skepticism, they realized that whatever is truthful should be heard and followed: to walk in the truth is to act on it. Hence one can "suppress the truth" by wickedness (Rom. 1:18) as well as by verbal denials.

Truth as reliability is a property of people, and derivatively of assertions, teachings, beliefs, and purported knowledge. It is a trust-worthiness that warrants belief and action. Do as he says! Believe it! Act on it! You can trust him! It's true! Truth is not something impersonal, purely theoretical, or impracticable. It is something we can firmly believe and confidently live by.

Knowledge depends on both objective and subjective conditions. The objective condition that makes knowing possible is an intelligible order of things created and made available to us by God. The subjective condition is the proper exercise of cognitive powers delegated to us and sustained by God. Thinking and learning are law-governed, like everything else in creation. Thinking is subject to logical laws, for I cannot contradict myself and talk sense, let alone construct a valid line of argument. Good logic is one of God's good gifts, and it is essential to thinking in this and any world. It issues in careful methodology, in respect for facts, in openness to others' criticisms and views. In handling the Bible it respects careful exegesis and good hermeneutics. There is no alternative to sound reasoning: such is our responsibility as the reflective beings God made us to be.

But thinking and learning are also subject to psychological conditions, for we cannot learn effectively and think clearly when fatigued, famished, or emotionally distraught. Emotional blocks may prevent my seeing what I ought, as do moral and spiritual blocks, for we are valuing as well as reflective beings. The New Testament notes that the god of this world blinds the minds of unbelievers to the light of the gospel (2 Cor. 4:4), and that some suppress the truth and refuse to retain God in their knowledge (Rom. 1:18–32). Jesus cited willingness to act on the truth as a subjective condition of our knowing the truth (John 7:17). Yet there is something in our psychological makeup that seems to hunger for a knowledge of God. Augustine says that our hearts are restless until they rest in him. Calvin says that the seed of religion in us is an unformed sense of the deity which nature suggests,[2] and which needs to be more fully informed. James Orr therefore suggests that as personal beings we need a personal God, as finite beings we need an infinite God, as ethical beings an ethical God, as intelligent beings an intelligent God.[3] If the way God has made us points us to him, then our knowledge of God is God-given.

Theism logically implies the possibility of divine self-revelation, for the living God is active in his creation, active therefore in relation to our knowing and especially in our knowing him. Since the whole creation bears witness, along with the way we are made, we can appropriately refer to this as general revelation of God. But God has revealed himself far more explicitly and fully in his redeeming work and most fully in Jesus Christ: this, along with the biblical record of it, provides a more specific revelation that is reliable and true.

Again, objective and subjective conditions are at work, and for both we depend on God. The objective conditions include the historical acts of God, the incarnate Christ, the intelligible and reliable biblical record. They are all necessary to the knowledge God intended. The subjective conditions include our God-given ability to read and understand, to perceive the truth about God and his grace, to respond believingly to the Christ. But this involves our values, for it takes an open heart and mind. For this, too, we depend on the goodness of God.

The Bible is crucial to human knowledge, but not just in supplying extra tidbits of information, nor even in adding a knowledge of theology to our knowledge of nature. It is crucial to our knowledge of God. In it we meet the God who acts. We meet the Christ, the living Logos, whose coming best reveals our maker, his purposes and his love. Our more general knowledge is fragmented by itself, hungry for unity and purpose. It provides the context in which and to which the Bible speaks—the backdrop of the biblical drama wherein our place in nature as both the glory and shame of the universe, along with the meaning of human culture, our sensitivity to people and their needs, our religious hopes and emptiness are all addressed. Scripture reveals the Maker of nature's splendors; it speaks

2. See the "nature psalms" such as Pss. 8 and 19; also Job 38–41; Isa. 40; Acts 14:11–18; 17:22–31; Rom. 1:18–32.
3. Orr, *The Christian View of God and the World*, 5th ed. (Edinburgh: Andrew Elliot, 1897), appendix to lecture III.

of his purposes that should shape our values and culture, of a new man as well as the old, and of a "pure religion and undefiled" that serves Christ in serving others. In revealing God in Christ it calls us to thought and life that is whole. Everything else then falls into place.

The theistic basis for knowledge, then, includes not only the *possibility* of divine self-revelation that is implicit in theism as such, but also its actuality. It is therefore completely consonant with all this to speak of Christ as the living Word of God, and of the Bible as God's word written. The Protestant Reformers spoke of Scripture as the only final and sufficient rule of faith and life, a decisive and unchanging point of reference to which we can be held accountable. As God's word its authority, like that of Christ himself, extends over every area of thought and life.

THE CHRISTOCENTRIC UNITY OF TRUTH

"All truth is God's truth," the church fathers asserted. Their point was not only that God is omniscient but also that truth is a unified whole, unified by its relation to God and his purposes in the creation. As Creator of everything in heaven and earth, he is its common focus, its ultimate point of reference, so that belief in God affords the unifying perspective we need.

All truth is about either God or God's creation and its possibilities, or about other things he thought but has never created. All truth about everything, then, bears witness to him. So the book of Ecclesiastes says that life and death, wealth and poverty, learning and even life's frustrations have meaning in relation to the Creator. In a world of that kind the popular division into sacred and secular activities finds no basis, for everything that relates to God is sacred.

The Bible pushes us one step further from a general theocentric view to a *Christocentric* unity of truth, for its unifying theme is the promise and advent of the Christ. Other themes are treated in this context, and so the whole of Scripture is properly read in this light. Yet if Christ is indeed the Logos of creation by whom and for whom all things exist, the same principle extends to general revelation as well. This is the theme of the prologue to John's Gospel and of Paul's Colossian epistle, and it is dramatically reinforced by the Incarnation itself. The Christ incarnated himself in nature, in history, in human culture, in all that makes up the human situation.

The entire creation, New Testament eschatology says, travails in hope of his triumph. So the truth about everything ultimately has a Christocentric focus.

The contemporary mind has lost this focus and either finds truth hopelessly fragmented or else tries to impose some artificial unity that lacks the same fit and coherence.[4] Those church fathers who tell us that all truth is God's truth accordingly go on to say the church must regather its fragments from wherever they are scattered and restore them to the whole from which they were torn. The pieces of learning we call "secular" must be brought back into relation with the "sacred." Science and religion, philosophy and religion, ethics and religion, art and religion, work and play and religion must all be seen again as a coherent whole. It is not enough to assert this in principle; it must be worked through in practice. Such is the mandate for Christian thought and action, a world view in which the many kingdoms of this world's knowledge become the kingdom of the Logos, Jesus Christ.

THE HUMAN NATURE OF KNOWING

In principle, because of its theistic basis, human knowledge should be both possible and unifiable. But in practice we have problems: we lack clarity, we lack concentration, we lack information, we lack time, we lack objectivity. All this is a matter of human finiteness and dependency. Lack of concentration, for example, reflects our emotional, physical, and social ties and limitations. Lack of objectivity is due to our personal and historical needs and involvements. Our finiteness shows all the time. We know in part. We see through a glass darkly. Human knowledge is at best a progress report, and, because we have to make judgments notwithstanding these limitations, it remains fallible. Our information may get outdated; our arguments may be invalidated; our interpretations and theories may be shot down.

Human finiteness is not a moral failing, however, and no guilt attaches itself to errors we could not avoid. Intellectual laziness is another matter; so is overly hasty judgment, careless logic, or the

4. This is the theme of Carl F. H. Henry in chap. 12, "The Living Logos and Defunct Counterfeits," in *God, Revelation and Authority*, vol. III (Waco: Word Books, 1976).

unthinking adoption of naturalistic assumptions. These reflect our fallenness rather than just finiteness. So do those moral and religious blocks that the New Testament speaks of as a spiritual blindness that prevents people seeing the light of the gospel. The effects of sin and disbelief on human knowledge and understanding are marked; they pervade the history of thought and the current marketplace of ideas; they color the mind of our culture and infect the thinking of Christians and non-Christians alike. Sin and error are not synonymous, but neither one is a respecter of persons; they infiltrate the best of institutions and contaminate us all.

Yet sin as such does not directly affect our knowledge of nature and its laws. It is primarily finiteness that hinders us there and only indirectly our fallenness, through the misdirection of energy, attention, and funds, through the misleading use of nontheistic assumptions, the rise of scientism, and the misuse of scientific technology. The knowing process is directly affected by sin in proportion to the proximity of its subject matter to the heart of a Christian perspective. Emil Brunner states it well in his "law of the closeness of relation":

> The nearer anything lies to that center of existence where we are concerned with the whole, that is, with man's relation to God and the being of the person, the greater is the disturbance of rational knowledge by sin; the farther away anything lies from this center, the less is the disturbance felt, and the less difference is there between knowing as a believer or as an unbeliever.[5]

Thus natural science is less affected than sociology, and sociology than literature or ethics or theology itself. In these terms, knowledge of many things remains viable for humankind in general.

Nor can we overlook the goodness of God in all of this. Considerable knowledge of nature, society, and people is essential for a life that is ordered and good, and increasingly so in the complex world of today. God's goodness to all (his "common grace") preserves the possibility of what we need, and in fact has advanced the

5. Brunner, *Revelation and Reason*, trans. Olive Wyan (Philadelphia: Westminster Press, 1946), p. 383. Abraham Kuyper also offers helpful suggestions as to the effects of sin in human knowledge in a section entitled "Science and Sin," in *Principles of Sacred Theology* (New York: Scribners, 1898), II.ii.

arts and sciences, and medical and other useful knowledge, with immense benefit to people. In the last decades disciplines have proliferated and knowledge has exploded in every direction. Yet the human nature of all this knowing is evident on every side: on the one hand, it is flawed, often shortsighted, fragmentary, tentative, ill-used, even disastrous; on the other hand, it is mind-boggling in both breadth and depth. Like humankind itself, it is both the glory and the shame of the universe.

This ambiguity affects religious knowledge, too, it will be said. There are few if any finally and irrefutably mustered lines of evidence or argument, and there is no one theology to end all the rest, because human knowledge is still in progress, subject to correction, change, and growth. But it is important to realize that from a biblical perspective the frequent lack of complete logical certainty is no surprise and no worry. The Greek ideal of human knowledge as indubitably certain and detachedly objective is alien to Scripture, for there knowledge is a God-given conviction and assurance of the truth, a knowing in which I am personally involved (*ginōskō* rather than the more philosophical *theōreō* or *epistamai*), and a wisdom for those who are teachable. It does not require the infallibility of humans and their knowledge, but the infallibility of God alone and of his word.

There are limits to reasonable ambiguity and doubt. The objective conditions of knowledge remain public, the same for all; and some at least of the subjective conditions (our cognitive abilities and psychological makeup) differ only in degree. So we can appeal to what is universal, as we did in Chapter Three: universal laws of thought, universal basic beliefs, universal scope. And the biblical revelation has the final word.

Yet the human nature of knowing reveals both finiteness and fallenness. We know in part and we see through a glass darkly, but know and see we do. Our subjectivity can distort our perception of facts and our interpretations of things; we can blunder in relating theory to practice, whether by unethical decisions or lopsided attitudes; and we shall look more at this in the next chapter. But thanks to the God who is true and reliable, the knowledge we need is possible. Creational tasks that require knowledge remain, and the responsibility persists to seek wisdom and understanding.

I speak of "responsibility to seek," because another pervasive factor in the human nature of knowing is the relation of personal commitment to rational activity. Whereas the existentialist and the rationalist might try to separate these two, a Christian view of knowing recognizes that separation is impossible. In fact, once the world-view dependency of epistemology is recognized, and once the effect of prephilosophical beliefs, attitudes, and values is seen, the separation of commitment from knowing breaks down.

By "commitment" I mean a whole-hearted and whole-life involvement such as any world view and any religious or quasi-religious faith entails. Commitment in this sense and rational activity are inseparable, for reasoning is a personal activity, inevitably affected by our most basic beliefs and values. That Christian commitment influences thought, and thought contributes to Christian commitment is evident in a variety of ways we have already observed.

(1) Christian commitment motivates inquiry: see the vast history of Christian thought.
(2) Christian commitment mandates inquiry.
(3) Christian commitment affects selectivity and perceptivity.
(4) Christian commitment includes assent to true beliefs, but is much more than that.
(5) Christian commitment brings unity to both thought and life.
(6) Christian commitment grounds confidence in knowing.
(7) Reason apprehends beliefs inherent in Christian commitment.
(8) Reason articulates and elaborates on those beliefs.
(9) Reason pursues cultural tasks mandated, illuminated, and informed by Christian commitment.
(10) Reason explores the justifiability of believing what Christian commitment affirms.

The point is twofold. First, other commitments are related to thought in analogous ways, so that what we have said provides a basis for developing a personalistic approach to human knowledge. This we shall do in the next chapter. Second, it underscores human responsibility in the quest for truth. Universal objective and subjective preconditions for knowing are largely given, and we are of course responsible for using such resources wisely and well. But commitment is an individual affair: commitments vary. We need to scrutinize our commitments and the perspectives they give lest we suppress the truth as the Bible warns. An unexamined life of learning is not worth living.

CHAPTER 9

TRUTH AND KNOWLEDGE: PHILOSOPHICAL

In the last chapter we drew some epistemological consequences of Christian theism, particularly in regard to the human nature of knowing, that are out of step with elements in modern philosophy. It is therefore important to face the problems that appear. We shall find, however, that in reality the problems are created elsewhere, and are largely resolved by a personalist view of knowledge such as Christian theism suggests.

Problems arise because of the extremes to which human thinking often swings. Enlightenment philosophy encouraged the view that we are capable of a knowledge that is completely objective and completely certain, and that consists in precisely verbalized propositions. Revelation, as John Locke put it, simply adds further propositions. [1] Current scientific humanism is an extension of that kind of rationalism, modeling all knowledge on a particular view of science.

Romanticists and existentialists, seeking a less one-dimensional view, have overreacted in the direction of subjectivity rather than objectivity, of feeling rather than reason, and of freedom from any logical necessity at all. Revelation has become a subjective and noncognitive experience, if it is acknowledged at all. Yet they need to recall that Locke also said, "He that takes away reason, to make way for revelation, puts out the light of both." [2] Marxist humanism also overreacted by making truth historically relative, because it

1. John Locke, *Essay on Human Understanding*, IV.xviii.
2. Ibid., IV.xix.

depends on socioeconomic conditions. The mistake of Enlightenment epistemology, then, was to stress the logical and propositional to the exclusion of the more human nature of knowing. The mistake of the reaction was to stress nonrational aspects to the loss of the logical and propositional.

This schizophrenia in modern philosophy finds expression in three problems we shall now address.

KNOWLEDGE AND BELIEF

The first problem is an exaggerated distinction between knowledge and belief that has its roots in Greek thought. In his *Republic*, Plato illustrated the distinction by the use of a divided line, the top half of which represents knowledge and the bottom half opinion.

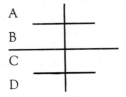

Knowledge is gained either (A) by dialectic, a careful conceptual analysis that pares away inconsistent or vacuous ideas so as to produce a direct contemplation of the truth, or (B) by deduction, mathematical-style, from the knowledge dialectic establishes. Knowledge is of transcendent and eternal forms and so is independent of sense experience; it is a recollection of unchanging ideas innate in the mind. In contrast, opinion depends on experience, and like experience it is changeable. Beliefs (C) about particular things may be assured for practical purposes but are far from being certain and objective. Illusions (D) are even more changeable and devoid of truth.

Knowledge, then, is an unchanging apprehension of universal truth with complete certainty, while belief assents uncertainly to opinions based on varying and incomplete experiences of a changing world. This Platonic distinction persisted in Western thought through the Enlightenment. With the rise of empirical science, it became somewhat blurred. Science yields knowledge by means of cause-effect arguments from indisputable sense data. Belief, it was said, is supported at best by low probabilities, and remains fallible.

To David Hume goes the credit for exploding the Enlightenment view. Knowledge was supposedly either a priori or causally inferred from experience. But he argued, the only a priori knowledge we have is not of matters of fact but of logical relations between empirically derived ideas, as in mathematics and in definitions like "a brother is a male sibling." Empirical knowledge invariably fails at the point of its causal arguments, because we have no assured knowledge of any necessary connections of a causal sort. Hume was a skeptic. What we have to live with, and can live with in practice, is belief based only on subjective habit and feeling. Something akin to Plato's level (C) prevails.

If Hume exploded the rationalist ideal, Kant approved. Concerned about the mechanistic science whose causal explanations undermined human freedom and religious belief, he undertook to "do away with knowledge in order to make room for belief."[3] Kant's critique of objective and certain knowledge pointed to our intrusion of subjective forms of perception and categories of thought that have no known bearing on things in themselves, so that the way we perceive and understand things is not purely objective, and can never be known with certainty to yield truth. At best we postulate beliefs that unify and complete the picture, satisfying both our intellectual and our practical demands.

Here, then, are two extremes. On the one hand, the Platonic and Enlightenment rationalist claims a knowledge that is completely objective and certain and disdains mere belief. On the other hand, the modern critic, heir to Kant and Hume, admits no logically certain knowledge and settles for subjectively based beliefs instead. From Hume it was a short step to the pragmatism and relativism of William James, and from Kant a short way to the greater subjectivism of romanticist and existentialist writers.

Interestingly enough, the same extremes appear in religious thought. On the one hand, natural theology and a rationalist kind of apologetic offer purely objective logical proofs to establish the truth with virtual certainty. On the other hand, the religious existentialist accepts a subjectively elicited faith devoid of appeal to objective controls.

Is there some alternative to these extremes? The knowledge-

3. Preface to second edition of Kant's *Critique of Pure Reason*. See p. 29 of N. K. Smith translation (New York: St. Martin's Press, 1965).

belief distinction cannot be drawn between the infallible and fallible, for the human nature of knowing does not admit infallibility. Nor should the distinction be placed between the rational and the emotive, as if knowing is completely rational and not at all emotive, while belief is emotive and not rationally based in any way. Nor can it be reduced to a simple conjunction that adds beliefs to what is certain. Somehow the two are more intimately related, more integrated with each other than that.

I think it important at this juncture to remind ourselves that the Bible makes no sharp division between knowledge and belief. Knowledge is assured, but so are beliefs. Both are held with personal conviction. Paul said he *knew* whom he *believed* and was *sure* (2 Tim. 1:12), an interesting admixture of words in the light of Platonic epistemology.

Whereas the concept of knowledge was the focus of discussion from Plato through the Enlightenment, the concept of belief has since received attention. One example is John Henry Newman's *Grammar of Assent*, which introduces an alternative distinction between certainty and certitude, the former being a logical matter, based entirely on evidence and argument, while the latter, still drawing on evidence, is a psychological state of confidence and conviction. William James' classic essay "The Will to Believe" is also very much to the point. When the evidence is indecisive but a decision is momentous and unavoidable, he suggested that belief may properly rest on more personal and practical considerations than scientific and logical arguments would normally allow.

Both Newman and James see that belief involves the human subject and is more wholistically personal than any detached and purely logical inquiry. This is the clue we need. It fits our personalistic model better than trying to fit human belief into the paradigms of Enlightenment or Platonic epistemology. The act of belief is the act of a person, related to all that a person is. Knowledge in the Platonic sense is an exclusively cognitive state, the result just of intellectual inquiry. The one is whole-personal, the other part-personal. The relation, then, is that of the whole to the part, not that of one part to just another.

Kierkegaard says this forcefully. He complained that the age of reason, the Enlightenment, was an age without passion. Passion is not just a passing emotion; it is whole-hearted, whole-personal concern and involvement. An age without passion, he declares, is an age without values—whether religious, ethical, economic, or political values, or intellectual for that matter. Unless I believe in truth and love the truth heartily, what intellectual values do I have? Will I give myself intensely to knowing?[4] Man does not live or even think by reason alone. Out of his heart comes his thinking.

If the two are thus related, then evidence and argument and degrees of certainty are admissible in belief. Recent epistemology does not continue the Platonic distinction, but sees knowledge as a subset of belief, part of a larger whole. Knowledge is defined as "justified true belief." Attention is on the cognitive content of belief rather than on the more whole-personal act; and within the cognitive content of belief some can be called knowledge, distinguished within the compass of belief by evidence that justifies one in believing. To prove a belief indisputably true may be asking too much of human knowing, but to justify believing it true is not. Fallibility is admitted, yet the evidence and argument may still be sufficient to justify belief.

These two developments, the whole-personal/part-personal distinction and the justification of belief, clearly provide a mediating alternative between the rationalist and skeptic extremes. It coheres much better with a creational point of view, for it combines the epistemic modesty of a fallibilist position with the epistemic hope of being sure.

THEORY AND PRACTICE

Closely tied to questions about knowledge and belief is the problem of theory and practice. Again our thinking has been shaped by the Platonic model and its successors in the Renaissance and Enlightenment. For Plato, knowledge was a matter of detached contemplation, an unchanging apprehension of eternal forms for their own sake, rather than an outcome of involvement with the changing world of everyday experience. Our word "theory" comes from the Greek verb for contemplating (*theōreō*), which, significantly, is also used of spectators: knowing as such was a spectator sport devoid of active involvement. It has uses, of course, in the world of partic-

4. Kierkegaard, *The Present Age* (New York: Harper & Row, Harper Torchbooks, 1962).

ulars, for particulars depend on the forms; yet the goal of knowing is itself not action but detached contemplation.

Aristotle also distinguished sharply between theory and practice. As experience is wiser than mere sensation, and the artist than the person of experience, so speculative and theoretical science is better than productive activity. Humans are distinguished from other animals by being rational, and reason's highest achievement is theoretical contemplation.

Descartes' "I think, therefore I exist" sums it up well. While initially he gives a broad definition of thinking that includes willing, doubting, understanding, and any cognitive state, his philosophy functions with a more limited notion of reason as thinking clear and distinct ideas and deducing logical conclusions. The ability for theoretical thinking is what distinguishes humans.

The philosophical revolution initiated by Hume and Kant gave primacy to the active life over the contemplative and to practice over theory. For Hume, belief rested on practical grounds. "Be a philosopher," he said, "but be still a man."[5] Kant distinguished between pure and practical reason. The former he criticized for its impotence, but the latter guides action and justifies belief. A person is at heart a free moral agent, and it is the practical demands of action that shape belief.

But extremes follow revolution. While John Dewey rightly criticized the spectator theory of knowledge, he inferred that *all* knowing has practical purposes and arises in addressing particular problem situations. Applying this view to education, he said that inquiry begins with problem situations that call for resolution; ideas are practical proposals for handling problems, not eternal truths. This was a welcome corrective to the purely theoretical approach of classical education, but it created difficulties. First, it provided a vehicle for Dewey's relativism. True beliefs and right values are relative to changing situations, for an idea becomes true only when it is put into practice and the consequences it predicts follow. On this account, truth has no transcendent locus at all. Second, by making knowledge pragmatic it tends to cut the ground from under pure research and theory and from the enriching value of contemplating ideas and art and life in general—even of developing an overall world view and gaining a transcendent perspective. Relativism and

5. Hume, *An Enquiry Concerning Human Understanding*, sec. i.

practicalism are both too anthropocentric, too purely humanistic, for a creationist approach.

Marxism is more influential now in the swing from theory to practice, claiming that ideas are shaped by the demands of praxis and must serve the class struggle. The task of philosophy is not to theorize about the world but to change it. Art should not reflect a fixed order or further the delights of aesthetic contemplation, but should concern social change and further the revolution. Praxis, not theory, is king.

From a creational standpoint the main problem with the practice-extreme is its anthropocentrism; and from that, relativism follows. But the theory-extreme has problems, too; its elitism, its lack of epistemic modesty, its failure to see that the creature and his knowledge exist in order to serve, and its tendency to reduce the person to one part of the person, the rational. Here again are the symptoms of the anthropocentric.

Is another alternative to this either/or possible? How can the two be better related?

First, we remind ourselves of a strength in the Platonic model, the recognition of a cosmic order that transcends all change. This gave epistemic confidence that unchanging knowledge of unchanging order is possible in principle, whereas unchanging knowledge of changing particulars is not. From a theistic standpoint, too, this is an ordered universe, a law-governed creation. Not everything is in flux; not every old order changes, giving place to new. The practicalist extremes see change with little uniformity, little order that we cannot change. The theist sees that order is the context for change, that it makes wise change possible, and that a theoretical knowledge that understands the order is requisite for purposeful action. She is committed to both order and change, the orderliness of creation and redemptive change. Both theoretical and practical knowledge are therefore needed: educationally, practice needs theory, and theory makes a difference to practice; and theoretical disciplines underlie our "how-to-do-its" in every walk of life.

Second, a human being is not to be distinguished primarily in Cartesian terms as a rational being but as a person, a responsible agent who acts. In the context of action thought and theory arise, but they are not always situationally addressed as they are for Dewey, for theoretical thought is itself a responsible activity for people in God's creation. We rightly explore the works of God and contemplate their maker. Contemplating, we stand in awe, though contemplation also equips for action.

Again we have a whole-part distinction. The Scottish realists of the eighteenth century seem to have recognized it. Their epistemology focused on "common sense beliefs" that are so necessary to the conduct of life that we cannot live and act without them. Such beliefs are established not by rational proofs but by virtue of the fact that God made both us and the world as he did.[6] Theoretical thought is a part, derived from the whole practice of life and serving it well, both by informing specific activities and by contemplating God and his creation. Belief is wholistic, arising from the practice of life and essential to action. So it appears that belief and practice are partners which knowledge and theory serve.

SUBJECTIVITY AND OBJECTIVITY

Related to the two preceding problems is the rationalist quest for a purely objective knowledge that admits of no subjective elements or influence. This ideal was most pronounced in the Enlightenment, which extended the mechanistic model to epistemology and regarded knowledge as an almost mechanical result of causal processes. The paradigm case was physical perception. Sense impressions are caused when physical stimuli to the sense organs produce changed brain states with a corresponding consciousness. Thomas Hobbes extended the causal explanation to our concepts, our reasoning, and our language. Thus all knowledge is produced by mechanisms unaffected by more personal and inward conditions. John Locke accordingly adopted the *tabula rasa* theory, that the mind is like a blank tablet of wax on which sense experiences leave impressions, which we then conjoin subconsciously according to fixed laws of association into larger concepts constituting our knowledge.

For many empiricists since then, sense impressions afford a hard core of irreducible and objective data on which rationalistic proofs can be built; for the scientific humanist it follows that the empirical

6. Eg., *The Works of Thomas Reid, D. D.*, ed. Sir Wm. Hamilton (James Thin, 1895), vol. I, pp. 108, 230, etc.

In developing the whole-part concept, I have benefitted from John Macmurray's *The Self as Agent* (London: Faber & Faber, 1957), chap. 4. For another approach see N. Wolterstorff, "Theory and Praxis," *Christian Scholars Review* 9 (1980): 317.

methods of science prove things beyond dispute. Objective facts are simply given in experience, and scientifically controlled observations make them doubly sure.

On this account, not only facts but also interpretations are considered foolproof. Initially, causal interpretations qualified, on the assumption that an observable regularity of antecedents and consequences proved a cause-effect relationship. Some scientifically oriented thinkers still jump to those causal conclusions; but philosophers have become more guarded, thanks to Hume's insistence that observable regularity alone can never prove that a causal connection exists. The philosophically chastened often settle instead for the positivist claim to empirical generalizations with predictive power. Thus, from Mill onward, the notion of general covering laws took hold, and both scientific facts and scientific laws were taken to be entirely objective and as certain as can be.

At the other extreme, all scientific objectivity was challenged when Hume traced beliefs to subjective habit, not to objective data. Kant argued that both the spatial and temporal forms of sense perception and such interpretive categories as causation are entirely subjective and without any known objective referents. How we perceive things and how we understand them depend on the knower, not on objective data. The German idealists pushed further the creative role of the human subject in constituting knowledge and belief. Psychological and sociological accounts followed. Marx's economic determinism was only one. The world, said Schopenhauer, is my idea. Friedrich Nietzsche treated philosophy as the projection of subjective drives for power, rather than as an objective inquiry. Sigmund Freud gave psychoanalytic accounts of religious beliefs, a ploy that Morris Lazerowitz has extended to all metaphysics.[7] Perhaps the latest example is that of Paul Feyerabend, a philosopher of science who reduces scientific argument to something subjective and relativistic, far outpacing the sociological account of Thomas Kuhn.[8] Thus science is deprived of objectivity altogether. Plainly the nineteenth-century developmental and relational model has displaced the mechanists' objectivity.

Analogies occur in biblical hermeneutics. At one extreme is

7. Lazerowitz, *The Structure of Metaphysics* (New York: Humanities Press, 1955).
8. See I. Lakatos and A. Musgrave, eds., *Criticism and the Growth of Knowledge* (Cambridge: Cambridge Univ. Press, 1970).

the view that biblical data are completely unambiguous and that from them one may draw equally unambiguous conclusions and a wholly objective system of theology. Interpretation is an entirely objective science with no subjectivity at all intruding. At the other extreme is the existential hermeneutic that replaces attention to objective truth verbalized in Scripture with concern for an existential self-disclosure triggered by the biblical witness. The one approaches interpretation mechanically, the other quite subjectively.

Tensions obviously exist between either extreme and our creational approach to truth and knowledge. On the one hand, the Greek distinction between knowledge and belief is reflected here, so that what we said earlier about human fallibility applies. Likewise, the relation between theory and practice implies that we cannot detach ourselves from active concerns and be entirely objective. The human knower is a being with inwardness, with values and interests and assumptions of which he may not even be fully conscious and which he can never completely suspend without ceasing to be the person he is. Complete objectivity is an illusion.

On the other hand, complete subjectivity is neither desirable nor logically implied. Fair consideration of all sides of a question, honest judgments, and careful assessment of evidence are morally obligatory, to whatever extent they are humanly possible. Individual prejudices, ignorance, and blind spots can be at least partly transcended, but the generic concerns of human subjects are with us always. And this is a good thing because it keeps us, as Kierkegaard remarked, from endless indecision whenever any shade of ambiguity persists. But if it were impossible to transcend our subjectivity at all, then not even the grace of God could enlighten the unbelieving mind and convince the unsympathetic of truth.

Some third alternative, then, is needed in epistemology other than the extremes of complete objectivity and complete subjectivity. We can take a first step toward it by adopting a distinction I introduced earlier between two very different senses of objectivity and subjectivity that are often confused, the metaphysical and the epistemological.[9] Metaphysical objectivity is the objective reality of a state of affairs independently of whether or not we know or believe anything about it at all. Thus sticks and stones and cabbages and kings exist objectively, and so does God: God knows it is so,

9. In Chapter Three.

whatever any of us mortals think, and his knowledge is the ultimate locus for all truth about reality. But unicorns and centaurs have no such metaphysical objectivity, at least in the sense of reality that we apply to cabbages or dogs. They exist only in our imagination and myths, in our minds, dependent on their being known. Another case is my own daughter, for I have none. Her status is entirely imaginary, in my mind, metaphysically subjective. The scientific humanist will claim that God, like Santa Claus and centaurs, is metaphysically subjective, too, existing only in mythology and imagination. Like some vague fear, he is "all in your mind"—he exists nowhere else independently.

On the other hand, epistemological objectivity is the knower's attitude of detachment, unconcern, uninvolvement in regard to an object of inquiry. Epistemological subjectivity is his involvement and personal concern with whatever it is he may know.

This distinction pays dividends. Some rationalists are concerned that any admission of subjectivity is a denial of metaphysical as well as epistemological objectivity, but that patently is not the case and does not logically follow. My knowledge of what is independently real may well be subjectively influenced and may involve me passionately, but that does not affect its metaphysical status. Metaphysical objectivity and epistemological subjectivity are quite compatible with each other and come ready-mixed all the time. Fears to the contrary were unfounded.

Again, the Romanticist complains that reason is cold and impersonal; this is equally unfounded. The Enlightenment may have idolized that sort of epistemological objectivity, but it is not necessary at all. If the pursuit of truth really flows from the love of truth, impassioned inquiry naturally follows.

Yet again, concern is heard that once we admit subjectivity, all objective controls are lost. Objectivity and subjectivity, both in the metaphysical sense, may indeed be incompatible and mutually exclusive, but not epistemologically. Objective controls do still operate—public evidence and logical arguments, for example—at the same time as such subjective influences as predispositions, fears, and hopes, and they can even make us change our minds, resolve our fears, and abandon some hopes. Knowing is in every case an individual mix of subjective and objective factors.

This fits well with the creational view of creaturely dependence and finiteness, for it is the not-so-simple nature of dependence that involves us subjectively in knowing. What leads us to ask questions, to inquire, to think, to need to know anyway but our disconcerting dependence on all that surrounds and affects our existence? Emotionally we are dependent, and dependency drives us to inquire. Physically, economically, socially, and in a myriad of ways our dependency shows. Our identity is at stake, our present security and future hopes, our values, our very selves. We need, we value, we hope and even vaguely believe, we think in a cultural and historical setting—all of this is our subjectivity and affects both how and what, as persons we are, we think and know.

A creational approach has further advantages here, for we are part of an ordered creation, our dependency and needs reflecting the balance and purpose of the whole. Subjectivity, then, need not be just a liability, it can also be an asset. There is meaning and purpose to those areas of need and value that all human beings inevitably possess—a universality to our subjectivity. Philosophers have attempted purely objective, causal arguments for the existence of physical bodies. But it is telling that our universal physical needs show subjectively the reality of our bodies and cry out for the reality of a physical world of which we are a part and on which we depend. Philosophers have argued too for the existence of other minds, trying to construct purely objective, logical proofs. But it counts epistemologically that our inner being yearns for other persons and that togetherness and empathy reveal us to one another for what in reality we are. Again, philosophers have constructed objective arguments for the existence and nature of God, but epistemologically it is significant that our hearts are restless, as Augustine observed, until they rest in God. Subjectivity is an asset as well as a liability in knowing.[10] Hence I have suggested universal subjective considerations, namely value areas and action spheres, that help justify belief (Chap. 3).

Yet in the sciences, would we not expect objectivity to prevail? Ask a scientist why he went into science, how his emotional and physical condition affects his work, why he works in the particular science he does, why the research project in which he is now engaged, and how he came up with his latest theory. Ask questions like this, and subjectivity is soon revealed. Michael Polanyi, sci-

10. See the development of this in C. S. Evans, *Subjectivity and Religious Belief* (Grand Rapids: Eerdmans, 1978).

entist turned philosopher, speaks of a tacit dimension and of personal factors in science and knowledge.[11] We always attend, he says, *from* something (the proximal) *to* something (the distal), and the former influences how the latter appears to us, what meaning it conveys, and how it is related to everything else. Subjective and peripheral factors, in other words, both preclude complete objectivity and focus attention in revealing ways. Regarding philosophy, I have elsewhere argued a similar point. Presuppositions and world perspectives influence philosophical methods as well as scientific, historical, and ethical knowledge. All knowledge is in this sense somewhat "perspectival."[12] Of course, Brunner's rule applies here, too, that a world view is more significant in proportion to the proximity of what is discussed to the world view's central perspective. Degrees of objectivity are present as well.

Likewise in literary and biblical hermeneutics, the objective and subjective combine. On the one hand, there are objective controls on interpretation, both historical, contextual, and linguistic. On the other hand, we have pre-understandings, expectations that we bring to the text, and an empathy for what the writer is thinking and feeling. In hermeneutics, as in science and philosophy, interpretations are not so much *deduced* logically from purely objective facts as they are *adduced* as hypotheses to be weighed and tried on for size and fit, and for their coherence with what we already know. Good judgment is required, a sense of what the subject matter and method as a whole require. Understanding any literature takes wholistic imagination.

Let us call this third alternative "interpretive realism." It is realistic in affirming the independent objective nature of the things known, their metaphysical objectivity. It is interpretive in affirming that to know is always to interpret the facts that are given, so that epistemological subjectivity is present.

What is a fact? Metaphysically, a fact is an objective state of affairs that pertains at a given time and place and in a given set of relationships, independently of whether any of us know it at all. Epistemologically, a fact is a "fact of experience," related to the whole complex flux of inner and outer experience of which it is a

11. Polanyi, *The Tacit Dimension* (New York: Doubleday, 1966) and *Personal Knowledge* (Chicago: Univ. of Chicago Press, 1958).
12. See *Christian Philosophy in the Twentieth Century* and *Faith Seeks Understanding.*

part. Subjectivity has intruded and shaped it. The facts we know, then, are not bare facts clothed only in a birthday suit of metaphysical objectivity, but "interprefacts" perceived and understood by a human person who clothes them in the habits of his human experience and perspective.

Both our interprefacts and our larger and more deliberate interpretations of things, being shaped in measure by what we are, are shaped as well by world-view perspectives and what we consider to be objectively real. Whether or not we believe in an objectively ordered creation makes a difference, as it does whether we believe that everything has value and theocentric focus, that this is a teleological universe rather than a blind concatenation of causal forces, and that a personal God is lovingly involved. How I perceive things, how I interpret things, how I actually experience life as well as what I do are all affected. If a world view has the selective and guiding functions we indicated at the outset, then it affects our knowing as well as other activities.
A hymnwriter said it this way:

> Heaven above is brighter blue,
> Earth below is softer green,
> Something lives in every hue
> Christless eyes have never seen.

A Christian views the world, experiences it and interprets it differently than a naturalistic humanist. Yet there are still relatively objective controls, universal basic beliefs, logical laws, and empirical considerations that both Christians and naturalists weigh in their thinking.

The naturalistic humanist's approaches to knowledge, I suggest, fall into the fallacy of taking a part for the whole. Scientific knowledge is only one kind of knowing, markedly different from our knowledge of other persons, for example, and as conceived in terms of Enlightenment objectivity it is only part of science. The Romanticist's subjective experience of nature is again but part of natural knowledge, and part of our subjectivity, too. He has reacted from one part to another, dwarfing the knower again. Likewise, the Marxist's claim that socioeconomic conditions shape knowing is but part of the story, sadly misleading alone. Taking a part as the whole is a reductionist mistake.

Epistemological subjectivity, I suggest, represents the whole of our being out of which we think and with which we believe and understand and seek to know. Epistemological objectivity is a move we make by momentarily and partially detaching ourselves from all we are and holding ourselves and the demands of our being in abeyance. We seek objectivity because of what we are subjectively, because of what we need and want and value. The same pattern holds here as with knowledge and belief and with theory and practice: knowledge with confidence, along with theory and objectivity, while unduly elevated in the Greek and Enlightenment traditions, is part of knowing—but it is not the whole. The necessities of our existence require more, for a man's life does not consist in the abundance (or scarcity) of the objective and logically certain theories he possesses. Subjectivity is more wholistic than objectivity and yields a fuller knowledge. The rationalist has not sold his birthright for junk food, as the Romanticist and existentialist declare; but he has sold it nonetheless for something of too limited value to one who tries to live and think as a divinely created and responsible person.

SOME CONSEQUENCES

Where does this whole-part pattern lead us? It suggests the proper role of reason in human life. First, beliefs arise from and are often justified by the demands of life as a whole, not on the basis of theoretical reason alone. Second, theoretical reasoning also arises from the demands of life as a whole, not independently as an autonomous activity.

Human life and action require beliefs. The generic nature of human beings and the ordered nature of the world in which we live tend to evoke very similar beliefs in all of us, which we have called universal beliefs. They include adherence to a law of noncontradiction, belief in an external world of orderly processes, belief in the existence of other persons who share our world and with whom we communicate and live, and belief also in some ultimate reality with which we must eventually reckon.[13] Beliefs such as these are a *practical* necessity if we are to think and to function at all. Yet while

13. Reformed theology teaches that unfallen man had the fuller idea of a personal theistic being, a belief of which human sinfulness has robbed us. Hence we construct particular god-substitutes that fall tragically short of what humankind needs both rationally and in fuller ways.

they are not ultimately based on *theoretical* reasoning, they give rise to further inquiry of a theoretical sort, science and philosophy included.

An interesting parallel exists in the more specific beliefs of a particular world view. They, too, arise and are often justified in the wholistic context of a lived world where, granted the particular experiences and values involved, they also appear as a practical necessity. "Here I stand, I can do no other," said Martin Luther. Then theoretical reasoning arises to expound and weigh such belief.

How, then, are the universal and particular related? First, universal necessary beliefs of the sort I have indicated, being quite skeletal by themselves, are fleshed out in particular ways in our life-world under the influence of various world views and conceptual models. They rarely if ever appear alone in all their vagueness, yet being garbed in some world view they are no longer presupposition-less, world-view neutral at all. They are articulated in particular historical forms, and the particular beliefs that arise both embody and unify the universal.

Second, universal necessary beliefs are prerequisite to particular beliefs, providing their backdrop and context. He who confesses that Christ is come in the flesh must believe that an external world of things and people exists. The universal may not logically imply a particular belief, but it is nonetheless necessary to it even if not sufficient. Christianity, along with other viewpoints, may therefore be seen as articulating universal notions of the world, of persons, and of values in more specific and unifying ways. The universal provides background and context for particular Christian beliefs that flesh out the universal in a more complete and coherent fashion.

Third, universal necessary beliefs contribute to the weighing of particular beliefs. They eliminate some options: those that turn out to be self-contradictory, for example, or that seem to contradict a universal belief: this is why Berkeley's mentalism seems so odd at first. Or if I take seriously the universal belief in other persons like myself, then to be consistent I should accord others the respect I claim as a person for myself, and this argues against certain political extremes. Universal beliefs provide theoretical thought with unchanging points of reference in our weighing and developing of more particular views.

Fourth, by the same token, more particular beliefs are necessary for thinking and acting in concrete situations. As human persons, reflective and responsible agents, we need beliefs that will ground our values and guide our actions. Consequently, the appeal we made in Chapter Three to universal human needs and value areas is warranted in attempting to articulate and justify particular beliefs. The heart has its reasons, said Pascal, that reason does not know. Reason is always a part, not the whole. It is not independent and autonomous, but is rooted in the commitments of life. Aristotle said that *by nature* we desire to know. By nature, too, we value the truth. So to the basis of values we now turn.

CHAPTER 10

A THEISTIC BASIS FOR VALUES

Persons are reflective and valuing beings. We have considered the knowledge and truth that human reflection seeks, and now we turn our attention to values. In every sphere of human activity, values are involved: moral values, aesthetic values, psychological values, political values, intellectual values, economic values, religious values, and so forth. Such values shape our lives, our society, our culture; and it is the pursuit of such values that is one of the major distinctions of human beings in this world. Yet ours is a pluralistic society in which no one set of values prevails, nor just one supreme good to integrate them all. Both agreements and disagreements exist: values we agree on, like peace and tolerance and liberty, enable us to live together; yet disagreement about values often divides Christian ideals from those of contemporary naturalistic humanism.

Values are good ends, ideals we ought to pursue.[1] Christian theists and naturalistic humanists could possibly agree on this definition, for both reject the Platonic view that values are objective realities independent of persons. The humanist rejects Platonism because of his anthropocentrism: things have value only to human beings and the human community, for our betterment, as good ends we ought therefore to pursue. The Christian rejects it because of his theocentrism: things have value ultimately to a personal God, for his purposes, and God's values are then the good ends we humans ought to pursue. The agreement is that values, to be valuable at all, must be of value to valuing beings, to persons. The disagreement

---

1. I word it this way, as students of ethical theory will recognize, to combine a teleological element ("good ends") with a deontological ("ought").

is over whose valuing makes something truly valuable and obligatory for us, whether ours or God's.

However, some humanists, those whom we identified as romanticist, might disagree. If in keeping with nineteenth-century Romanticism they romanticize all of nature, then they will value nature for its own sake rather than just for its value to persons, either human or divine. Otherwise, we are told, the door is wide open to exploitation and rape of the environment and its natural resources for selfish, pragmatic, and shortsighted ends. The Romanticist therefore either depersonalizes values or else personalizes nature: either he rejects the claim that values have value because of valuing beings and goes the Platonic route of impersonal values independent of any persons, or else he adopts a vitalism and panpsychism that personify all of nature as if it were alive, responsive and concerned, a quasi-valuing thing in its own right. In either case, animals and plants, as well as the landscape itself, have value of their own.

The Christian theist is dissatisfied with both of these options. Regarding the first, neither values nor anything else are independent of a God who is Creator and Lord of all: their source and ground is in God and what he values. Regarding the second, humans are uniquely in the image of God, demarcated from other earthly creatures as responsible and valuing beings: the personification of nature obscures this uniqueness of persons. But while Christian theism is thus at odds with Romanticism, it does not follow that nature's value is entirely anthropocentric, for humans are not the only persons involved. God cares about his creation more than humans do, and for more ultimate and inclusive ends than ours: he values nature's splendor and fecundity for himself. We should not be exploitive and selfishly pragmatic, then, for nature has further potentials, and we have other ends that would better honor the Creator and respect his handiwork. So to say that values have value only for persons neither denigrates nature nor invites its abuse. Whether or not some humanists open the way to environmental rape, theism does not.

The difference between a Christian and a humanist understanding of values is profound. First, the naturalist claims that our obligation to pursue certain values rather than others, whether individually or in the context of social institutions such as marriage and government, is based simply on human interests, or on the social conventions and contracts that arise in the course of history. Thomas Hobbes, for instance, regarded moral obligations as contractual, based on enlightened self-interest; a sophisticated version of this view appears in the recent work of the Harvard ethicist John Rawls.[2] Defining justice in terms of fairness, he bases the obligation to seek justice on a hypothetical contract that is adopted because we like the consequences of fairness, and because it seems the most reasonable way to go.

But the obligation is entirely self-imposed; and the self-imposed obligations of man and society, like New Year's resolutions, can too easily be neglected or changed. Without some independent standard, enlightened self-interest might well find cause to override the interests of the community. Even if humans have a natural altruistic tendency, as some have tenuously generalized, how can we infer altruistic obligations from that? Does *is* imply *ought*? Would it do so also if unbridled rather than enlightened self-interest marked us all? Would unbridled self-interest then be the good end we ought to pursue? What does make values obligatory? Whence comes the binding force of unchanging moral duty, if there is no independent authority transcending local interests and social change? Has the humanist an adequate basis for obligation to the values we ought to pursue?

Ethicists since David Hume have wrestled with this separation of "is" from "ought." Elizabeth Anscombe rightly complains that it is due to the lack of a *law* conception in ethics, and claims that it is not possible to have a law conception unless we believe in a divine law-giver.[3] In this regard, the humanism of twentieth-century academic philosophy and social science stands in marked contrast to the moral traditions of the West that are rooted in Judeo-Christian thought.[4]

Second, the difference between humanism and Christian theism involves the anthropocentric claim that the highest end integrating all of our values is the human community itself, and that all other values should flow from this. The theist, meantime, claims that

2. John Rawls, *A Theory of Justice* (Cambridge: Harvard Univ. Press, 1971). pt. 1
3. Elizabeth Anscombe, "Modern Moral Philosophy," *Philosophy* 33 (1958): 1–19.
4. This claim is elaborated by Alan Donagan, *The Theory of Morality* (Chicago: Univ. of Chicago Press, 1977), chap. 1.

God is our highest good, that what integrates life and gives rise to other values is the supreme end of glorifying, enjoying, and serving him in all our creaturely activities.

In the giving of the law, as recorded in Exodus 20, the source of obligation is plainly God himself, and to "have no other gods" before him means that he is our highest good. We therefore need to explore the idea that God is both the ultimate source of obligation and our highest good; this will help us see more fully what a Christian world view contributes regarding human values.[5]

A TRANSCENDENT SOURCE OF OBLIGATION

As in every aspect of a Christian world view, we must start with the God-creation distinction and relationship.

(1) *The eternal God is completely and unchangingly good.* He exists of himself and needs none other than himself in order to be or to be satisfied. He creates for his own ends, and his glory he can share with none other. He is his own highest end. In all these regards God is unique, transcending all other valuing beings.

Because he created *ex nihilo* and all creation continually depends on him for its existence and order and destiny, God is of supreme importance to everything in creation. He makes everything else possible and anything else worthwhile. We, by contrast, do not exist of ourselves. We need God in order to be and to be satisfied, for "in him we live and move and have our being" (Acts 17:28). We do not exist for ourselves but were created for God's good purposes, to glorify God and enjoy him forever. It is this which integrates all of life and gives lesser ends their worth. Because God is our highest good and we are obligated to him in all things, his purposes for this creation are the good ends we ought to pursue.

In moral philosophy, divine command theories have recently renewed this theme, relating ethical concepts like good and right to what God wills for us, and bad or wrong to what he forbids.[6]

---

5. Theological differences show up in different approaches to Christian ethics as in other aspects of a Christian world view. For an account of some such differences, see James Gustafson, *Protestant and Catholic Ethics* (Chicago: Univ. of Chicago Press, 1978).

6. See Ian Ramsey, ed., *Christian Ethics and Contemporary Philosophy* (London: SCM Press, 1966); Philip Quinn, *Divine Commands and Moral Requirements* (Oxford: Clarendon Press, 1978); Robert Adams, "A Modified

Two emphases appear here. First, the *content* of our moral obligations is coextensive with what God wills for us. This follows from the sovereignty of God over the whole creation, and is almost a truism for the theist. The second emphasis is that God is the ultimate *source* of our moral obligation, the only one who properly has authority over us all, and whom all of us should obey. This, too, is virtually a truism for the theist. Consequently, I take it that the divine command theory is in these two regards correct.

But while truistic, it is not insignificant. Ethicists have long asked whence comes the moral "ought," pointing out that natural facts and empirical consequences do not as such command us. Their "is" does not seem to imply any "ought"—that is, unless they reveal the will of a personal being with authority over us. The divine command theory points, therefore, to the authority of God, and in doing so identifies the ultimate source of moral obligation. In terms we have previously adopted, we all stand first and in everything else in relationship to God as his creatures. The obligation to do his will is simply a corollary of that.

It should be emphasized that a divine command theory of this sort says nothing about the sources of our moral knowledge. In the final analysis, as indicated in Chapter Eight, it is God who makes possible all the knowledge we can ever have of anything at all, but this does not foreclose epistemological questions about the means and sources of knowledge. The Christian regards Scripture as his final rule in moral matters as in doctrine, yet this by no means precludes other sources of moral knowledge. In fact, Scripture itself suggests our responsibility to some sort of general revelation in ethical matters (e.g., Rom. 1–2). Various attempts have been made to spell this out. Some, like Bishop Butler and the Scottish realists, have adopted an intuitionist approach, holding that we are endowed with the ability to directly grasp what is right. Others, like Augustine, believed in innate moral knowledge. Others again, like Aquinas and John Locke, developed natural law theories that draw moral knowledge from the nature of humankind as God made us. And

Divine Command Theory of Ethical Wrongness," in *Religion and Morality*, ed. Gene Outka and J. P. Reeder, Jr. (New York: Doubleday, 1973), pp. 318–47. See also the following anthologies: J. M. Idziak, ed., *Divine Command Morality: Historical and Contemporary Readings* (New York: Edwin Meller Press, 1979); Paul Helm, *Divine Commands and Morality* (New York: Oxford Univ. Press, 1981).

still others have attempted a kind of utilitarian approach. We shall return to this epistemological question.

One traditional objection faced by divine command theories is that they make God's will an arbitrary imposition doing possible violence to our every moral sensitivity. But for at least two reasons this could not be: first, what a person wills reflects his values and character. Second, in a good and wise being it reflects his knowledge of others' real needs. God's law, then, far from being arbitrary or capricious, expresses both his character and his concern for his creatures.

(2) *Values reveal character.* What God values for his creation and what he asks of us in his law reveal what he is like. In the biblical record, the two most inclusive moral concerns are *justice and love*, and these concerns characterize God himself in all he is and does. They underly the moral law; they are reiterated by the prophets; they are demonstrated in the gospel and exemplified by Jesus Christ. They should therefore be the overarching principles of all human morality, both personal and public. The good ends we ought to pursue, in business, politics, education or whatever, will then be both just and loving ends, and we should pursue them with justice and love.

"The Lord works . . . justice for all who are oppressed" (Ps. 103:6), and so ought we. Righteousness and justice are the foundation of his throne (Ps. 89:14), and so should they be for human governments and every human authority in whatever social context or institution. "What does the Lord require of you but to do justice . . . ?" (Micah 6:8). Just laws and just government, a just economy (just balances, just wages, etc), and an equitable relationship between husband and wife are therefore good ends we ought to pursue. Justice means treating equals equally, distributing benefits and liabilities equitably without favoritism, prejudice, or "respect of persons," in every sphere of life.

The God of love is also called "merciful and gracious, slow to anger and abounding in steadfast love" (Ps. 103:8). So the Lord requires us both "to do justice and to love kindness," and to walk humbly with God (Micah 6:8)—this last clause putting justice and love in the God-creation context that makes them obligatory. Jesus the Ideal Man exemplifies it all, dramatically revealing the kind of love intended—compassionate, unceasing, self-giving love that seeks nothing in return.

This love, *agapē*, differs from Greek ideals. Plato, for example, talked of *eros* in a broad sense of desiring the good for oneself. Aristotle thought friendship must always be reciprocated. Neither seem to have envisioned a love that does not seek first its own interests but is concerned rather for others. Yet Jesus makes *agapē* mandatory: the first and greatest commandment tells us to love God with all we are and have, the second tells us to love our neighbors as ourselves. Thus, work is to be a loving service to others as well as an exercise in economic justice, and we are to go the second mile beyond what society requires and even love our foes.

Plainly, justice and love merge. Justice is tempered with a love that does not always insist on one's own rights, and love's gifts are equitably distributed. Justice stresses more the outward ordering of life, while love is an inner and more personalized concern for the benefit of others. The theistic basis for values thus obligates us to pursue God's good ends with justice and with love, whether in politics, education, art, or business. [7]

(3) God created with purpose and declared what he made to be good, of value to himself. A relation exists, therefore, between what "is" and what "ought" to be, between *fact and value*. The physical world is not without purpose, value-free or value-neutral, to be manipulated at will for whatever we might desire, nor is its worth altogether relative or anthropocentric. Fact and value are united by God's purposes in creating.

Christian theism here contrasts with value-neutral views. The mechanistic science of the Enlightenment saw matter as inert, without inherent tendencies of its own but acted on by blind, external forces. Values then had to be located elsewhere than in the world of such facts, and were given either a subjective basis in human feelings and sentiment, or else an objective basis in Platonic fashion, independent of people or things. This separation of facts and values allowed them both to be objects of empirical study, whether in natural science or in social and behavioral science. Psychology and sociology purported to do value-free studies of human values, describing human values without judging what ought universally to

7. On the relationship of justice and love, see Henry Stob, *Ethical Reflections* (Grand Rapids: Eerdmans, 1978), IV. Also Emil Brunner, *Justice and the Social Order* (New York: Harper, 1945), I; William Frankena, *Ethics*, 2nd ed. (Englewood Cliffs: Prentice-Hall, 1973), pp. 43–59; and Gene Outka, *Agape* (New Haven: Yale Univ. Press, 1972), chap. 3.

be, and political and economic science followed the same route rather than remaining the extensions of ethics they were before. In such a world of value-free sciences, it makes no sense to call this a moral universe, or to appeal to natural laws that are right or good. Values, rather, are relative to us and anthropocentric, and the positivist and scientific humanist from Comte and Mill to the present day has followed this path. The existentialist agrees that the world is without value or meaning as it is, for meaning and value are something we ourselves create. Value-neutrality prevails.

On the other hand, the optimist, romantic idealist that he is, sees everything in rosy hues with full value-actuality already, as if life is naturally so good that we can bask in nature's warm light, preserving and enjoying it as it is.

But the theist accepts neither the pessimism and subjectivism of value-neutrality nor the overoptimism and romanticism of value-actuality. The one ignores the biblical claim that the creation was good, the other is unrealistic about natural and moral evil. Yet the value inherent in God's purposive activity, affirmed by a value-judgment at creation, was reaffirmed by the Incarnation of Christ in this world. Creation, even in its present state, has value-potentiality. The kingdom of God is at hand, among us now only partially and in its fullness still to come. The creation holds potential for good, for it was ordered by God and is law-governed as a means to his good ends. Moral law is God's law, not in legalistic fashion as if law is an end-in-itself, but in order that people and society should be as God intended, just and loving, imaging God himself. Both the principles that underlie the law and the ends to which the law is directed, then, have a claim over us as the Creator's principles and ends, possible by virtue of who he is and the way he made things to be. Moral law and natural law command us because the lawgiver is God: as his creatures we are obligated to him, his authority and his purposes, and to actualizing value-potentials in the way his law commands.

Evil is also possible, of course, for the potential of creation for God's good ends is not yet fulfilled. This is not yet the best of all possible worlds, for the achievement of good is in many ways thwarted. Realism about human finiteness and sin underscores that fact; yet value-potential persists, some of it already actualized in human society and culture, some of it not. What *is* continues to attest what *ought* to be, and we shall see that it contributes to our moral knowledge.

(4) In delegating powers to his creatures, God has given us *a creation mandate* to pursue his purposes, actualizing values he intended. Our task, according to Genesis, is to replenish and subdue the earth: this implies untapped possibilities in nature from its very beginning, the stewardship of which is entrusted to man. Value-pursuits therefore pervade our relationship to nature, as well as to God and to each other. Responsible action is mandated in every sphere of life.

This is not the evolutionary optimism of nineteenth-century idealists or of some contemporary humanists. Theirs is an immanent teleology, where forces at work in nature itself conspire to produce a classless society or a rational world at peace. The Christian, while he recognizes the immanent forces at work in nature, finds them insufficient ground for hope, and in a twisted and fallen world he knows such forces can alienate us further from the Creator's ends. Nor is the Christian's optimism a trust in human freedom. He recognizes that we transcend in measure the processes of nature and by our actions direct some of nature's forces and give shape to our own history, but this too is insufficient ground for hope. Out of ignorance, we bungle. Out of inordinate self-interest, we corrupt. Human action indeed actualizes value-potentials, but some are actualized in positive ways and others negatively, negating the possible good by the evil we do.

Rather than affirm an immanent teleology alone, the Christian affirms a transcendent teleology, one in which value-possibilities are actualized by a transcendent God who continually acts in creative ways. In his providence he preserves possibilities and actualizes some. In his judgment he corrects perversity, and in his grace he restores possibilities that seem otherwise lost. God's grace frees people from sin's twisted ends to act again as God's representatives on earth, stewarding resources, seeking justice, loving kindness, and whatever else is of value to God. Hope inspires effort.

This sort of note is sounded by Moltmann's theology of hope, which stimulated Latin American liberation theology. But for him, hope focuses on the revolutionary implications for present history of Christ's resurrection. That is important, yet the biblical hope looks not only for what God might do now, in history, but also and even more confidently at what he will do to fulfill his purposes in the future. Teilhard de Chardin's writings look more to the future, but his hope focuses on a process of human evolution in which Christ is an immanent force drawing all creation into loving union with God. He gives no clear place to the special redeeming acts of a transcendent God or to the tragedy of a historical human fall, and his immanentism seems to blur the God-creation distinction, viewing the fulfillment of things in nineteenth-century fashion as a matter of time rather than the soverign intervention of God.

But the God who is the sovereign source of obligation is also the sovereign source of hope. He acts in revelation and redemption in ways that transcend by far the natural course of events. The coming kingdom depends on that. So also do our efforts now: our present obligation to the values God sets before us is matched by hope in his providence and grace.

The transcendent God is thus the basis for all value, the basis for both obligation and hope, and the God-creation distinction and relationship speaks eloquently to the values we ought to pursue. In sum:

(1) God the creator is our highest good, and we ought to pursue his good ends.

(2) God the Creator is just and loving, as we ought to be in all the ends we pursue.

(3) The ordered creation has potential for God's good ends; what *is* attests what *ought* to be.

(4) God mandates the pursuit of these ends through his providence and grace, which is our hope.

A BASIS FOR UNIVERSAL VALUES

If theism gives a transcendent basis for value-obligation, by the same token it should give us a basis for universal values, normative for all humans in God's creation in whatever time, place, or condition.

The fact, however, is that people disagree not only over the highest end of man, for not all are theists, but also over the other ends we ought to pursue. When world views differ, values differ. When they are similar, values are likely to be similar. While some variation is to be expected within a pluralistic tradition such as Christian theism in the light of theological and philosophical differences, the relativist denies there are any unchanging and universally binding values; everything is relative to the conditions and beliefs of people and societies.

It is important to distinguish descriptive from normative relativism. Descriptively, relativism is far from complete, for all human beings have much the same needs, hence the same value areas and spheres of action; anthropologists point out that all cultures seem to have taboos against incest, distinguish murder from war or execution, have some sort of family obligations, and establish some rules related to the economic necessities of life. Moreover, it does not follow that different value systems are equally valid and *ought* to differ as much as they do, nor that they would in equally enlightened societies. Normative relativism, then, does not automatically follow. And a complete normative relativism is self-refuting: for if no values are universally binding, neither is the value of tolerating different values. A more limited relativism therefore follows. [8]

But even the limited normative relativism of naturalists (to the effect that values *ought* to vary individually and culturally) assumes that values depend on individual and cultural causes, that they are anthropocentric and have no transcendent basis. How far does Christian theism change this? What knowledge can we gain of God's law and purposes that will help identify good ends that ought universally to be pursued?

(1) By virtue of the God-creation distinction and relationship, one and the same *supreme good* is equally normative for all humankind. The Bible puts it in various ways: it is to love the Lord God with all one's being, an exclusive devotion that allows "no other gods"; it is to seek first the kingdom of God and his righteousness (Matt. 6:33; 22:36–38; Exod. 20:3). The catechism says likewise: to glorify God and enjoy him forever.

While this is implicit in our creatureliness and is virtually a truism for theists, it stands in contrast to all naturalistic and anthropocentric conceptions. Our highest end is neither personal fulfillment, nor happiness, nor even building community among people, valuable as these may be. For theism the highest end is theocentric—to honor and serve God in and through everything we are and do.

To state it thus makes evident God's "highest" place. No ob-

8. On this debate see John Ladd, ed., *Ethical Relativism* (Belmont, CA: Wadsworth, 1973) and, for a briefer treatment, Paul W. Taylor, *Principles of Ethics* (Belmont, CA: Dickenson, 1975), chap. 2.

ligation can be greater than our obligation to him. No being has greater importance than he. And since he is the maker of heaven and earth, all other ends serve him: aesthetic, political, economic, social, and other values. Everything in creation has purpose in relation to God.

(2) In this world, the unique *value of persons* in God's image marks us off from other creatures. This value God places on persons is evident in the biblical law: the Decalogue first commands respect for God (the first four commandments) and then respect for other persons (the remaining six). The Incarnation of Jesus Christ reaffirms the value of humankind, and as the "second Adam" he calls us back to what the first Adam was intended to be. Second in importance only to love for God is that we love others as ourselves. On these two commandments, said Jesus, hang all the law and the prophets (Matt. 22:37–40). Augustine therefore spoke of justice as giving to each his due, to God first and then to fellowmen, but always a justice pervaded by love. Justice and love, these overall two attributes of God himself, are requisite to our respect for human persons. As moral values they are universally binding.

In his famous categorical imperative Kant affirmed that we should always treat other persons as ends of value in and to themselves, not just as means. On this principle he built his whole approach to ethics, his theory of human rights, and his plea for "perpetual peace." And Alan Donagan has recently shown that major ingredients of Judeo-Christian morality can be drawn from this respect for persons.[9] In its biblical context, this principle is the basis for humanism of a genuinely Christian sort.

(3) What we have said about the nature of persons can now be brought to bear in identifying more *specific values*. Not all legitimate values are universally binding, for some (like economic security) are culturally relative. But God made us all responsible agents in relation to himself, to nature, to other persons, and to ourselves. As W. D. Ross points out, relationships bring "trailing obligations."[10] Relationships are value-laden, and it is possible to identify in them universal value-areas and action spheres that are essential to being human. Within these action spheres we seek to actualize

9. Donagan, *Theory of Morality.*
10. Ross, *The Right and the Good* (New York: Oxford Univ. Press, 1930), chap. II.

the values we deem important—intellectual, aesthetic, economic, social, sexual, familial, and so on.

While each of these areas is essential to a fully human quality of life, the specific values people pursue vary. A first list might include intellectual values, like understanding and truth; aesthetic values, like beauty and creativity; physical values, like life and health; psychological values, like happiness; economic values, like meaningful work and growing wealth; social values, like friendship and prestige; political values, like justice and liberty and power; and religious values, like knowing God and finding overall meaning for this life and hope for the next. But are all these *essential* to human existence and *universally* binding in whatever culture? In the intellectual sphere, some people might prefer to satisfy a morbid curiosity or inflate their pride. In the aesthetic sphere, not all creative art seems beautiful, and naming beauty the highest ideal in art may well be Platonic rather than Christian. In the economic sphere, meaningful work may be essential—but with *what* meaning? And why a *growing* wealth for oneself rather than contributing to others' economic needs? Among social values, why prestige? Among political values, surely equal justice must take precedence over power. Is power a good end we ought to pursue for its own sake, or just a means to other ends? We need to identify as *good* ends those universal values we all ought to pursue.

If universal values are God's good ends, then we have two ways of trying to identify them: by what Scripture indicates about the intended purpose of each human action sphere, and by moral indicators in the very nature of that kind of activity itself. The one requires a world-viewish theology of every human activity—a theology of politics, of work, of play, of health, of sex, of learning, of the environment. The other requires further exploration of the fact-value relationship discernible in these human action spheres. The former is often more explicit and decisive, while the latter helps us see underlying reasons and address issues that fall outside the biblical purview.

Some, like William of Occam, rest moral law on God's free choice alone, rather than on any reasons at all. Occam was a nominalist who rejected real universals lest they infringe on God's freedom, and he therefore found no objective grounds for moral reasoning to consider. As the issue was sometimes stated, does God will something because he knows it is good, or is it good because he wills it? Could God have made stealing or murder right?

Occam's concerns, however, are well protected by what I have said. This is indeed an ordered and purposive creation, but its order and potential are God's doing, not in the least independent of his freedom in creating. Ours is one of many possible worlds God might have created, but his choice in creating it included the choice of inherent value-potentials.

Of course, if God were arbitrary and capricious, changing his purposes for no reason at all, then neither creational indicators nor biblical theology would help us at all. We would be condemned to a skepticism from which only frequent special revelations could save us. In an ordered creation, however, not everything is equally possible: in economic relationships, for example, it is as counter productive and even self-contradictory to allow stealing to go on and promises to be broken as it is unloving and unjust.

Moreover, Scripture itself (e.g., Rom. 1–2) suggests that the creation bears witness to moral law, and moral failure is traced to religious roots, when people worship and serve the creature rather than the Creator. To so mistake our highest end mistakes other ends, too, and ignores God's purpose in making us the way we are. For example, the apostle speaks specifically of homosexual acts as contrary to nature, implying that heterosexuality is indicated by its potential for reproduction. The creation is structured according to God's law, and bears witness to it even without the biblical law on such matters.

Some ethical intuitionists have taken this to imply that we have a moral faculty enabling us, under appropriate conditions, to judge alternative actions and spontaneously recognize the good and the right. Bishop Butler called it "conscience," the term Romans 2:15 employs. Yet moral sensitivities vary considerably from culture to culture, even from person to person, and are notably subject to change. And the biblical use of "conscience" suggests neither innate moral knowledge nor an infallible moral sense, but points rather to a moral sensitivity that has to be informed and guided, and so can be misinformed, perverted, and dulled. Ethical intuitionism, if it is to be a viable theory of moral knowledge, must stand on other than exegetical grounds.

The plainer sense of Romans 1–2 in tying moral law to the God-creation relationship and in distinguishing natural from unnatural activities is that the moral law is somehow written into the creation, into the very heart and essence of our being. The reference is not to what comes naturally to some but not to others by virtue of individual differences, but to what is natural or unnatural in some universal sense for all humankind, by virtue of what God intended in the way he made us all. So the moral law summarized in the second table of the Decalogue speaks of universal obligations regarding human life, human economic needs (stealing deprives others of needed resources), human sexuality and marriage, and the truth about people.

The Christian natural law ethic of Thomas Aquinas built on this kind of interpretation. It drew knowledge of the good ends (final causes) we ought to seek from what was understood to be the essential nature (formal cause) of the human species. Self-preservation, bearing and raising children, knowing God, and building a justly ordered society are Aquinas' initial examples of universal ends, and from such as these a more detailed ethic developed.

Enlightenment formulations of natural law drew more on the Roman Stoics than on the Greek Aristotle. John Locke followed Cicero in taking as his starting point the rational nature of man. Since rational beings are capable of self-determination and of ruling nature, Locke inferred that God gave us natural rights to life, to liberty, and to the property needed for a human quality of life. These are rights to good ends we ought to pursue, and from them flow our moral duties to preserve life, to safeguard liberty, and to acquire and use property justly. The basis for all this and more is the distinctive value of human persons as rational beings in God's image.

Within a creationally based approach to moral knowledge, God's law is in no way arbitrary, but addresses the essential nature of human persons. As relational and responsible beings, we share universal areas of value and activity whose inherent ends bear witness to universal values God intended. We shall pursue this further in the following chapter with regard to social institutions, and in Part Three in regard to a variety of other activities. For an initial example at this stage, therefore, we will briefly consider some implications of human sexual relationships. What moral indicators exist in this sphere of human activity, and how do they point beyond general moral concerns to particular questions that arise regarding sexual activity?

In its biological nature sex is potentially reproductive. In its psychological nature it is potentially unitive. I say "potentially" in both cases, first because not every sex act, in the nature of things, is actually reproductive nor is it intended to be, and because not every sex act automatically unites persons in a bond of love and commitment, although the overall sex life of a couple has the psychological potential to do so. But I say "potentially" also because these are "value-potentials" to be "actualized" in a responsible relationship. Actualization of the unitive potential of sex requires a context of equal respect for one's partner as a person; that is, it requires a context of just treatment and mutual loving service. Within that context the unitive value-potential of sex can be realized. Without it, that value-potential is frustrated, sex loses an inherent part of its meaning, and persons tend to become sex "objects" rather than "partners" in the fullest unitive sense of the word. Unitive potential, therefore, points to the proper context for sex in a marriage of mutual love and respect between both persons.

Reproductive potential is a moral indicator, too. Since not every sex act is naturally reproductive, it does not argue against responsible uses of contraception, although entirely selfish and other irresponsible uses are in any case wrong. Reproductive potential indicates that the sexual relationship is properly heterosexual. Combined with the unitive intent, this means that heterosexual marriage is the intended context for sexual relationships, and that within a marriage that is actually unitive, the possibility of reproduction can be a privilege to be enjoyed, not a burden to be avoided. Thus Scripture speaks not only of marital joy and fidelity, but of raising a godly heritage, thereby serving God's larger purpose for marriage and the family in his kingdom on earth.[11]

The sexual relationship must be related to these ends for which it was created, but it must also be conducted with justice and love. This precludes not only rape but any other practices that victimize a person or even "use" someone simply as a means for self-gratification. It therefore speaks against pornography. It speaks also against extramarital intercourse, which disrespects the marriage partner, for respect for persons is what underlies just and loving concerns. And a self-centered marriage is not enough, for like the self-cen-

11. For analogous approaches to sexual ethics, see Lewis Smedes, *Sex for Christians* (Grand Rapids: Eerdmans, 1978), and Peter Bertocci, *Sex, Love and the Person* (London: Sheed and Ward, 1967).

tered individual it neglects responsibilities in the other human relationships that make up our lives and calling. Self-centeredness is but a version of the anthropocentricity in a humanistic view of life. The Christian views life in theocentric fashion, its values to be realized in relationship to God, the sexual relationship included.

On sexual ethics, the Bible is sufficiently explicit that other moral indicators seem simply to parallel and reinforce what it says. But on matters that Scripture does not directly address we can lean less on exegetical procedures. Take as an example the moral issue of abortion, to which the Bible does not explicitly speak.[12] To ask about God's purposes in this area, we must start with God's purposes for sex, and so with its reproductivity. Responsible sexual relationships will reckon seriously with this God-given potential, and treat fetal life as a gift of God to be stewarded responsibly with justice and love to all concerned, not something man-made and of actual value to the parents alone. Anthropocentricity, the view that we create our own values, cannot prevail if a religious view of life is fundamental.

The fetus is not yet actually a human person, in the sense of a rational being, consciously and responsibly relating to God, to nature, and to human persons. It does not yet reflect and value. But it is a human life on its way to becoming a person, potentially a person, and this value-potential must be regarded. It has value not primarily because of its biological functions, but because of that potential for personhood which actual biological functions indicate. Christian ethicists therefore look for moral indicators in fetal development, giving different moral weights to conception, implantation, detectable brain impulses, viability, and so forth. No clear line can be drawn after conception, yet personhood as such is due to more than simply genetic causes. An early conceptus thus has less actualized potential, and therefore less moral significance, than a full-term fetus; but it has moral significance nonetheless, and the further a pregnancy proceeds the greater the potential for actual personhood and the greater the moral problems with abortion.

Similar approaches are possible for work and play, politics and

12. Exodus 21:22–23 is talking about an injury that leads to either a premature delivery or a spontaneous abortion, not about voluntary abortion. Abortifacient drugs were used in antiquity; some think the New Testament term *pharmakeia* refers to them. But even so there is no discussion of therapeutic abortion.

education, art and science, and every human activity. The basis for universal values is found in the purposes and character of God. So two questions must constantly be asked: (a) What is God's purpose for this activity, its value-potential in his creation? (b) How may these values be pursued with justice and with love? The first question directs us to the biblical law, to a biblical theology of the particular activity, and to natural indicators of its inherent value-potential. The second question insists on respect for persons, both divine and human. We must love and respect God with heart and soul and mind, and our neighbors as ourselves.

A structure for our thinking has thus emerged that moves from (i) theological and philosophical *bases* (God and his creation) to (ii) overaching *principles* (justice and love) that apply to every area of human responsibility, to (iii) *area rules*, reflecting universal values, the good ends intended for each action sphere, to (iv) *case decisions*, which bring the above to bear on more particular kinds of situations. This thought structure can be traced in biblical teaching—indeed, I have tried to pattern it thereon—as well as being applied to matters on which Scripture is silent.

One might well complain, however, that this structure does not always provide complete logical certainty, but leaves a lot to wise judgment. But what we saw earlier about truth and knowledge anticipated that objection: a true statement is one that is reliable for its purposes, and a true belief is sufficient to act upon. Human knowledge affords little by way of logical certainty on matters of fact and substance, but it does provide sufficient reasons to justify belief, and in moral matters the combined witness of Scripture and nature leaves us, as the apostle says, "without excuse."

A FINAL CONCERN

Theorizing about the basis and universality of values as we have done is not enough, nor is it enough to pursue the key questions that lead to the values we ought to pursue, nor even to know what those values are in every area of life. As valuing beings, we not only think about values and conceptualize ideals, we also value them. To value what is valuable is to love it: to love justice, to love mercy, to hunger and thirst for righteousness, to love truth, to yearn for every good end ordained by God, and, for the theist, to love the

Lord God with all one's heart. To simply objectify values is not enough; we must also interiorize them and make them our own.

Valuing, then, is larger than knowledge of values. It involves all I am as a responsible human being. The "whole and part" model proposed in the last chapter applies here, too. There we suggested that the relationship of belief to knowledge, of practice to theory, and of subjectivity to objectivity be viewed in each case as the relationship of a whole-personal involvement to one of its parts. Belief involves the whole person as a responsible being, as do human practice and subjectivity. Knowledge is more part-personal, less wholistic, and so are theory and objectivity. The knowledge of values we have now discussed is likewise only a part and not the whole of human responsibility. We need to value, to love, to do the good wholeheartedly. This is why love goes further than justice, for it is a whole-personal concern extending beyond what objective fairness requires. This is why we must *love* justice, if we are to do it, and *love* what God intends for us if we are to actualize the value-potential he has packed into his creation. The highest end of man is, after all, to *love* God, by serving and enjoying him forever.

CHAPTER 11
SOCIETY AND HISTORY

Marx called religion the opiate of the masses, as if Christianity is
too detached from earthly concerns and too absorbed with heavenly
things. But we have already seen that this is theologically mistaken.
The God of the Bible is the living God, loving and just, creatively
involved. In taking human form, he incarnated himself in an under-
developed and repressed people. He became a suffering servant,
despised, rejected, and killed. Consequently Christianity is no oth-
erwordly, mystical religion, no opiate of the masses. God's mandate
to us involves our neighbors and the life of the community; it extends into the institutional structures of society and their need for
change.[1]

Consider the scope of the kingdom of God. The Old Testament
law and prophets addressed every aspect of life, social institutions
as well as social conditions and individual conduct. Jesus spoke
about family problems and economic problems, and about political
as well as ecclesiastical concerns. He blessed people's lives with the
word "peace," *shalōm*, the expectation of a joyous peace with justice
and compassion for all, and when John the Baptist asked if he was
indeed the Messiah, Jesus pointed to the benefits of the kingdom
he had already bestowed (Matt. 11:2–6). The apostles wrote about
our responsibilities in economic and political matters as well as in

---

1. The implications of this are the intriguing subject of the current
Christian-Marxist debate. See, for instance, José Miguez Bonino, *Christians
and Marxists: The Mutual Challenge to Revolution* (Grand Rapids: Eerdmans,
1976); J. Andrew Kirk, *Liberation Theology: An Evangelical View from the
Third World* (Atlanta: John Knox, 1980); Dale Vree, *On Synthesizing Marxism and Christianity* (New York: John Wiley, 1976).

family and church, and the early church well understood what this implied for its life as a community. Finally, the millennial hope that runs through the Bible is one of justice, peace, and compassion fully actualized in the end. The kingdom of God is all-embracing.

Society is made up of social institutions, not just of individuals, and we can neither think about society and social ethics nor engage in social work or social action without considering those institutions. They are essential to who we are: I identify myself by my *family* name, my *national* origin, my *work*, my *religious* affiliation. The problems I have are in large part problems associated with such institutions when they are disorganized or disrupted or tend to disintegrate, for social institutions do malfunction.

The Romanticist might blame it all on institutionalized society and prefer his own Walden instead; the scientific humanist might call for a modern management approach; the Marxist, glimpsing the specter of class conflict in the very structure of things, will want to change that structure in revolutionary ways. Yet these paths, if taken exclusively, are but naturalistic solutions and plainly anthropocentric, for the question never arises about a transcendent basis for the values that social institutions promise, and hope centers entirely in what human art and science can achieve. The Christian obviously does not want to minimize the role of creaturely means, but he sees that there is more involved in society and history than natural processes and human endeavor alone.

In this chapter I want to suggest a Christian view of society that takes these things into account, and is an outgrowth of what we have said in previous chapters about God's involvement in his creation, as well as about man and values.

WE CANNOT LIVE RESPONSIBLY IN PURELY INDIVIDUALISTIC FASHION

Individualism under any name is self-centeredness, an aberration on what God intended. The quest for individual fulfillment independently of others, the desire to "do my own thing" of whatever sort, like the narcissism of our day, focuses on the self. When freedom is equated with the liberty to pursue my own self-interest regardless of others, it is perverted. Enlightenment thinkers reduced society to a collection of independent individuals, isolated atoms joined together under the laws of reason in a man-made contract. They were Robinson Crusoes, each individual on an island alone with his goats and his God, isolated from other humans, ruling irrational Friday by force until Friday was enough ruled by reason to enter the social contract himself. As a social philosopher, Daniel Defoe advocated this individualistic view. Since the model was that of a mechanistic science whose particles of matter were conjoined by external forces, social institutions as such had no place in the state of nature: family and civil order are not indigenous to us, but are artifices overlaid on the natural associations of individuals.[2]

Undoubtedly this view came as a welcome corrective to the medieval absolutisms that gave potentially repressive authority to the head of a family, the head of state, a feudal lord, or a papal head of the church. Absolutism adopted a hierarchical model built on the Greek notion of an unchanging hierarchy of being. Yet neither the hierarchical nor the atomistic model has a Christian origin and, despite the fact that both at times are imported into Christian thinking, I am not satisfied that either does justice to a biblical view of man and society. Nor am I convinced that the natural state of affairs is either hierarchical or atomistic.

On the one hand, the basic biblical ideal is one of interdependence and mutual service, each submitting to the other, rather than a hierarchical one-way street or a contractual arrangement. On the other hand, God created us as relational beings who both are and are who we are by virtue of our relationships to God, to nature, and to other persons, and for these relationships we are indelibly responsible. Reinhold Niebuhr points out that even the physical impulses of humans take on wider significance than anything known in the animal world. Sex, for instance, serves not just the survival of the species but also has unitive potential: it helps create, reaffirm, and sustain family relationships and the larger human community.[3]

By speaking of marriage in terms of a social contract, Enlightenment thinkers, like John Locke, unwittingly opened the way to making it a purely voluntary and human device rather than a divine

2. This individualistic and contractual view is evident in John Locke's famous *Second Treatise on Civil Government.* On Defoe's views see M. E. Novak, *Defoe and the Nature of Man* (New York: Oxford Univ. Press, 1963). The contrast in the biblical view of society is evident in Russell Shedd, *Man in Community* (London: Epworth Press, 1958).

3. Niebuhr, *Faith and History* (New York: Scribner's, 1949), p. 17.

ordinance rooted in the relational way we are made. The very nature of marriage and family, in fact, seems designed to undo our individualism and teach us about living altruistically with others. Any individualism whose quest for liberty decries our interdependence and mutual servanthood is a perversion of the Creator's intention.

The contrast between Christianity and naturalistic humanism can peak here. Is marriage a man-made device to be modified at will, or is it part of God's law-governed creation, its purposes therefore essential to the good ends for which we are made? Is government entirely a man-made device, or is it, too, in its basic purpose part of a law-governed creation and essential for the actualization of values God intended? And human work with its concomitant institutions? And the church? Are these simply products of social evolution without any purpose other than what we humans vest in them? Given such a view, it is not surprising that authority becomes egotistic or tyrannical rather than a means of service, and that we see economic exploitation, political corruption, broken marriages, abused and unwanted children, and religious personality cults. Social institutions by human device too easily become devices for self-aggrandizement and ego-satisfaction, abuses of power for individualistic ends. And hierarchical authority that loses equal respect for all persons itself evokes cries for liberation and revolt.

The issue today is much the same as in ancient Greece, when the Sophists debated whether morality and social institutions are based in social convention (*nomos*) or in human nature (*physis*). Plato and Aristotle vigorously argued the latter, relating human nature to eternal and universal ideals. "By nature," Aristotle insisted, humans are social and political animals. Neither the family nor the *polis* is a voluntary association of individuals, for each has an organic unity and nature of its own. The European tradition in political theory has continued an organic kind of view. At times it is overdrawn, as in Hegel and Marx, but the emphasis is nonetheless valid that social institutions are native to human history, and that the social unit is not an optional association of individuals but has a life and character of its own. In biblical perspective, some social institutions are said to be ordained by God and rooted in the nature of his human creatures. They are his idea, his doing, not ours. In making us relational beings, he ordained that we live our lives in such contexts.

AT LEAST FOUR KINDS OF SOCIAL INSTITUTIONS ARE ORDAINED BY GOD

Among the many kinds of social institutions that arise in various cultures, four are said biblically to be ordained by God and rooted in the created nature of humankind: marriage, work, government, and religion. Each is embryonic in the Genesis account of the Edenic community, in the activities and relationships involved: marriage and work plainly, and a community of faith, and the beginnings of a law-governed society. Even apart from human vices, a significantly large population would require some form of regulation to safeguard the mutual interests of all, and with developing technology traffic control would be needed even in an Eden. The complexities of living together require organization for the sake of distributive justice.

Particular forms of organization, of course, vary greatly and are a product of history. Other kinds of institutions also arise, embodying various human interests and tasks. Education, art, and science are obvious examples, and in our culture institutionalized recreation and play may be included. All of these represent human action spheres and serve human needs. In some cultures institutions are not as differentiated as they are in industrialized societies. Aristotle, for instance, treats the family as a domestic economy involving slaves and servants as well as husband, wife, and children. The extended family and clan can play a more prominent role than in the West today. Social stratification and castes impose economic expectations and limitations, and tend to perpetuate frequently gross inequities.

Yet every kind of institution has its task complicated by sin. In the family we see domineering spouses, broken marriages, prodigal children. Thorns and thistles retard the good fruits of our work: needless extremes of wealth and poverty, labor problems, unjust employment practices, economic recessions. In government we need to control civil violence, and to protect human rights from abuse by others; retributive as well as distributive justice is called for, criminal as well as civil law. And the church must now give itself to evangelism (which would have been needless apart from sin) as well as to worship; it must cope with church splits as well as serve people in need.

Each kind of institution can also be touched redemptively by God's grace. The history of the church in the world, in fact, tells of marked changes in the status of women from Greek and Roman times to the present: contrast, for instance, Aristotle's claim that women lack the ability to rule themselves rationally and must be ruled by others, with the New Testament's refusal to distinguish preferentially between male and female, any more than between Jew and Greek, or slave and freeman. History tells, too, of the changing conditions of labor from slavery until now, and of governments enlightened by the influence of Christian ideals and values.[4] It is a mottled picture, of course, because people and their institutions contain possibilities for evil as well as for good, and even the church is marred; yet the salt of the earth has been at work, and the lights of the kingdom have not been hidden. One can still envision the potential impact of the Christian message on family and work and government and church, on art and technology and education, and the *shalōm* that can yet come to them, and will come in the fulfilled kingdom of God.

The biblical conception of vocation now comes into play, for if social institutions are rooted in the order of creation then the creation mandate sets us within such structures, to live and to serve. In New Testament terms, our calling is to love and serve God in all that we do. My vocation, then, is not just the work I do for a living, although it includes that. My vocation is the entire network of roles I play in various social institutions: it is the vocation of a husband, father, homeowner, neighbor, taxpayer, citizen, churchman, teacher, scholar . . . and so on. All this is my calling from God, my part in his kingdom to be exercised responsibly with justice and with love. Social institutions are vehicles of God's work on earth and the locus for responsible human activity. The living God creates with purpose, and is still active through means such as these which he made.

EACH KIND OF INSTITUTION EMBODIES OUR RELATIONSHIPS TO GOD, TO NATURE, TO OTHER PERSONS

In the case of the family, interpersonal relationships are obvious, and our relation to nature is seen in its biological basis and economic

4. Kenneth Scott Latourette summarizes the historical impact of Christianity in the final chapter of his work, *A History of the Expansion of Christianity*, vol. VII, *Advance Through Storm* (New York: Harper and Bros, 1945), pp. 490–505.

support. This much the humanist readily admits. But one thing that distinguishes a theistic view of marriage and family is the relation to God it involves. Marriage was purposefully ordained by God, symbolizing God's love for his people and Christ's for his church. Children are "a heritage from the Lord," reminding us of the loving fatherhood of God, and providing a context in which we can learn to serve others with unselfish love, and continue a godly heritage that will honor both God and one another.

Work involves our relationship to nature through its physical effort, its possible creativity, its materials and products and benefits. It relates us to other people, employing and being employed, buying and selling, and providing services. This much again the humanist recognizes, and he too wants just and humanizing economic relationships. But the theist sees work also as a divine vocation, a service to God through the service of others, a sacred stewardship and an act of thanksgiving.

Government meantime provides a structure of laws to order relationships equitably for the common good. Social justice that respects the rights of all is essential, affording equal and peaceable opportunity to enjoy what nature provides for human needs. It means preventing abuses and holding offenders accountable to society for their misdeeds. Government is rightly concerned with retributive as well as distributive justice. This much the humanist might well affirm, too. But the theist sees political power as divinely ordained and subordinate to God's authority, so that we practice our relationship to God in the political arena. A law-governed society is one of God's ways of achieving his good ends on earth.

The church's primary concern, for its part, is our relationship to God. Thus it is a community of faith, hope, and love and, in the words of the Apostles' Creed, a "communion of saints" worshiping and serving together. But the church also images our relationship to nature by its use of the physical: its music and architecture and art, its ordinances and hymnody and liturgy. Its central symbol is a cross, whose meaning is tied to the bodily death and resurrection of a physically incarnated Lord. The church's symbols thus speak about the transcendent God and his grace in ways that remind us of both our calling in the natural world and God's activity.

But does the Christian theist simply add to what the humanist already sees? He does add, to be sure, but what the Christian sees in relationship to God changes the way he sees relationships to nature and other persons, and changes the way he sees the institutions of society. To see nature as God's creation is to see ourselves as responsible to him for how we treat and use it. To see that people are created in God's image is to respect them for what God made them to be, rather than molding and manipulating them for our own self-interest. To see marriage ordained by God is to respect its integrity and God's purpose for it: we may rewrite the wedding ceremony, but we cannot remake the concept and purpose behind it. To see work and governmental authority as ordained by God similarly affects the sanctity of work and the uses of power. A Christian view of social institutions is such that our relationship to God affects every other relationship and the institutions in which those relationships function.

My relationship to myself is affected, too. In these institutions I find personal satisfaction and growth, a potentially meaningful context for purposeful living. In valuing the self God has made me to be, then, there is reason for personal dignity and the kind of self-image that will free me to accept those roles in society which make up my life's vocation, through which I can serve God's purposes and contribute to the good of others.

THREE FEATURES MAY BE DISTINGUISHED IN EACH KIND OF INSTITUTION

These three are: first, God's purpose; second, the moral quality of relationships; and third, the organizational and authority structure.

The *first* follows from our recognition that God creates with purpose. God's good ends for social institutions are the overriding values we ought to pursue in and through institutional functions: in the four basic institutions they are familial values, economic values, political values, and religious values. A Christian view of family, then, will speak of its distinctive value-potentials, and not just in biological and economic terms. Family life involves dependency, generates affection, and provides a context for growth and for mutual service. In learning to give of ourselves to others, we learn also to give ourselves to God and so to continue a godly heritage that will contribute to God's purposes in the world. So the Bible likens our relationship to God to a family in which we are his children, he is like a father to us, and his love is like a mother's; again, we are like a bride, and he the bridegroom. Familial values, then, include growth in mutual love and service that extends beyond the family as such, while bearing witness to its maker. When sin mars human existence, it diverts the family from these ends, and perversions of family life result.

Inherent in work are economic values that benefit employers and employees, their families and the entire society of which they are part. Work makes possible not just physical existence but also a human quality of life through education, art, technology, government. It serves other people, it serves the common good, and it does so by stewarding nature's resources. Individual self fulfillment may be another potential value, but to take it as work's ultimate end would be narcissistic. Nor is profit itself of value except as a means to other ends: by itself profit is simply self-interest, but as a means it can contribute to the service of others and to providing a more human quality of life that bears witness to the Creator in whose image we are made. Work was ordained by God from the beginning for these ends, but the sin that infects humankind turns it from serving to self-seeking, and from humanizing to dehumanizing outcomes. Burdensome toil is sin's curse (Gen. 3:17–19). Work should ideally be a joyful calling, something addressed heartily to God.

We could speak similarly of God's purpose for human government in terms of peace and justice, the *shalōm* envisioned for his kingdom. Anything less results from sin. We could speak of God's purpose for the church in terms of the worship and fellowship that gratefully dedicate every aspect of life to God, and so to God's purposes in this world. "Civil religion" that adds worship to business as usual falls as short of religious values as the "politics as usual" that disregards social injustice falls short of true political values, as the unbridled pursuit of profit falls short of true economic values, and as a self-centered marriage falls short of true familial values. God's purpose for each kind of social institution must come first.

The *second* feature is the moral quality of relationships within institutional life, where the overarching principles of justice and love should prevail. A marriage whose *eros* has not been penetrated and changed by *agapē* is likely to be possessive. A marriage without concern for justice will fail to respect each partner's independent interests and needs; it will fail to treat its members equitably.

In larger institutions, where interpersonal relations are overshadowed by organizational structures, justice is of paramount importance. Fair employment practices, just pricing, honest advertising, nonmanipulative sales practices, and a concern for the wider effect of one's work on society at large, a concern that respects everybody's rights and respects the natural environment—these are all essential. So too in politics, a just society is the end and just laws the means. The moral quality of relationships must always be preserved.

I am always my brother's keeper, for he has a right to expect that I treat him as a fellow human being, as I myself would want to be treated. I must do to him as I would that he would do to me. Mosaic law therefore sought to protect the helpless from unfair abuse: the poor and fatherless, wives and widows, workers and slaves. The Old Testament prophets pointed an accusing finger at nations that failed: just judgment, for example, was to mark the rulers of Israel, for they were not to take wealth or power unjustly to themselves.

Since the seventeenth century, this concern for social justice has been expressed in terms of equal human rights, a tradition that has roots in Roman jurisprudence as well as in the Judeo-Christian Scriptures. Human rights are natural rights, ours by nature, not by virtue of human law or decree or by historical fortune; and from a theistic perspective they are God-given rights, rooted in the fact that God made us all in his image. This in turn means that human rights are inalienable and cannot be denied to humans by anyone. The human right to self-determination is the basis for any particular government's authority, for while political authority in principle is ordained by God, ideally the people decide who in particular will exercise that authority.

Yet no individual's rights are unlimited, for we live in relationship to others. John Locke pointed out in regard to settling new lands that since the earth was given for the benefit of all, an equal right to property requires that we leave enough to benefit others— a rule that applies to many other specifics as well. Moreover, an individual's rights may justly be suspended when he abuses the rights of others, so that criminal punishment deprives the offender of his full right either to property (by fines) or to liberty (imprisonment) or even to life itself if capital punishment be applied. Yet even punishment must be equitable and just, rather than vindictive or disproportionate to the crime. The Old Testament *lex talionis* ("eye for an eye") seems in this light to be a limiting principle, restricting punishment in proportion to the crime and prohibiting the excesses of the day. Equal justice is always important, but is should be tempered by love rather than stretched by a vengeful hate. The moral quality of relationships is always important.

The *third* feature in any kind of social institution is different from the first two, for, while God's purposes and moral principles are uniform and do not change, institutional structures vary greatly. Their historical development is largely left to responsible human creativity. Patterns of family life, forms of government, economic systems, church government—all these change. One factor that has affected this historically is changing conceptual models. The medieval hierarchical model of reality was reproduced in the feudal system, in the ecclesiastical hierarchy, and in the authority structure of the extended family or clan. The source of authority is at the top, a fact that led some to claim divine right for each particular king, or divine appointment for a pope. Analogously, the atomism of mechanistic science was reproduced in individualistic and contractual views: in democratic ideals, in the congregational form of church government, and in the contractual view of marriage. Again, on the evolutionary model, historicist approaches emerged: laws derive their validity from historical precedents, an economic system from the historical dialectic that preceded it, and a particular family structure from social trends. Thus the Nazi ideology presupposed the biological evolution of an Aryan race, and Marxism depends on the economic evolution of human society.

Obviously not every kind of structure is equally compatible with the values at stake. Yet we often tend to argue more vigorously over institutional structures than we concern ourselves with unchanging purposes or the moral quality of relationships. We argue like legalists about the authority of the husband and father or about sex roles in egalitarian marriages more than we address the purpose of marriage and what justice and love mean in its operation. We dogmatize about our own economic system without attending enough to God's purpose for work and to the application of justice and love in economic relationships. We laud one political system, forgetting that the kingdom of God is not a representative democracy, and paying too little attention to God's purpose for government and to the practice of justice and love in the exercise of power.

No one form of government is mandated in Scripture. Historically, patriarchal rule gave way to judges, then to a monarchy, and in New Testament times to a combination of Roman governors and local Jewish authorities. When Paul says in Romans 13 that we should submit to the authorities since they are divinely ordained, he is not speaking of particular *forms* of government but of governmental authority in general, whatever its form and whoever is in office. Under whatever form of government we live, our duty is to cooperate—unless, of course, higher duties conflict.

Likewise, in economic matters no one economic system is mandated: land redistribution was part of the Year of Jubilee, but is not even mentioned in the New Testament; slavery appears to be a different kind of institution in the Old Testament than in the New; and a modern money system is nowhere envisioned. Moreover, the biblical writers enjoined cooperation within the existing economic structure, even while the law restricted abuses. The runaway slave is even expected to return to his master, while the master must now treat him as a brother.

In religious organization, too, things vary. Many of Israel's institutions differed considerably from the early church, and the church itself varied locally: Timothy appointed both elders and deacons, while Titus had elders only.[5]

Similarly, no one family structure is explicitly taught or consistently practiced. While monogamy may be implicit in the beginning of the Genesis account, Abraham and Jacob were polygamists, as were David and Solomon, and polygamy is not explicitly repudiated when adultery and many other sexual sins are condemned. In some families the father appears dominant, in others the mother, and scholars are far from agreed about the meaning of "headship" in marriage (Eph. 5:22–24).

This suggests that we are not told to adhere to one particular form of organization, but to participate in a specific form of organization in which historically we find ourselves. This does not imply that all structures are equally good, and that there is nothing to choose between them; for while cultural variants and human creativity are legitimately involved, from a biblical perspective all organizational structures stand under the judgment of God. The concern again and again is whether a structure serves God's purpose for that kind of institution, and whether it best contributes to just and loving relationships. That is where the case for monogamy must

5. See H. J. A. Hort, *The Christian Ecclesia* (New York: Macmillan, 1914).

rest, and for or against democratic government and modern capitalism, and any particular form of church government. An egalitarian marriage may be loving and just, a union of mutual loving service that extends its benefits to the surrounding world, or it may perpetuate a self-centered individualism that denies the meaning of *agapē* and the very purpose of marriage itself. So, too, may representative government become a power struggle between competing self-interests. Moreover, as individualism misunderstands the value of individuality, so collectivism misconstrues the meaning of community: neither extreme is good. In the final analysis, as Abraham Kuyper observes, there may be only "a gradual difference in practical excellency" between one form and another,[6] for no form is best in and of itself, but only as it serves God's ends in morally good ways. God's purpose for social institutions is paramount, and the moral quality of relationships within them.

That a particular institutional structure can serve both good and evil should not surprise us, if nature and history have a potential for evil as well as good. Christianity plainly asserts that no outward structure, however law-enforced, can ensure virtue. A different institutional structure may or may not help, but it will not cure the problem. The revolutionary is far too idealistic, for the actual purposes people and institutions serve and the actual qualities that make human relationships do not necessarily change when structures change. Structural change without changed people might as well lead to something worse as to something better, and structural change itself tends to have unfortunate concomitants. The history of revolutions makes that plain.

Sin is as evident in institutional life as it is in individual relationships, and sometimes it may be harder to control, for institutional structures tend to perpetuate practices and cement attitudes. Institutions assume a life of their own, with parameters of possibility established by their structure and methods. They can take over people's lives, shape our values, influence our destiny, mold history: so President Eisenhower back in the 1950s wisely warned of "the industrial-military complex." Some writers even identify the evil "powers" of which the New Testament speaks with social and political roles assumed by demonic beings in the institutional struc-

6. Abraham Kuyper, *Lectures on Calvinism* (1898; Grand Rapids: Eerdmans, 1931), p. 83.

tures of society.[7] But by the same token Christ's kingdom will triumph over "the powers"; in measure it triumphs even now through the reassertion of his purposes for our institutions and through the moral quality of relationships that God's grace affords.

The problem is one of power, the power for evil that people and institutions exert in our lives. On the one hand, some would say that Christians should renounce the use of power, yet we all exercise it in a variety of ways—the power of the press, the power of persuasion, even the power of love. What we need, rather, is an ethic of power that places moral limits on power and guides its use. On the other hand, some would renounce all appeal to ethics in their uses of power, like Machiavelli or Nietzsche. At a more moderate level, Reinhold Niebuhr's "Christian realism" claims that justice and love alone cannot control institutionalized power, as the liberal idealists supposed; power then must realistically be used against power, beyond what justice and love alone would allow. While this echoes Luther's rhetorical "sin boldly," without moral parameters it implies too unprincipled a pragmatism.

Power must rather be kept within moral limits that are defined. Thus the apostle Paul speaks of governmental power and its use of the sword in a context that emphasizes love and peace, renouncing vengeance and retaliation in favor of concern for one's foes (Rom. 12:9–13:7). Hence the need for constitutional limits to power, and even for "rules of war" and a "just war" ethic. On what principles should these limits rest? In the light of what we have said two kinds of limitations appear: the divine purpose for which the kind of institution exercising power exists, and the respect for persons that underlies justice and love. Power should only be used with proper purpose, and it should always respect the rights of persons. Power should restrain power that is outside of these bounds, and might even change the structure of an institution in which power is repeatedly and unrestrainedly usurped.

In practice, power may be limited in a variety of ways. First is a system of checks and balances within a particular institution: the division of powers in American government, patterns of account-

7. Eph. 2:2; 6:11–12. See H. Berkhof, *Christ and the Powers* (Scottdale, PA: Herald Press, 1962); John H. Yoder, *The Politics of Jesus* (Grand Rapids: Eerdmans, 1976), pp. 85–116; S. C. Mott, "Biblical Faith and the Reality of Social Evil," *Christian Scholars Review* 9 (1980): 225–60. C. S. Lewis seems to capture this possibility in *That Hideous Strength*.

ability in management, regular audits of finances, and the like. V. A. Demant argues for the separation of economic and political powers in contrast to socialism.[8] And even the family needs the checks and balances of "help meets," for God appoints husband and wife to balance out each other, and both to be equally answerable to himself.

A second way is the balance of powers we are familiar with in international affairs, or in Adam Smith's claim that a free enterprise system can balance competing self-interests. Self-limitation is surely far more desirable, on the basis of moral principle and limited goals, for power struggles seem invariably to develop and get out of hand. Yet, tragically enough, a balance of powers arrangement too often prevails not only between nations and businesses but also within an institution itself. The tactics of some political pressure groups amount to an unprincipled struggle for power, and one shudders to think of the havoc wrought by power struggles even within the family and the church.

A third way seems much closer to God's intention, namely that different kinds of institutions by their very existence should limit each other. The family has functions that government may not usurp, and so does the church. This kind of pluralism places built-in limitations on institutions of every kind.[9] But the ideal goes beyond mutual limitations to mutual cooperation: government should respect family, church, and business activity, protecting their integrity and their freedom to pursue their proper ends aright. The church should encourage participation in family, government, and industry, extending its prophetic voice and redemptive role to their activities as well. God's kingdom, and the Christian humanism that goes with it, embraces all of life's tasks.

SOCIAL ACTION

Granted this view of social institutions, and granted the need for social change, what means toward change can moral uses of power take? The answer rests in part on how one sees the theological

8. Demant, *Religion and the Decline of Capitalism* (New York: Scribners, 1952).

9. This is implicit in the Kuyperian theory of law spheres. See Gordon J. Spykman, "Pluralism: our last best hope?", *Christian Scholars Review* 10 (1981): 99–115.

alternatives on the relation of Christianity to culture, which we noted in Chapter Three.[10] But I also find some guidance in a pattern that is evident in biblical history: the roles given to law, prophet, and gospel. Law serves two purposes: to enforce a minimal justice in society, and to be a pedagogue, a teacher, in helping to shape the conscience. In a pluralistic society laws cannot enforce the particular morality of any one group, but they can prescribe what is necessary for civil order and the common good. And their pedagogical value may be seen, for example, in the gradual effect of human rights legislation on racial attitudes in the United States since the 1950s.

The prophetic role was to reaffirm moral law and apply it to the life of the land, calling people to repent, to do justice, and to love mercy. Law and prophets together prepare people for the gospel of God's forgiveness, which teaches us to forgive, to love as God loves, and to give of ourselves for the sake of others.

Yet law, prophets, and gospel are not the whole biblical pattern: there is also the millennial hope that sets before us the unchanging goal of shalōm, with its perfect peace and justice throughout the world. Drawn together into a pattern, these themes call for participation in what God himself is doing in society, by working redemptively in the institutions of our times and so changing the direction of things.[11]

This is illustrated by the biblical treatment of slavery. The Old Testament law sought to limit its injustice and cruelty, and to prevent permanent bondage. It banned physical abuse, protected the lives of slaves, preserved their families, and ensured recompense upon their release. The prophets meantime called people to uphold the purpose and not just the letter of the law. Then, in the spirit of the gospel, Paul talked of love and respect between master and slave, and urged Philemon to receive his runaway slave Onesimus

10. See also Augustus Cerillo, Jr., "A Survey of Recent Evangelical Social Thought, *Christian Scholars Review* 5 (1975): 272.

11. Jacques Ellul claims that the Christian is called to change the suicidal direction of history by acting in accordance with the "eschaton," the goal of God's kingdom. I find his view of man and history too deterministic and too pessimistic, and his ethic is situational, without unchanging moral law. Yet he is surely correct about the task. See *The Presence of the Kingdom* (New York: Seabury Press, 1948); *To Will and To Do* (New York: Pilgrim Press, 1969); and *Jacques Ellul: Interpretive Essays*, ed. Clifford G. Christians and Jay. M Van Hook (Champaign, IL: Univ. of Illinois Press, 1981).

as a brother. Justice and love can erode the evils in society and reconcile people to one another.

A similar picture is evident in regard to the evils of war. The Old Testament law placed clear limits on its conduct, requiring that negotiation be attempted first, and that women and children be spared. Scorched earth policies were forbidden because of their long-term consequences in an agrarian society (Deut. 20:10–20). The prophets then railed against excesses of violence (e.g., Amos 1–2), and the New Testament spoke of loving one's enemies, even in contexts where it admits that the power of the sword is indeed entrusted to governments. Reconciliation is at work.

Within this kind of biblical pattern, what can be done to produce change for the better? The means available in today's world are many. Consider the following list:

(1) The life of a community that bears witness to a better way.
(2) The preaching and teaching of the church.
(3) Social work.
(4) Education.
(5) Publication, and use of the media.
(6) Political pressure groups to affect legislation and regulation.
(7) Campaigns to influence decision makers.
(8) Entering power structures (e.g., public service, management, stockholders' meetings) to change things from within.
(9) Holding elective office and electing better representatives.
(10) Boycotts.
(11) Strikes and sit-ins.
(12) Acts of civil disobedience, with the intention of being arrested in order to have a law tested in the courts.
(13) Threats of force.
(14) Selective uses of force against serious injustices.
(15) Nonviolent revolution.
(16) Violent revolution.

I have listed these in order of increasing seriousness and moral ambiguity. Some Christian traditions will of course reject the threat and use of force altogether. But my point is that while all these means have at times been used by Christians and are available in today's world, they are all exercises of power and must be kept within moral parameters.

For example, two views of revolution are current today, one

based on the Marxist dialectic and one on a Christian natural law tradition. The former sees confrontation as essential to change, making necessary the destruction of existing institutions. The other sees revolution as a last resort to be used only in the most extreme instance of tyranny after all other means have been tried and have failed. In this tradition, moreover, the use of force is severely limited; it belongs only to governmental authorities and not to private parties. Hence, said John Locke in his famous *Second Treatise on Civil Government*, if a tyrant so usurps his trust that the just ends of government are hopelessly thwarted, then the people may establish another government on whose authority force may then be used against the tyrannical "usurper." Power can only be used within clear ethical limits, and the moral rules governing revolution are analogous to the better known rules of the just war theory.

A parallel situation exists in regard to civil disobedience. As worked out in ethical theory and in the careful practice of Martin Luther King, Jr. and others, civil disobedience is permissible only against extremes of injustice where lesser recourses have failed. I must operate within the law in all regards, except that the unjust law is disobeyed. I may suffer arrest and trial, but the injustice goes on trial thereby: legal appeals and public sentiment can produce legal correction. Just cause, just means, and just ends are equally essential.

In a law-governed creation made for good purpose but now corrupted, yet entered by one who suffered arrest and punishment in order to redeem people and bring a kingdom of justice and love, the restraint of power within the limits of justice and love is essential, even at the cost of suffering. Less extreme measures than armed revolution and civil disobedience are usually possible, and very often effective. Yet even then moral limitations on power must be observed. The power of the pen, the influence of the media, the words of the preacher, the rhetoric of the politician, the kinds of pressure exerted, the nature of an educational process—all these must be fair to all sides, considerate of persons, and morally restrained.

A CHRISTIAN VIEW OF HISTORY

Reinhold Niebuhr finds three markedly different approaches to history in the West: the classical Greek view, which equated history with natural process and sought an escape from its purposeless cycles;

the biblical view, which distinguished history from nature, because in history human freedom causes both evil and good; and the modern approach, which looks to the historical development of human power and freedom for the solution of every problem.[12]

This modern approach underlies humanistic world views today. Eastern thought in many cases may be closer to the historical Greek outlook in its distrust of progress and its mystical religion, but Western thought is through and through a product of Renaissance and Enlightenment optimism. The utopian literature of the Renaissance set the mood, eighteenth-century confidence in the rule of reason over man and nature gave it philosophical basis, and nineteenth-century evolutionary concepts made progress seem inevitable. Rousseau, Kant, Hegel, Comte, Mill, Marx—all of them saw history moving toward universal human concord, a theme further elaborated nowadays by process theologians in terms of the "consequential nature of God." History relentlessly actualizes the good.

Woven through such optimism is a focus on, almost an obsession with, freedom. John Locke affirmed the equal right to freedom for every individual to act as he or she chooses. Kant claimed that the rule of reason frees us from the causal determinism of natural impulse and inclination. Hegel saw the sovereignty of the State as an embodiment of free Absolute Spirit; for Hitler it became the sovereignty of a race; and for Marxism it is liberation from repressive social structures. Freedom is the goal of history, and history is relentlessly achieving it.

Contemporary humanism obviously shares the dream with romanticist and Marxist humanism. The scientific humanist sees technology as the liberator, giving us freedom to modify the genetic inheritance of future generations, freedom to modify the environment, freedom to control unacceptable behavior. But this "illusion of budding omnipotence"[13] replacing a powerless providence offers, for the existential humanist, the sickening prospect of a dehumanized society where passion and free individuality are repressed. Freedom is still the existentialist's ideal, but it is so individualized and unmanaged that optimism about history has become illusory.

Emil Brunner calls this modern outlook "the bastard offspring of an optimistic anthropology and Christian eschatology."[14] It has at least two Christian genes: the distinction it implies between man

12. Niebuhr, *Faith and History*, pp. 14–15.
13. Ibid., p. 88.
14. *Christianity and Civilization* (London: Nisbet, 1948), p. 55.

and nature, and the belief that history has meaning. Since history is the story of human freedom, Arnold Toynbee replaced cause-effect explanations with the theme of "challenge and response." And since, contrary to the classical Greek conception, history is the arena of hope, there are messianic expectations of various sorts.[15] Yet the modern outlook is also a Christian heresy. It is often too optimistic, as if history's potential for good is inherently far greater than its potential for evil. It can also be too pessimistic, as if history's potential for evil clouds out any other hope than history itself holds. Yet it is still naturalistic and anthropocentric: humankind and history are closed in to their own possibilities, to an immanent teleology with no outside sources of hope. Man is his own messiah.

But how can naturalism be optimistic? How can it suppose that history is amenable to the good ends we ought to pursue? Is history really productive of a freedom that is good? A bevy of problems arises here. If naturalism supposes that physical processes completely cause whatever happens, in what sense can we be free? If history is shaped by other conditions in addition to human action, what guarantees have we that human action can prevail? Is history altogether amenable to meanings we want to impose? What logical right has the naturalist to messianic expectations?

A Christian approach to history, on the other hand, is logically entitled to expect meaning and hope, for it is part of that larger world view whose contours we have been examining.

(1) *The God of history is the God of creation*, continuously active, purposive, the living God who is always with us. The Logos of history is the Logos of creation, ordering events for his good ends, and biblical history is not primarily the history of human freedom but the history of God's activity in social and national affairs. He directed the history of Israel, incarnated himself in a historical setting, and established the church to continue his work. This God-creation relationship is the overall context of history.

History, therefore, is not cyclical as in the classical Greek outlook, nor is it understood naturalistically as a self-contained process with wholly immanent causes. The leading actor throughout is God; his supporting cast changes but the same drama continues, and it gives indications of a hope that will be fulfilled in the end. So the psalmist recites the mighty acts of God and the prophet looks even

15. Reinhold Niebuhr develops this theme in *The Nature and Destiny of Man* (London: Nisbet, 1943), vol. II, chaps. I, II, VI.

at historical catastrophies in the light of God's purpose. History for them affirms the sovereignty of God, not of man and not of the state. It is God's freedom of action that gives meaning, nor ours.

(2) *History reveals the accountability of persons* as responsible agents in relationship to God as well as to nature and other persons. Old Testament history portrays this in the lives of the patriarchs and the nation of Israel. Rather than economic or political explanations of events, it gives moral and religious explanations, for these are the focus of God's purposes.

Human sinfulness, not just freedom, accounts for a great deal of what occurs. Back in the nineteenth century when nationalism was at its height throughout Europe, the Dutch statesman and theologian Abraham Kuyper traced the division of humanity into separate nation-states to sin. Nations and nationalisms are products of unnatural causes that violate the organic unity of humankind: race, self-interest, power-seeking, alienation.[16] This may be an overstatement, but the point is clear: national self-centeredness that alienates people from people is sin. Nationalistic chauvinism is sin. The biblical story of the tower of Babel says it aright: sin is a disintegrative force where God intended community. He made all peoples to live as one on the face of the earth (Acts 17:26).

(3) *History actualizes value-potentials* inherent in human existence, potentials for good that can be turned to evil ends. The Bible pictures it as a process in which wheat and tares grow together intermingled until the harvest. In his famous *City of God*, Augustine similarly describes a parallel growth of the heavenly and the earthly cities, Jerusalem and Babylon. As with the wheat and tares, history does not itself produce the triumph of good, but rather good and evil grow together until God finally achieves his purpose through judgment. Underlying the two cities are two kinds of love, two kinds of relationship to God and others, *caritas* (*agapē*) and *cupiditas* (self-interest), for people are governed ultimately by what and how they love. But Christian love (*agapē*) tempers justice in the service of people in need.[17]

What sort of progress, then, does history achieve? It is a mixed picture, a dialectical opposition of good and evil. Here is a major

16. Kuyper, *Lectures*, pp. 79ff.
17. Historian Kenneth Scott Latourette developed this theme that love affects history in his presidential address to the American Historical Association in 1948, "The Christian Understanding of History," reprinted in C. T. McIntyre, ed., *God, History and Historians* (New York: Oxford Univ. Press, 1977), pp. 46–67.

point of contact with Marxist and Hegelian views, for they, too, perceive a dialectic in history. Yet in the Christian view this dialetic is not by nature inherent in all processes, as it is for Hegel, but it is, rather, a corruption of things; and while it is a dialectic of good and evil it is not basically socioeconomic, as it is for Marx. In fact, the dialectic being caused by sin, goes on in each one of us as well as in the history we create.

Nobody is free from the inner conflict of good and evil, neither Hegel's world-historical figures, nor Marxism's proletariat. Nor will the dialectic be resolved by an emerging synthesis that blends opposing forces into one better whole; rather, the biblical hope is that good will triumph over evil by God's own intervention in history. The resurrection of Christ from the dead is offered as the guarantee of his eventual kingdom (1 Cor. 15). The Christ of history is indeed the Christ of creation, the alpha and the omega as well.

But does progress meanwhile occur, and in what sense? Indeed it does in art, in discovering new forms and sense qualities that enrich our lives with aesthetic delight, and in science, technology, and medicine, and in humanizing working conditions, and so on. The history of every field of human endeavor gives such evidence. The human lot is in many regards vastly improved over what it was only a century ago. These value-potentials are inherent in God's creation, and are actualized by his continued creativity in providence and grace. Yet evil and ugliness often grow, too—in tyrannical government, nuclear threats, repressive social systems, pollution of the environment, rape of natural resources, decaying ghettos of an inner city, discrimination, and every inhumanity of man to man. The explanation is human fallenness and irresponsible self-seeking, which, while restrained by the providential activity of God in history, still pervert the potential of God's creation.

(4) *History is about human culture and social institutions*, instruments of God's purposes, that ideally nourish good and restrain evil. History is not human history until it includes the role of economics, politics, family, and church, of art and science and ideas.

Such perspectives as the foregoing affect how we read history and how it is written. What was said about knowledge and truth should make this plain. History is no more an objective, empirical science than any other science, and less so than some because it comes so close to the beliefs and values of those who read it and write it. How we see human existence and social institutions, and what basis we give for values, affect the selection and interpretation of historical materials. John McIntyre, for instance, defines history as "meaningful occurrence, and more particularly occurrence the meaning of which is a construct out of certain categories, namely, Necessity, Providence, Incarnation, Freedom and Memory."[18] Necessity refers to the parameters of what is possible in natural conditions and the nature of man. Providence includes the judgment, mercy, and purpose of God in history. Freedom is included, but not as the main key to meaning it was for the Enlightenment. In a Christian view of history neither freedom nor nations are the principle thing, as if God were just a helper dragged in to assist from time to time. That sort of a God is easily excluded by the humanist who thinks that nature or humankind—or nothing at all—is ultimately in control. Rather, in a Christian view freedom exists only "under God," and sovereignty is always delegated by him. The majesty of God is the principle thing, and the nations are as a drop in a bucket and small dust on the scales (Isa. 40:15).[19] A Christian view of history, as of anything, is theocentric from beginning to end. God is with us.

Of course, an overall perspective of this sort does not of itself predict the outcome of a historical crisis or say why particular things happened. It may unmask self-deceptions and expose some myths. As an overall point of view, it suggests what we should emphasize in our reading of the past, and what should concern us most as we watch history unfold and participate in shaping our own future. If the moral quality of relationships within institutional life and God's purpose for certain kinds of social institutions are paramount in history, then they should be the basis for our assessment of things, and for our own involvements.

In Part Three, we will look at some of these involvements in the overall perspective of a Christian world view.

18. *The Christian Doctrine of History* (Grand Rapids: Eerdmans, 1957). Analogous accounts of Christian categories that illumine history's meaning are given by Herbert Butterfield in *Christianity and History* (New York: Scribner, 1950) and by J. V. L. Casserly in *Toward a Theology of History* (New York: Holt, Rinehart & Winston, 1965). See also the 1967 paper of the World Council of Churches, drafted by Hendrikus Berkhof, "God in Nature and History," reprinted in C. T. McIntyre, *God, History and Historians* pp. 292–328; for comparative studies of Christian and non-Christian views of history, see Reinhold Niebuhr, *Faith and History*, and D. W. Bebbington, *Patterns in History* (Downers Grove: Inter-Varsity Press, 1979).

19. See Kuyper, *Lectures*, p. 81.

PART THREE
A WORLD VIEW IN ACTION

CHAPTER 12
HUMAN CREATIVITY

Having looked at the contours of a Christian world view, we want now to suggest more briefly some differences it makes to various cultural activities. Culture is alive, growing, cultivated; it requires creativity. Going beyond biological necessities, it brings a distinctively human quality to life through work and play, art and science, education and government. First we shall define what we mean by creativity, then look at its world-viewish significance, and finally offer a series of theses to summarize a Christian view.

WHAT IS CREATIVITY?

Psychologist Rollo May calls creativity the encounter of an intensely conscious human being with his or her world.[1] As a working definition, this points to three elements: the human subject, an objective world, and the encounter between them. All three are important: what we think of the human person, how we explain the amenability of the world to human creativity, and how we describe the encounter. While the first two obviously will be affected by different world views, they also affect our interpretation of the third.

What kind of encounter is involved? Obviously it goes beyond the routine and superficial in bringing something new to light, some new ideas or perceptions, some new form that things can take, some new reality. Such an encounter occurs first in the imagination,

1. Rollo May, *The Courage to Create* (New York: W. W. Norton, 1975), chap. 2.

often before anything is said or done overtly, and it issues in the experience of possibilities that have never before been actualized. Art, says Jacques Maritain, "catches hold of the secret workings of nature in order to produce its own work—a new creature."[2]

Yet creativity is not altogether spontaneous and intuitive. It requires a rich soil of experience for seed thoughts to germinate and grow, as well as a perceptive eye, a flare for words, a ready mind. And when creative ideas arise, they must be carefully developed, experimented with, or researched before they are translated with measured steps into anything like their final form. It takes conscious effort on the part of "an intensely conscious" person.

Nor is creativity confined to what we traditionally call the arts. It may work with colors and sounds and words that evoke feelings, yet it may also work with theoretical ideas, with scientific investigation, with technological developments, with institutions and organizations. Nor is creativity confined to the genius. It is in varying degrees characteristic of all human beings, for all have a capacity to imagine what is not yet but could be, and to work for its realization. Creativity sees value-potentials in the objective world, and seeks their actualization. That is of the very nature of persons.

Examples can be given from every field of endeavor.[3] Mathematicians, theologians, scientists, athletes, and businessmen can all identify with the kind of description we have given, for creativity is a distinguishing feature of a person *qua* person, not of a person *qua* artist alone. Everyday uses of language can be creative, in the puns and metaphors and verbal surprises we enjoy. Everyday work can be creative, in new ways we find of organizing a job or getting it done. Social life can be creative, and so can love and hate, for creativity may be a force for evil as well as good. It is, after all, the encounter of a very human subject with a world of varied possibilities.

Moral questions therefore arise concerning the direction creative powers should be given. No human activity is entirely value-free, nor is it ever completely amoral; there are always values we ought to pursue, the good ends that reflect God's purposes for his creation. Thus surfaces the larger issue of the proper place of creativity in meaningful human existence.

2. Jacques Maritain, *Creative Intuition in Art and Poetry* (New York: Pantheon Books, 1953), p. 65.
3. See, for instance, the accounts given in B. Ghiselin, ed., in *The Creative Process* (Berkeley: Univ. of California Press, 1952).

CREATIVITY AND WORLD VIEWS

Creativity first attracted careful attention in the age of Romanticism. How did that come about? The Renaissance, we have observed, tended to dignify human powers independently of Christianity, and the Enlightenment idealized human freedom as if it were the very highest end of man. Romanticism simply picked this up, finding the fullest freedom in creative genius.

The Enlightenment, moreover, took the imagination to be a purely cognitive faculty, the imaging of mental pictures, and art to be a contemplative activity of the mind. Both were cousins of the free theoretical thought and logical inquiry that most concerned the age of reason, and they could be seen and appreciated only in relationship to that. It was the age of essayists, not of poets; it produced the meticulously organized music of a Mozart, not the seemingly wild or out of bounds music of a Wagner.

But the essayist Addison began to glimpse an affective element. By picturing in the mind, the imagination satisfies an inner human need, and in an impersonal mechanistic world the pleasures of metaphor and fancy keep us in touch with ourselves. But it was Immanuel Kant who made the imagination count for itself. The human subject brings form and order to things as they appear, imaginatively projecting structured possibilities that satisfy an inner need for a unified world with purpose. Coleridge picked up on this with his claim that imagination creates symbols of something beyond the immediate horizon, worlds created after our own images.[4] The freedom of self-expression through creative symbolism soon came to characterize the romanticist age.

The distinction between creative imagination and theoretical reason was indeed a valuable achievement for the arts, and it freed the human mind for discovery and innovation. Art is not just a decorative imitation of things we already know, any more than are discovery and innovation. But if creative activity itself requires informed and thoughtful work, then the divorce of reason from imagination would mean an end to art. For we do not create out of nothing—only God does that—but by discovering possibilities that reside in what God has already made. To comprehend the possibil-

4. See E. Tuveson, *The Imagination as a Means of Grace* (Berkeley: Univ. of California Press, 1960); and Mary Warnock, *Imagination* (Berkeley: Univ. of California Press, 1976).

ities we glimpse and to bring them to reality takes understanding and measured steps, a wedding of reason and imagination.

The major problem with Romanticism, however, is more than its distrust of reason: it is a tendency to enthrone human creativity, exalting the exceptionally creative genius and giving unreined freedom to novelty and feeling. Creativity for creativity's sake is anthropocentric. Give creative energy a purely biological basis and it becomes naturalistic. Add an elitist cast and it becomes racist as well, as the Nazi ideology showed: the idealization of freedom led via the idealization of creativity to the repression of the supposedly less privileged. If I am creative, and creativity is the highest good, then whatever creative thing I do is good. Creativity can do no evil, and moral distinctions are lost. Thus the enthronement of creativity becomes a deification of self wherein the fundamental God-creation distinction is lost. Prometheus is unbound.

It is little wonder, then, that some Romanticists talked pantheistic language. According to Schelling, Emil Brunner reminds us, "it is the creative mind, the work of the genius, in which the divine creativity of nature, identical with God-head, reaches its culminating point."[5] And Abraham Kuyper warned against late-nineteenth-century aestheticism that rated itself of at least equal value with the Reformation.[6]

Art is not creativity's only expression though. Work is, too—and science and technology and even play. These likewise can become religion-substitutes: play can supposedly save us from dehumanization, and technology can bring in a secular millennium.[7] Technologism, like aestheticism, must be avoided, for the one is the religion of scientific humanism and the other that of romanticist humanism; the underlying question is whether God or human creativity gives lasting meaning, unity, and hope to human existence. A Christian view of creativity, like a Christian view of knowledge, must combine modesty with confidence—modesty because we are

5. Emil Brunner, *Christianity and Civilization* (London: Nisbet, 1948), p. 149. His chapter X, entitled "The Problem of Creativity," is one of the finest things written on the topic. See also Reinhold Niebuhr, *The Nature and Destiny of Man* (1941; New York: Scribner's, 1964), chap. II, "The Problem of Vitality and Form in Human Nature."

6. Kuyper, *Lectures on Calvinism* (1898; Grand Rapids: Eerdmans, 1931), p. 143.

7. See further in the following chapters on "Play" and "Science and Technology."

finite creators and creatures ourselves, and confidence because the image of God in us opens up possibilities that God purposed for the world he made.

So far our emphasis has been on creativity as an encounter between the human subject and an objective world, but evidently we are now at the point where we must look more directly at what our understanding of the human subject and the world contribute.

The doctrine of creation provides the overall context, for we are first creatures, and only because of that are we in any sense creators, too, yet created creators at best. Elizabeth O'Connor therefore writes of human creativity under the title *Eighth Day of Creation*,[8] as if God, having himself created, gave us time to see what we could do. The objective materials we work with are divinely created, and it is their orderedness and amenability to new forms that make possible the things we imagine. They have capacity for giving concrete shape to abstract ideas, for uniting aesthetic interest with useful function. Since aesthetic and technological value are both implicit in creation, we have God to thank for a world that is responsive to our creative work, a world pregnant with all sorts of possibilities that we can bring to birth. A Christian view of creativity parts company from every naturalistic view at this most basic point.

But what about the human subject? It is customary to start with the image of God, for some analogy exists between God's creativity and ours.[9] Creativity is an expression of our freedom and partial transcendence of nature, for we remain relatively independent of what we create and it remains relatively independent of us. As God delegates creative powers to us, so we in a sense delegate creative powers to the materials with which we work. We create with purpose, whether like God for our own good pleasure, or whether to serve people's needs, or as an offering to our maker. And while we are part of the human community, a creative community if ever there was one, yet our respective styles remain relatively individual, characteristically our own.

Yet the analogy between our creativity and God's breaks down, for while God creates *ex nihilo*, plainly we do not. Some prefer to say we *make* rather than create, yet one can make things by follow-

8. Waco: Word Books, 1971.
9. Dorothy Sayers develops an extensive analogy to the creative work of the divine Trinity in *The Mind of the Maker* (London: Methuen, 1941).

ing instructions, with little imagination at all. Others prefer to talk of *discovery*, as if in a sense the statue already exists within the marble, the painting within the pallet, and the organization within confusion, and we just discover them there; yet even that is not quite accurate, for they don't already exist in the materials, but only their possibility is present—along with a myriad of other possibilities. It takes creativity to imagine alternative possibilities, to understand what makes them possible, to select one that will serve our purposes, aesthetic or otherwise, and to find ways of bringing it about. Compared to *ex nihilo* creation, our work moves in the direction of discovery, but our creative work still goes beyond what is actually there to find; in that it does something that is not part of the "otherwise" process, it is indeed more analogous to what God does than what mechanically happens.

The important thing to remember, however, in the light of romanticist extremes, is that only God creates out of nothing, only his imagination is unlimited, only he is not limited by available materials, only he is absolutely free to do as he will. That glory he shares with none other. Yet he has still made us in his image, creators of culture with all its varied possibilities for art and science and the structuring of social institutions.

The naturalist tends to explain this in terms of genetic and environmental conditions, for he finds correlations between such conditions and the incidence of creative persons. Yet even should these conditions prove sufficient, he has yet to explain the remarkable value-potential of the materials for what creative people do. However necessary genetic and environmental conditions are, and undoubtedly a creative environment and hereditary factors do contribute, the theist (as distinct from the deist) might still think them insufficient. A world amenable to human creativity, and human creativity itself, bear witness to their Creator. These are living God's good gifts, evidence of his continued creativity in human affairs.

Creativity in a human context, then, involves our relationship to God as well as to nature and to oneself, and also to other persons. Nicholas Wolterstorff argues that the primary Christian consideration regarding the arts is not our creativity, important as that may be, but that we are responsible agents. Art and other creative enterprises are part of the creation mandate to order nature for good ends, part of our stewardship of life. God's overall purpose for us is *shalōm*, a just peace with joy in God's creation, and *shalōm* includes aesthetic satisfaction and delight.[10]

If human responsibility is the overarching biblical theme about persons, then it is surely applicable here. Creativity may be part of the larger image of God in us, but the larger image in our humanness is of responsibility to God for all our actions. Creativity is not the whole.

Yet it takes creativity for us to sin; it takes a kind of free transcendence of the created course of events. We sin by misdirecting creativity to ends other than those God intended. We sin by irresponsibly creating what does not benefit humankind. We pervert creativity and so pervert people. We repress it and dwarf people. We interpret it naturalistically or exaggerate it romantically and so turn truth into error.

If the paradigm of creativity that we finitely image is God's creativity, then we must also take into the picture the creativity of his forgiving and redeeming love. Peter Bertocci develops this theme, pointing out that God first allows our exercise of creativity in sinning, and then handles it creatively. He allows creativity, Bertocci suggests, because no other good is as good as it might be without creativity, even if it could be gained independently: with all its risks, creativity is less a risk for humans than would be dehumanization. Then at the root of a truly mature person God's grace places the creativity of redeeming love that suffers risk and loss to serve those in need.[11] A Christian approach to creativity in God's image will then take God's grace as its model and responsible action as its watchword, rather than the exaltation of human genius.

It is not surprising in the light of all this that different theological emphases affect attitudes to creativity. Traditions with a strong emphasis on the physical in creation, incarnation, and sacrament, like the Roman Catholic and Anglican, have generally been productive in the arts. Traditions that stress a law-governed creation, such as the Reformed, have put creative energies into government and work. The Anabaptist tradition, emphasizing God's provision for human needs, has attended to work and to works of compassion and healing. American evangelicalism's theology focuses largely on sin and grace, and its most creative outlet has

10. Wolterstorff, *Art in Action* (Grand Rapids: Eerdmans, 1980), pt. 3.
11. Peter Bertocci, *Religion as Creative Insecurity* (Westport, CT: Greenwood Press, 1973).

therefore been in evangelism and missions.[12] Theology naturally gives direction as well as meaning to creativity. But a complete and balanced theology should direct it into every area of responsibility: art, science, society, and church.

Finally, then, *some theses toward a Christian view*:

(1) Human creativity derives its value from God's creativity and his creation mandate to us; I respond to the revelation of his creativity with mine.

(2) Human creativity manifests God's image in our humanness: creative imagination is vested in a physical world, along with a capacity for sensory, intellectual, and emotive delight.

(3) The practice of creativity and the development of culture requires both creaturely modesty and confidence in God-given possibilities and powers.

(4) Creativity is a cultural capacity to be developed in all persons, not just an elite; yet some are more gifted than others. Because genetic and environmental conditions contribute to creativity, being creative cannot be regarded as meritorious of itself.

(5) Creativity also depends on objective possibilities inherent in a law-governed creation, possibilities for values that we can often actualize.

(6) Creativity therefore extends to all cultural activities, both art and science, work and play, thought and action.

(7) Creativity can be repressed or exalted beyond measure, and exercised in irresponsible ways.

(8) A creative community can nourish creativity, but it can also become snobbish, self-centered, elitist, and therefore repressive.

(9) Creativity and culture are not enough to define the distinctive in being human, nor to define the good in good art, good science, good work, good play, good thinking.

(10) Developing creativity will require valuing it, accepting our capacity for it, mastering materials and skills so as to imagine and act freely, and directing it to good ends.

(11) Human creativity exists for the glory of God and for *shalōm* among all people, with responsibility for consequences as well as the character of what it achieves.

12. I am indebted for these observations to historian Mark Noll.

CHAPTER 13

SCIENCE AND TECHNOLOGY

Culture arises as a fruit of human creativity, and the first cultural enterprise that inevitably commands attention nowadays is that of science and technology. While it was of course present in simplified fashion in earlier years and was given fuller rein by the scientific revolution of the Renaissance and by the industrial revolution, the past fifty years have witnessed a knowledge explosion and ushered in a technological age of unprecedented magnitude.

In this chapter I propose an agenda for reflection on science and technology in the light of a Christian world view. Three concerns will occupy us: attitudes toward science, the nature of science, and the bearing of ethics on science and technology.

ATTITUDES TOWARD SCIENCE

Scientific humanism, as we saw in Chapter Two, adopts an extremely optimistic attitude toward the scientific enterprise. Echoing Francis Bacon's "knowledge is power" and Auguste Comte's humanistic proposal for a scientifically governed society, it translates the Enlightenment's rule of reason into a rule of science. Science alone affords reliable knowledge, it is said, and science alone can assure a future in which suffering and disaster are overcome. But when a technological mentality takes over, whatever scientific technology makes possible must be done. In effect, science becomes both savior and lord.

Romanticist and existential humanists may well react against modern technology, but the world's vast population cannot now withdraw into the simplicity of a pretechnological age. We can neither escape technology nor realistically do without it. The question is, rather, whether it is to be master or servant, whether it will determine our values and our future, or whether our values will shape both it and the future instead.

From a biblical standpoint, the "savior and lord" attitude is idolatrous. As we noted earlier, the Genesis creation account and the Exodus story of the plagues in Egypt both repudiate mythologies in which people worship and serve creatures rather than the one Creator of heaven and earth. At this end of the twentieth century, scientism and technologism are mythologies that must be repudiated,[1] a scientism that sees science as savior and a technologism that would make advanced technology the master of our lives. C. S. Lewis spoke of them as *That Hideous Strength*, a most appropriate title.

But when we demythologize science and technology by viewing them as servants rather than masters, then they find a proper and valued place as cultural activities. Like other creative enterprises they are possible because the human person in God's image is endowed with powers of imagination and action that can actualize valuable possibilities inherent in nature. Subjectively, science and technology are possible because of the uniqueness of persons; objectively they are possible because this is an ordered creation of law-governed processes and delegated powers. Science and technology are indeed worthy enterprises, part of the cultural mandate given by the divine logos of creation at the outset of human history.

Modern science began in a culture that believed this and practiced it. Some writers claim that the Judeo-Christian view of God as Creator made possible scientific and technological progress, for by insisting that the world is neither divine nor evil, it set people free from superstitious fears, both about meddling with nature and about unleashing demonic fates. We can therefore experiment without fear of malicious reprisal. And in a well-known series of articles, Michael Foster has argued that the Christian view of nature's laws as contingent on God's will, rather than independently and logically necessary as in Greek science, freed early modern science to pursue empirical research. If things do not logically have to be the way

1. On this theme see Alasdair MacIntyre's essay, "Scientific Theories and Scientific Myths," in *Metaphysical Beliefs* (London: SCM Press, 1957), pp. 13-81.

they in fact are, then we must examine them as they actually are and see what is the case.[2]

Yet biblical perspectives not only underscore the possibilities of science and technology, but also accord them value. That the creation itself is good encourages us to value its resources. All nature bears witness to the great goodness of God and praises him, and our stewardship of its resources should be a glad service of vast benefit to humankind. In fact, Francis Bacon regarded science as God's way of restoring to us that responsible oversight of nature which sin has corrupted.

Here is an attitude that avoids the idolatry of scientism yet values science, and that avoids the antitechnological mentality of the Romanticist yet values technology. In epistemological matters we suggested an attitude combining epistemological modesty and epistemological hope. A truly Christian approach to science should exemplify this: a modesty that realizes our own limitations and places limited hope in science and technology, yet a hope that values possibilities that a loving Creator provides through them. Science and technology, after all, are functions of both human knowledge and human creativity.

THE NATURE OF SCIENCE

The extravagant claims of scientism and technologism, due in large measure to an overconfident humanistic spirit, may be traced to Enlightenment epistemology. Scientism is a recent version of its rationalism, and so the epistemological foundations of science should place high on our agenda.

Enlightenment rationalism bequeathed an exclusive claim to knowledge by purely objective methods that can be extended equally to every area of inquiry. Not only nature but man and God were subjected to the same approach: witness Kant's *Religion Within the Bounds of Reason Alone*. Consequently the scientism of the nine-

2. M. B. Foster, "The Christian Doctrine of Creation and the Rise of Modern Natural Science," *Mind* 43 (1934): 446; 44 (1935): 439; 45 (1936): 1. See also R. Hooykaas, *Christian Faith and the Freedom of Science* (Grand Rapids: Eerdmans, 1972); Ian Barbour, *Issues in Science and Religion* (Englewood Cliffs: Prentice-Hall, 1966), chap. II; Stanley L. Jaki, *The Road to Science and The Ways to God* (Chicago: Univ. of Chicago Press, 1978), chap. 3. A. N. Whitehead argues in parallel fashion in *Science and the Modern World* (New York: Macmillan, 1925), chap. I.

teenth and twentieth centuries made claims that science itself need not make:

(1) the exclusiveness of science, as the only path to reliable knowledge;

(2) the unity of science, so that the methods of physical science are equally applicable to every area of inquiry; and

(3) presuppositionless science, completely objective and requiring no nonscientific assumptions.

Oddly enough, these claims do not themselves result *from* science but are a priori claims *about* science, and hard to substantiate scientifically. The exclusiveness of science is challenged by claims from the humanities, claims about common knowledge, claims about moral knowledge and our knowledge of other persons, and the claims of religion. Can all these counterclaims be dismissed by scientific examination? The unity of science is challenged by the human sciences that deal with persons and society, which are neither as manipulable nor predictable as physical variables. And the presuppositionlessness claim is challenged by recent work in the history and philosophy of science that highlights subjective and sociological influences and the role of models or paradigms in the construction of both theories and experiments.[3]

These are standard philosophical objections to scientism, but further objections arise from a Judeo-Christian standpoint. Our knowledge of a self-revealing God belies the exclusiveness of science. Our knowledge of the uniqueness of the human person in all creation defies the unity of science. Our recognition of our own creatureliness and the theistic unity of truth undermines the possibility of presuppositionless science. The Christian, in fact, welcomes the rich diversity of God's creation and freely admits that, because human knowledge presupposes things about nature, God, and man, it is never fully autonomous.

Science, then, is not as scientism claims. But neither will it do to swing to opposite extremes, from scientism to fideism, from the unity of science to Romanticism, from presuppositionless science to relativism. Science is an interpretive activity, therefore somewhat

3. See, for example, T. B. Kuhn, *The Structure of Scientific Revolutions* (Chicago: Univ. of Chicago, 1962); Michael Polanyi, *Personal Knowledge* (Chicago: Univ. of Chicago, 1958); and Stephen Toulmin, *Foresight and Understanding* (London: Hutchinson Univ. Library, 1961).

provisional and still fallible like all human knowledge, but insofar as it represents a coherent and cumulative body of theoretical understanding with reliable predictive power it offers a modest but tremendously worthwhile hope for which God is to be thanked.

ETHICS, SCIENCE, AND TECHNOLOGY

The rise of modern science and technology has proved both a blessing and a bane.[4] Medical advances have eliminated extensive suffering and increased longevity; automation and cybernation have eased human toil and are eliminating some of the monotony of work; modern communications have distributed the benefits of travel, learning, and the arts much more equitably than ever before. Yet biomedical technology holds ominous possibilities for playing God with life and death and earth's genetic heritage; a technological society's insatiable thirst for nonrenewable energy threatens the future of our civilization; political technology and modern communications manipulate public opinion, the popular vote, and the national destiny; military technology threatens the very survival of the human race. At the everyday level we face questions about abortion and euthanasia, about economic consumption and distribution, about environmental pollution and control—questions posed by scientific and technological advance. Technology is power, the power to manipulate, the power to exterminate, the power to proliferate, the power to create dehumanizing futures and to destroy our very selves.

The blessing and bane that technology brings can clearly be seen in environmental concerns. Two viewpoints dominate the literature: on the one hand, Paul Ehrlich traces the problem to the finiteness of nature's resources, in the face of which technology could end up helpless; on the other hand, Barry Commoner traces the problem to human abuse of things. Finite resources mean that we must adapt our values to the hard facts, limiting material prog-

4. See Ian Barbour, *Science and Secularity* (New York: Harper & Row, 1970), esp. chap. III; David Ehrenfeld, *The Arrogance of Humanism* (New York: Oxford Univ. Press, 1978); and F. Ferre, *Shaping the Future* (New York: Harper & Row, 1976). Jacques Ellul has been the most persistent critic: see *The Technological Society* (New York: Knopf, 1964). Alvin Toffler elaborates the possible banes and benefits in *Future Shock* (New York: Random House, 1970) and *The Third Wave* (New York: William Morrow & Co., 1980).

ress, limiting population growth, abandoning hankerings for a technological millennium on earth. But our abuse of nature also means we must change our way of thinking: we are part of nature and limited by it, not apart from it and independent. Technology must be governed by this realization.

Two philosophical viewpoints also emerge, a romanticized monism that unites man with nature, as in process philosophers like Charles Hartshorne and in Eastern religion, and a dualism of man and nature that has its roots in Descartes, and even earlier in Plato and the Manichees. The dualist, it is said, exploits nature by trying to rule it, while the monist respects nature as himself. One's philosophy affects his environmental stance.[5]

But a biblical view fits neither of these paradigms, neither the dualist nor the monist. A Christian understanding of the human person is of a responsible agent who is part of nature and yet transcends it, a unitary being, not a dualistic one. Here is no anthropocentric claim to dominate nature for our own ends, but an admission of finiteness and interdependence. Since our relationship to nature is an inherent part of both our being and our responsibility, it argues against any exploitation of nature, against an unqualified dependence on natural resources, therefore against any unqualified reliance on technology. The problem is not with technology but with us, for we have not realistically reckoned either with our own dependency or with the finiteness of nature, but have been misled by the rule of reason and of science into supposing that we can always make a way out. But the Christian doctrine of sin and Christian eschatology combine to deny that we can. Sin has cosmic consequences, and the whole creation groans under its weight (Rom. 8:18–23). Redemption has cosmic consequences, too, and Scripture speaks of both the resurrection of the body and a new earth. In the final analysis our hope lies not with technology but with the living God, the Logos of all creation, for nature is finally his, not ours, and science and technology must function as means to his good ends.

5. See Kurt Baier and Nicholas Rescher, eds., *Values and the Future* (New York: Free Press, 1969); and W. T. Blackstone, ed., *Philosophy and Environmental Crisis* (Athens, GA: Univ. of Georgia, 1974). For Christian approaches see Ian Barbour, *Western Man and Environmental Ethics* (Reading, MA: Addison-Wesley Publishing Co., 1973); Eric Rust, *Nature: Garden or Desert?* (Waco: Word Books, 1971); and esp. Lauren Wilkinson, ed., *Earth-keeping* (Grand Rapids: Eerdmans, 1980).

Technology is applied knowledge. So, like knowledge, technology is power. The ethics of power must therefore apply to technology. Starting with a theistic basis for values (as in Chapter Ten), we need to insist that nature is neither primarily nor ultimately of value to us for our purposes, but is of value to God for his good ends. On that basis we need to develop an ethic of responsible technological power that includes the following in its agenda:

(1) The value of *all creation*. We are obligated to respect the creation order, its beauty and fecundity as well as its utility. We are forbidden to prostitute its resources for such unstewardly ends as needless wealth, power, or prestige.

(2) The value of *all life*. This is neither a romanticist personifying of living things, nor a purely utilitarian approach that treats life as expendable whenever it serves our ends. We must reject irresponsible uses of technology, whether in germicides, in disposal of radioactive wastes, or in genetic manipulation. We must value living things as essential to the ecosystem God made.

(3) The value of *human persons*, such that all persons have equal rights and correlative duties. An ethic of power will keep technology within just limits, in the distribution of limited resources and in respect for our aesthetic and recreational dependence on nature. Technology must not dehumanize, but by just distribution must contribute to the human quality of our earthly existence.

(4) An *ethic of hope*. A transcendent God is not tied to nature's resources alone, but is free to act creatively in this world and to change an expected course of events. Usually he does so through human creativity, science and technology included, for we do change the course of history and we can avert evils. We must therefore nourish responsible human creativity. By this as well as other means, he who made the heavens and the earth and changed water into wine renews our hope.

CHAPTER 14

WORK

The technological mentality of our times operates in the economic realm as well as in the scientific, but here it affects people more directly. In production, in management, in advertising and sales, technology contributes to efficiency and productivity. Computerized inventories and accounting, sophisticated management techniques, systems analysis, modern advertising, and distribution networks all involve technology. Yet problems arise when an amoral mentality takes over, implying that utilitarian considerations must overrule other values. Profit, productivity, efficiency, or corporate growth can easily become not just an important factor but the overriding goal to be considered.

This kind of mentality marred the industrial revolution. The earlier work ethic lost its religious roots in the secularization of economics, and utilitarianism prevailed. Vast industrial empires exploited labor, devoured natural resources, polluted the environment, and determined the destiny of millions who toiled out of necessity in dehumanizing ways. The supposed rule of reason had produced a nightmare. Marx the humanist understandably cried out about alienated labor toiling in onerous ways, exploited by others for their own advantage, and robbed thereby of the satisfactions that come from working freely for results that the worker himself can enjoy.

The Greek attitude toward work has also fed into our thinking. Aristotle wisely distinguished natural from unnatural moneygetting, and limited gain to what is needful for a human quality of life. Avarice and unbridled profit for its own sake he denounced as unjust, for they contravene the natural ends of work and commerce.

Yet this ethic was offset by an aristocratic premium on the leisure free men enjoy as against the labor required of servants and slaves. The physical was often depreciated in ancient Greece, so that while political activity became a noble occupation, more mundane tasks were often disdained.

The Renaissance humanists echoed this classical view, and we have not escaped it yet. We value professional and political life over manual labor, and maximize leisure by shortening the work hours or taking an early retirement. Work itself has become an ambiguous thing whose meaning and value is in doubt; even a casual observer can notice the diffidence with which some treat the conception of "career." In part it is a reaction against the material-minded self-interest and utilitarianism that surround us, but in part also it reflects a Greek dichotomy of work and leisure in which work simply makes possible the activities of leisure, and the intrinsic value of human work is lost.

Understandably, therefore, Father Frances Connell insists that if the purposes of work are to be drawn from the overall purpose of human life as a divine gift and calling, then we should introduce theology into business education[1]—and, let us add, into career preparation in general. Literature professor Joyce Erickson proposes that understanding the meaning of work should be one goal of a liberal arts education, since it involves questions about values and personal identity and relationships.[2]

A world-viewish understanding of work cannot help the graduate get a job or tell employers how to run their businesses, but it can provide understandings and values that the workplace should embody, it can identify the proper ends of economic activity, and it can point out goals that conflict with these ends and relationships that are unjust.

A THEOLOGICAL CONTEXT

Within a Christian world view, work finds meaning in relationship to things of ultimate concern. Because the God-creation relationship is the basis for our values, we can affirm that all creation, the

1. Connell, *Business and the Liberal Arts*, ed. J. J. Clark and B. J. Opulenta (Jamaica, NY: St. John's Univ. Press, 1962), pp. 81–98.
2. "Career Education in a Christian Liberal Arts Setting," *Christian Scholars Review* 6 (1976):167.

physical as well as the political, is of worth. Our work keeps bringing created potentials to fruition. "The earth is the Lord's, and the fullness thereof," said the psalmist. It has value to God, and we therefore take up our work as his servants, responsible to him, and the living God who is still creatively at work in his creation is active through us. We are both his servants and his coworkers in the economic sphere.

The myth of the self-sufficient individualist is thereby banished. The autonomy of economic activity is equally mythical if work is a divine calling implicit in the very structure of our being. Productive work, like creativity in general, is only possible because nature's resources are responsive to our interests and needs.

If the doctrine of creation speaks to the objective possibility of meaningful work, the doctrine of man speaks to the subjective conditions it requires. We are creative beings in the image of God, finite creators who bring into actuality possibilities that God envisioned. Work ideally is to be creative; at least it should be in its overall nature and its impact on people and their lives. Yet this is where the industrial revolution took its toll—because, for all the material advancement it produced, it too often routinized work and reduced it to mechanical tasks devoid of and even deadening to imagination and originality. Technology can sometimes now take over routine jobs and thereby allow more creative specialization, but the need remains to humanize all of work with creative satisfactions.

We are relational beings, and it seems to me that this is where job satisfaction is found, in how work relates us creatively to nature and its resources, to other people and their quality of life, to ourselves and our own capabilities, and ultimately to God. Whether the job itself is creative or routine, it provides the occasion to work imaginatively at serving other people, at improving the quality of life, at developing constructive social relationships, and at serving God.

We cannot work, anymore than we can live, in purely individualistic fashion. Aristotle was correct in saying that we are social beings, and that not all "getting" is right even when it is legal. John Locke was correct in saying that property rights are not unconditional, for they are related to the work we do to develop nature's resources. According to Locke, these are resources God gave to all people, so we should leave enough for others to develop, too. Relationships put limits on property, profit, and wealth.

Work is ordained by God, but, like every human activity and institution, sin has twisted it from its original shape and diverted it from its original purpose. Plato addressed the problem of human acquisitiveness in the *Republic*, devising a social and governmental structure and an educational program to bring it under control. But the history of slavery is a classic example of economic sin, and slavery can exist under other names in any economic system that unjustly demands labor without regard to the ultimate meaning of work or to justice for all involved. A capitalist economy cannot ensure justice if free enterprise becomes unqualified self-interest. Competing self-interests do not automatically balance each other out as Adam Smith supposed, for competition is the exercise of power, a power enhanced by technology; and power without an ethic of power spells disaster. The Christian should know that laws alone, even economic laws, are not enough to make people just.

Nor is public ownership or massive governmental regulation the solution, for corruption shows its ugliness and power is abused in public office, too. In politics we value the checks provided in the division of power between branches of government. A similar division of power between the political and economic orders is needed so that the one can help offset the failures and vices of the other.[3] Indeed, that God ordained a variety of social institutions has led some to argue for a pluralistic social philosophy that would give a high degree of sovereignty to each kind of institution, whether family, education, business, or government.[4] No economic system and no overall social structure can avoid the problems of self-interest and power.

This kind of realism underlies the biblical pattern of law, prophet, and gospel we noted in Chapter Eleven. "Thou shalt not steal" stands as a general moral rule in the whole economic area, in the value it ascribes economic rights as well as the specifics of property and work. In the Mosaic legislation it applies to a wide range of things:

3. The point is developed at length by V. A. Demant in *Religion and the Decline of Capitalism* (New York: Scribner, 1952).
4. This underlies the Kuyperian doctrine of law spheres, and is proposed by Gordon J. Spykman in "Pluralism: our last best hope?", *Christian Scholars Review* 10 (1981):99.

(1) Respect for other people's property, whether stolen (Exod. 22:1, 4), damaged (Exod. 22:5–6; 21:33–36), borrowed (Exod. 22:7–14), or lost and found (Deut. 22:1–4).

(2) Business life, both transactions (Lev. 19:11–15; Deut. 25:13–16) and wages (Deut. 15:12–14; 24:14–15).

(3) Concern for the underprivileged, including loans to the poor (Exod. 22:25–27), the rights of slaves (Exod. 21), and the rights of the poor and of foreigners (Exod. 23:6–9). The Jubilee Year provided a redistribution of land that would restore equitable opportunity as against discriminatory monopolies on work and resources.

The wisdom literature reminds us that he who loves money never has enough, and that a happy home, wisdom, and a good reputation are preferable to wealth and property. The Gospels record the repentance of Zacchaeus for acquiring wealth unjustly, and tell of the rich young ruler who loved his riches too much. That wealth counts for less than work itself, and that work is ordained for one's own needs and for helping others, is plain in all of this. Paul's advice to masters and servants (Eph. 6:5–9; Col. 3:22–4:1) makes it doubly plain, for he insists that justice and fair treatment come first.

A similar picture emerges in the history of Christian ethics. In the early church, some rejected private ownership of property altogether, maintaining that it resulted from the fall. A doctrine of two vocations developed, the spiritual and the earthly, and those who embraced the former refused to participate in war or government or to accumulate wealth. The medieval church confined this spiritual calling to religious orders, and referred the earthly calling to those in "secular" work; yet moral strictures remained in regard to pricing, usury, and avarice.

By rejecting this dichotomy of sacred and secular, the Reformers repudiated the extremes of both the mendicant orders and self-indulgent luxury. They extended the concept of divine vocation to all kinds of work and all orders of life, calling on Christians to persist in their present callings rather than moving from pillar to post out of self-interest. Work has other ends than that.

In Puritan New England, the Massachusetts colony controlled self-interest by regulating prices and interest rates and establishing a minimum wage. And a Boston minister denounced as false those suppositions which today's business community takes for granted:

(1) That a man might sell as dear as he can, and buy as cheap as he can.

(2) If a man lose by casualty of sea in some of his commodities, he may raise the price of the rest.

(3) That he may sell as he bought, though he paid too dear, and though the commodity be fallen.

(4) That, as a man may take advantage of his own skill or ability, so he may of another's advantage or necessity.[5]

The underlying principles in this theological and historical recital are clear: the earth is the Lord's, not ours, so we are responsible to him both for our work and for the moral quality of relationships therein.

MEANING IN WORK

What, then, should we say about the purpose of work from a Christian perspective? First, it becomes apparent that loss of meaning and purpose in alienated labor is related to the loss of a biblical view. Without the God-creation relationship and the relational nature of persons in God's image, work loses both its religious and its truly human context and is taken over by competing self-interests. These may be the interests of individuals or classes or corporations, but they must in any case be controlled and larger ideals restored if work is to regain its meaning and the worker his dignity. And lack of moral self-control invites outside controls that too easily confuse the situation and repress creativity.

Second, meaning and purpose are to be found in what God intended work to be and to achieve in his creation. This takes precedence over questions of private or public ownership, over rhetoric about a simple life-style, and over the choice of a job, for our purposes in working should obviously align with the purposes of the Creator.

I suggest that the purpose of work is to provide for human needs, one's own and others', and for a truly human quality of life. This seems both to capture the underlying intent of the biblical literature on the subject, and to follow from what has been said about the place of man and society in God's creation. Since work

5. R. L. Tawney, *Religion and the Rise of Capitalism* (New York: Harcourt, Brace, 1926), p. 131.

is then a vocation given to us by God for this end, the satisfactions of work begin with an acceptance of this call and continue with the devotion of our labors to him. We work in response to God's call.

Provision for human needs is obviously intended, others' needs as well as one's own, the needs of family, of those unable to provide for themselves, and of those who provide services to us in a myriad of ways. Provision for a distinctively human quality of life is essential, too, for as creative beings made in God's image we have capacities that should be developed and stewarded well. Directly or indirectly, our work contributes to the development of culture, to art and science, to government and recreation and education, and to other enriching things.

This purpose affects work itself. Work that is not recompensed sufficiently to meet family needs and to provide a human quality of life is a kind of work that violates God's intention and is ill conceived. Work whose conditions dehumanize those who labor, whose products are dehumanizing or in any way endanger a human quality of life, are kinds of work that also violate God's intention and are ill conceived. The actual work itself should contribute directly and not just economically to God's purposes, and should even be morally uplifting.

Thomas Aquinas interestingly notes four goals for work: to obtain food, to remove idleness and the problems it creates, to curb concupiscence by afflicting the body, and to provide for charitable giving to others.[6] The first and last of these concern basic human needs, the other two bear on the moral quality of life that is proper to humans. Calvin's benediction might then appropriately be given:

> there will be no employment so mean and sordid (provided we follow our vocation), as not to appear truly respectable, and be deemed highly important in the sight of God.[7]

Since the basis for values is in God's own valuing, what more ultimate meaning could one want?

We need to recover this concept of vocation. Work is not only, not even primarily, a matter of productivity; for all his lack of a constructive alternative, Herbert Marcuse aptly underscored the dangers of an unqualified productivity principle for both East and

6. *Summa Theologica* II.2, Q. 187, Art. 3.
7. *Institutes*, trans. John Allen (Philadelphia: Westminster Press, 1949), Book III, ch. 10, p. 791.

West in his *Essay on Liberation*. Productivity, in fact, is not the end at all, but only a means to the ends for which in the final analysis we work. Nor is profit the purpose: profit is necessary in our economic order, necessary to the survival of a business, to research and development, to a just reward system for employers, employees, and investors alike, but it is still only a means to proper ends. Work is service, serving God and our fellow men. If, then, we are concerned with morality in work we should seek to transform the profit motive into a means of responsible service to others.

WORK AND ETHICS

But what does the moral quality of work relationships entail? Respect for persons is the basic concern when we talk about human values and the practice of justice and love. Fair pricing and just wages for an honest day's work are but the beginning. The freedom and dignity of the worker mean, as Dennis Munby points out, that one should be treated according to due process under contractual agreements, and be consulted about conditions of employment and other things that affect one's attitude to the task and to one's well-being.[8]

Not all work is in itself creative, fulfilling, or even satisfying. Some will be, but there are always unpleasant and frustrating jobs that require self-sacrifice for the sake of others. And the thorns and thistles that curse the work of a fallen race cannot be defoliated out of existence. Yet if such work is necessary and is part of our calling, then sacrifice can be accepted. Even if the work itself inhibits personal growth and satisfaction, other work-related satisfactions can still be provided: fringe benefits, opportunity for advancement, in-service training, educational opportunity, and constructive social activities.

Work relates us to other people, for it is a social activity. In the household industries and guilds of the past, this was much more to the fore than with the decentralized industry and suburban living of today. But while the technological and industrial revolutions have changed things, work remains the single most time-absorbing activity of most adults; it can still be an entrée into, if not the locus

8. Munby, *Christianity and Economic Problems* (New York: Macmillan, 1956), pp. 252–55.

of, an enriching social and cultural life.[9] Work relates us not only to ourselves and other people but also to nature: moral responsibility in that regard is essential, too. But most fundamental from a Christian perspective is that we work before God, and participate in work's other relationships before him as well. The apostle therefore talked of working to please and serve God, not just the humans we serve. This vocation above all else gives dignity to it all, for if God is with us in our work then work is both noble and ennobling, and as great a pleasure as we often find in leisure and play.

William Temple, former Archbishop of Canterbury, declared years ago that Christians have the task of reforming the economic order into closer proximity to Christian principles.[10] At the very least their own economic activity should model a new order for a new society, a kingdom of justice and *shalōm* that is yet to come.

9. Alvin Toffler (*The Third Wave*, chap 16–17) envisions the enrichment of family relationships by virtue of the vast amount of work that can be done in the home, as computer terminals become more readily available.

10. Temple, *Christianity and the Social Order* (Harmondsworth: Penguin Books, 1942), p. 47.

CHAPTER 15

PLAY[1]

A citizenry unprepared for leisure will degenerate in prosperous times—as Sebastian deGrazia says of ancient Sparta.[2] Ours is an increasingly leisured and playful society in which four-day work weeks, once beyond the wildest dreams of labor, are now becoming a reality. Early retirements are common: some retirees find new careers, while others lapse into an idleness relieved only by fishing or TV. In the case of youth, equipment for sports like skiing and for high-fidelity stereo music, which a few decades ago were regarded as the luxuries of the rich, have become common expectations and in their judgment almost a social necessity. Since the 1960s the productivity principle of a distorted work ethic has been challenged by an idea of play not yet embodied in a clear-cut ethic. Self-indulgence and narcissism have therefore come to mark the games people play.

On the other hand, workaholism blights the home, one's work, and even life itself. We need recreation and the capacity to enjoy life. But we are caught between the two extremes of self-indulgent play and compulsive work, and have no adequate map of the road we should tread.

A Christian view of play must rest on a Christian understanding of human persons as God made us to be. In calling for such a view, then, I want first to show how pervasive play is by pointing out different kinds of activity that play includes, then to inquire about

1. An earlier version of this chapter appeared in *Christian Scholars Review* II (1981): 41–48. It is used here by permission.
2. *Of Time, Work and Leisure* (New York: Twentieth Century Fund, 1962), pp. 11–14, 426.

the place of play in relation to the nature of persons, and finally to identify some needed ingredients in a theology of play.

Play is customarily defined as nonproductive activity. This is not strictly correct, for play can be economically productive for professionals, quiz-show participants, and many others. The intent of the definition is that the purpose of play is not to be found in elements extrinsic to the activity, as supposedly with work, but is to be found in the activity itself and its enjoyment. Yet even this is unsatisfactory, since it presupposes that the purpose of work is its extrinsic rewards, while a Christian view of work also stresses work's intrinsic dignity and values. Similarly, if we define play as free and voluntary activity in contrast to the necessity of required work, then we fail to consider those who work voluntarily, not of necessity, and those who play for a living. My point is that to set work and play in antithesis, as has traditionally been done, does not help. Some people work harder at play than at work, while others of us have a ball at work.

My thesis, then, will be that play is best seen as an attitude, a state of mind rather than as a distinguishable set of activities, and that the separation of work from play is a historical disjunction consequent upon the fall of humankind from its intended estate.

THE PERVASIVENESS OF PLAY

Playing with words can help us make the point. We play *with* words and play *on* words. We play with ideas, play music, play ball, play back, and play the fool. We have play-boys, play-bills, play-schools, and play-suits. We play act, play down, play up, play off, and role-play, until we are quite played out, or else out-played by others.

Two kinds of play emerge in this list. The first includes games, sport, and athletics (e.g., play with words, play ball, play-schools, etc.), but many of these are games for the sake of something other than play (e.g., play-school, play therapy, play with ideas). The second includes art, imagination, and fantasy (e.g., play music, play-bills, role-play), in which play becomes aesthetic activity. Some examples fit neither of these two categories (e.g., play back, play down), but are metaphors that can function in almost any area of life.

Consider some related concepts, brothers and sisters of play, and cousins by the dozen: leisure, free time, recreation, relaxation, games, sport, humor, jokes, teasing and pleasing, fun and pun, contests and competitions, joy, adventure, pageant, festivity, celebration, ritual, imagination, contemplation, fantasy, myth, drama, art, creativity. Notice that sheer frivolity, utter waste, complete idleness and indolence, if relatives at all, are the prodigal children of play, the black sheep of the family. Even the term "vacation," taken literally as "emptiness," is a misfit here in comparison with the literal meaning of "holi-(holy)-day."

The relatives who are in good standing, however, fall into several groups: not only games and art, but also celebration, ritual, festivity. Play then takes at least three cultural directions: the first includes games, sport, and athletics (notice the increasing organization, technique, and professionalization in that trilogy); the second includes art, drama, fantasy (notice here the increasing creativeness and play of imagination); the third includes festivity, ritual, and celebration (notice how they all replay the past, but with increasing structure). The three are not mutually exclusive, for there is art in sport, and in ritual, too. But our point is that we play both for present enjoyment (games), and in creating new worlds of experience (art), and in reliving the past (celebration). That is indeed pervasive.

Academic disciplines tell a similar story:

—in anthropology, we have Huizinga's *Homo Ludens*,
—in sociology, Goffman's dramaturgical theory of the roles people play, and the sociology of sport,
—in economics, money games and "playing the market,"
—in political science, the presidential "race" and its "front runners" with their "game plans,"
—in psychology, Freud on dreams and play,
—in education, we read how children learn through play,
—in history, Erasmus' *In Praise of Folly*, a title that puns on its dedicatee, Sir Thomas Moore (Latin, *moror*, to be a fool), the imaginative author of *Utopia*,
—in literature, we have Hesse's *Magister Ludi*, Beckett's *Endgame*, Sartre's *Les Jeux Sont Faits*,
—in philosophy, Wittgenstein introduces "language games,"
—in mathematics, we find game theory,
—in religion, the theology of play.

Here we find not so much play-activity, but rather the study of play and analogues to play, even extensions of it, in every area of inquiry. Someone has suggested that play is the root metaphor that gives overall meaning to life in the mythologies of our day. "All the world's a stage, and all the men and women merely players," said Shakespeare, "and one man in his time plays many parts." Play pervades every department of life, and cannot be kept on the fringes. Playfully man acts in everything he does.[3]

Play is thus all-pervasive, and extends beyond isolable kinds of activity. It does not lie just on the fringes of life, as if games were spare parts we don't really need in the main business of the day. On the contrary, we work playfully, joke with colleagues, and even tease our readers along (as I have been doing). The old disjunction between work and play breaks down.

PLAY AND THE NATURE OF PERSONS

In the light of play's pervasiveness, what shall we say about its proper place and purpose in human life? Two antithetical attitudes exist. Some see play as essential to human nature, even our defining characteristic: a person is *homo ludens*, and human kinds of play distinguish her from other animals. Leisure, says Joseph Pieper, is the basis of culture; and sociologist Sebastian DeGracia documents it at great length.[4] Piaget finds play essential to the cognitive development of children.[5] Harvey Cox claims that essential to retaining our humanity is the festivity that links us to our past, and the fantasy that links us to possible futures.[6] But some have outdone themselves: Nietzsche went so far as to reduce all of life and thought to masks in a play, taking nothing seriously except the will to power—in effect, the will to win—so that all of life is a biologically driven power play. The flower children of the '60s said it more ironically, and today a self-infatuated narcissism speaks. On this view everything is play, self-centered play, but still no play ethic exists.

3. Cf. "artistically man acts," Nicholas Wolterstorff's phrase in *Art in Action* (Grand Rapids: Eerdmans, 1980), pt. 1.
4. Pieper, *Leisure, The Basic of Culture* (London: Faber and Faber, 1952), and Sebastian DeGrazia, *Of Time*.
5. Piaget, *Play, Dreams and Imitation in Childhood* (New York: W. W. Norton, 1962), pt. II, cited in David L. Miller, *Gods & Games* (New York: Harper and Row, 1970), p. 122.
6. This is the thesis of his *The Feast of Fools* (New York: Harper and Row, 1969).

On the other hand, the human being is defined as *homo faber*, the maker of things. Work, not play, is the meaning of life. Play may be an escape valve, providing relaxation or recreation to help us work harder when vacation time (viz., empty time), with its escape from responsibility, is over. So nonproductive play becomes productive in the end. We commercialize sport and bring the latest medical technology to heighten athletic prowess, until the human meaning of play is forgotten in the technology of medics and trainers. Bruce Haley traces this trend among nineteenth-century Victorians who required sports in school "for moral self-improvement." The battle of Waterloo was won on the playing fields of Eton, for a wealthy playing class absorbed itself in such games as war and commerce as eagerly and resolutely as in field sports and athletics. Their pursuit of more wealth, said Ruskin, was a game "absolutely without purpose": London, the center of British finance and commerce, became "a great city of play; very nasty play, and very hard play . . . a huge billiard table without the cloth, and with pockets as deep as the bottomless pit."[7] They turned play into work, and work into the worst of play, with unbridled competitiveness.

The lack of playful play is evident today in the Vince Lombardi slogan, "winning isn't the main thing, it's the only thing," a slogan that at times seems true of the political and business worlds as well as on the football field. Institutionalized play is no longer festive and free, but has become big business. Play for its own sake seems to have lost meaning, as if, in the words of Bernard Shaw, "hell is an endless holiday: nothing to do, and plenty of money to spend on doing it."[8] So really work is all that counts.

This attitude may well have arisen in reaction to the overplayfulness of Romanticists, themselves in reaction to the Enlightenment's rigid rule of reason in all of life. But *homo faber* is a child of the industrial revolution, close kin to technologism, scientism, positivism, and utilitarianism, where the "ism" marks a value judgment of an exclusivist sort. Today's *homo faber* has inherited these reductionist extremes, to the loss of imaginative play and the celebrative spirit. He sees art works as financial investments, and has little

7. Bruce Haley, *The Healthy Body & Victorian Culture* (Cambridge: Harvard Univ. Press, 1978), p. 253.
8. Quoted by Robert Lee, *Religion & Leisure in America* (Nashville: Abingdon, 1964), p. 25.

room either for playful work or playful play, for the work has swal-
lowed up play.

Sam Keen contrasts *homo faber* and *homo ludens* as the Apol-
lonian and Dionysian views of life.[9] For the former, life is all work,
ruled by reason, law and order, and play is only a means to that
end. For the latter, life is all play, ruled by feeling and sensation,
given over to life's enjoyments.

In Christian perspective, however, the meaning of being human is found in neither work nor play. In the final analysis a human
being is neither *homo faber* nor *homo ludens*. So it is not play that
will rehumanize work but something more basic than either that
rehumanizes both work and play. The task of a play ethic is not to
revert to Aristotle's nonproductive activity, nor to separate work
from play as in his aristocratic society where slaves worked while
the wealthy could enjoy unproductive leisure. Play is not the key
to being human, but being human is the key to play.

A person at the heart of his being is *homo religiosis*, his life to
be lived in responsible relationship to God, and it is worship that
is his most distinctive activity, not work and not play. Of course,
there are aspects of play in the celebration of worship, but more
fundamentally it is the religious meaning of life that gives purpose
and meaning to both work and play. This must ground our play
ethic, for a responsible relationship to God includes play. Hence we
need a theology of play, so that we might see more fully its purpose
in relationship to God.

THEOLOGY AND PLAY

Three ingredients for a theology of play stand out in my proposal.
More may well be needed; in fact, it would be valuable not only to
consider how each classical topic of systematic theology bears on
the subject, but also to review the social history of Old Testament
Israel with this in mind. My three ingredients, then, are only a
beginning.[10]

(1) *The image of God in play.* Play cannot be forced, but in

9. Keen, *Apology for Wonder* (New York: Harper & Row, 1969).
10. I am indebted in this section to ideas and stimuli from David
Miller, and from Sam Keen (both cited above), also Hugh Rahner, *Man
At Play* (London: Herder & Herder, 1972); Jorgen Moltmann, *Theology of
Play* (New York: Harper & Row, 1972); and Lewis Smedes, "Theology &
Playful Life," in Orlebeke and L. Smedes, *God and the Good* (Grand Rapids:
Eerdmans, 1975). Like most human efforts, this chapter combines some-
thing old and something borrowed with relatively little new.

order to be truly playful it must be voluntary and with a free spirit. These very characteristics mark the activity of God. Before creation the eternal Trinity was, from the *homo faber* standpoint, strangely unproductive: the divine being enjoyed leisure for eternal conversation, with endless time to imagine possible worlds that might not be created.

The "work" of creation itself was not necessary, neither logically required nor morally obligatory nor economically needful nor inwardly compulsive, but was voluntary and entirely free. God did not have to create at all, let alone to create the actual worlds he made. He created things, we are told, for his own good pleasure. On the seventh day he rested and enjoyed its goodness. The work of redemption, too, was voluntary and freely engaged in, not forced on God by an economy out of control. No necessity, internal or external to God, drove him to it. God redeems for his own glory and pleasure.

Calvin calls the world the theater of God's glory. So perhaps Shakespeare was right, and all we men and women are merely players, playing our many parts for God's pleasure and honor. Our chief end, according to the Westminster divines, is to *glorify* God and *enjoy* him forever. Life, then, is celebration.

This theme appears in Ecclesiastes. Amid the frustration and apparent emptiness of life, the enjoyments of life are still God's gifts. "There is nothing better for a man than that he should eat and drink, and find enjoyment in his toil. This . . . is from the hand of God" (2:24). "I commend enjoyment, for man has no good thing under the sun but to eat, and drink, and enjoy himself" (8:15). The New Testament likewise talks of joy in life and work, of serving with gladness. Its ideal of servanthood is not one of maximizing productivity but of the liberty to serve joyfully, even playfully, from the heart.

(2) *The Sabbath.* For one day in seven, the people of God were told to forget their work and *rest* in God's gracious provision. Even in the wilderness, where subsistence depended on collecting manna before it rotted, the day of rest applied. It was a holiday, holy before God, not a "vacation." Celebrating God's creation and his deliverance, the people gathered festively to recall the past and to anticipate the future which Sabbath rest prefigured. Because of God's provision, work need not be compulsive. Ultimately life depends on God, not on our work. The Sabbath is a symbol of that, and of the God-creation relationship of which our dependence speaks.

Likewise, for one year in seven the land was to lie fallow, at leisure, unproductive, resting in God's provision and anticipating his kingdom. The Sabbath pictured life in a time frame between creation and the eschaton, a life embraced by God. Hence there need be no fear of wasting time in celebrating; nor need we take ourselves too seriously.

The same idea appears in God's words to Job, when everything seemed lost and all the fruits of his labor gone.

> Behold, Behemoth,
>   which I made as I made you;
>   he eats grass as an ox. . . .
> He is the first of the works of God. . . .
> For the mountains yield food for him
>   where all the wild beasts *play*.
> Under the lotus plants he lies. . . .
> Behold, if the river is turbulent he is not frightened.
>   (40:15–23, emphasis mine)

It is a picture of leisure and play replacing fear of what will happen if we are not productive, a picture echoed by the birds and the lilies of the Sermon on the Mount which neither toil nor spin. For *homo religiosis*, too, meaning and hope in life are not focused in work. We can afford to rest and play.

William Henry Davies, intentionally or not, suggests the same idea in a poem I was told to learn as a boy in school:

> What is this life if, full of care,
> We have no time to stand and stare,
> No time to stand beneath the bough
> And stare as long as sheep and cow,
> No time to wait 'till her mouth can
> Enrich that smile her eyes began?

(3) *The Kingdom of God.* "The streets of the city shall be full of boys and girls *playing in the streets*" (Zech. 8:5). The promise of the kingdom, as Lewis Smedes observes, is of restored playfulness. The Year of Jubilee was another foretaste, with its economic justice, joyful liberty, and peace. The Old Testament concept of *shalōm* is at work here, and the psalmist's confidence:

> Thou dost show me the path of life;
>   in thy presence there is fullness of joy,
>   in thy right hand are pleasures for evermore. (Ps. 16:11)

The Heidelberg Catechism (day XIX) accordingly teaches that "God will take me to himself into heavenly *joy* and *glory*."

Play and its relatives find meaning and purpose, then, in a place reserved for them in God's kingdom. There is time to laugh, time to dance, time to embrace (Eccles. 3:1–8). Like Tevye in *Fiddler on the Roof*, we can play and sing even in a strange land. Scripture begins with life in a garden and ends with a city at play; so play—art and celebration and fun and games, and a playful spirit—is part of our calling, part of the creation mandate. It is not the play of self-indulgence, nor of shed responsibility, but of gladness and celebration in responsible relationship to God. Play requires a free spirit rather than "free time," a spirit freed from thinking and acting as if life itself depends altogether on me. The Christian can afford to play.

So I say that play is first an attitude of mind, and only secondly is it various kinds of activity. It is a free spirit, celebrative and imaginative because of the possibilities God has for us in this world. It is an attitude that carries over into all of life, finding joyful expression in whatever we do, productive or not.

A PLAY ETHIC

A Christian ethic must take this theological understanding of the meaning and purpose of play, and ask how we can exercise its meaning and achieve its purpose with justice and with love. As a result of sin, work has become toil, workers are exploited, and economic life is perverted. As a result of sin also, leisure has become laziness and play self-indulgence; players are exploited, and the playful life is perverted. We live in responsible relationship to God, or we fail to do so, in work and in play. Sin and grace extend into both these mandates of creation.

Thomas Aquinas therefore expressed three cautions that we would do well to observe nowadays. First, do not take pleasure in indecent or injurious play. Second, do not lose your mental or emotional balance and self-control. Third, do not play in ways ill-fitting either the hour or the person[11] Stated positively, play should have positive moral and other consequences, it should be properly controlled, and it should be both timely and worthily human.

11. *Summa Theologica*, II. ii, Q. 168, Art. 2.

One way to develop a Christian play ethic is to explore what playing in responsible relationship to God, with justice and love, should mean for playing in the other relationships of life. In relationship to nature and its resources, questions of stewardship and respect for God's creation necessarily arise. We can play responsibly in these regards or we can play destructively and profligately, spending our natural resources on riotous living. I question the use of scarce energy resources in auto racing. I question the stewardship in roaring around a placid lake in a gas-guzzling motor boat that exhales noxious fumes. I question not only bullfighting and cockfighting, but also hunting animals for "sport alone" rather than for food or other responsible purposes. I question play that heedlessly defaces nature's beauty or upsets its ecosystem. Such "games" disregard the stewardly purposes and consequent limitations of man's "dominion" over nature.

Play is a social activity. Playing alone can become narcissistic. Playing together can build community. "Playing in relationship to God," then, will forbid games and jokes that tend to dehumanize people created in the image of God. Aquinas' words about indecent and injurious play are well taken. The early church rightly objected to the Roman circus, and Christians since have protested violent sports, dueling, and sadistic games; a movie like *Rollerball* is a sad commentary on our times. Christians protest pornography, and they have censured the theater and entertainment world, for not everything can be justified in the name of art any more than it can in the name of other kinds of play. Play that makes sex objects out of people, play that shatters self-respect, play that stifles growth, play that is unloving, unjust, unfair, or needlessly violent must be challenged. I object to boxing as a sport, and I have some moral reservations about football (as well as both economic and educational reservations about the overly large place it sometimes takes in college and high school). We need to reinforce in sports as well as in art and celebration the kinds of values society should have. We need to ask what Christian servanthood means in competition. "The family that plays together stays together," we quip; the point in this is that play can relax hard feelings and recreate togetherness, the sense of a shared existence we so greatly need. It can, but it is far from automatic.

In relationship to oneself, it is customary to talk of the psychological, physical, and re-creational values of play, and so we ought. But it also has aesthetic and intellectual potential, and leisure incubates ideas in art and science and society. Play can socialize us. It can discipline. It can develop precision and grace with aesthetic delight. It can produce transferable qualities of cooperation, persistence, and self-denial. But it can also produce sadistic, self-indulgent, self-exalting, self-abusive, even masochistic people utterly drained of other interests. Plato says that too much physical exercise without other things can make one an uncivilized beast, and too little makes one indecently soft.[12] No kind of play by itself can build character—how could a Christian claim it does? But it can provide an arena of possibilities, both good and bad, for personal development.

Objection is properly raised to cutthroat competitive sport that aims to win at all costs and delights in humiliating opponents. Such competitiveness, unloving in purpose and unjust in method, often extends into business and the professions. By stressing technological rather than human development it can dehumanize play. Emotional stress too easily erupts in violence. Commercialization highlights winning more than the creative art and ability involved. Understandably, then, some groups have reacted against competition altogether, and avoid competitive sports. More appropriate, it seems, would be attempts to harness the competitive spirit and direct its energies constructively. "Friendly competition" that stretches participants and evokes the finest efforts of which we are capable, efforts in which one ultimately competes with oneself—this sort of competition is always most demanding within the parameters of rules and of moral principle, and is most appropriate to human creativity.

Yet that is not enough. Play should indeed contribute to humanness, to health and well-being and work, but like everything else in life it has a religious significance that is more basic than all of these. If play is properly enjoyment of God, if play reminds us that we rest in his provision, if it expresses the *shalōm* of his kingdom, then I can no longer take myself with utmost seriousness, not even my theories about play. Play reminds me of this. It puts me in my place, win or lose. And so it gives perspective on life, on my life in relation to God. Winning is not the only thing; it isn't even

12. *Republic*, 410D.

the main thing. The playful attitude of the believer is more important by far.

In God's world we can afford leisure and play. We can playfully work and playfully play, playfully teach and playfully learn, playfully live and playfully love. Like Disney's dwarfs, we can whistle while we work. For even now we anticipate the kingdom of *shalōm* that is sure to come.

CONCLUSION

We have traced the major contours of a Christian world view and glimpsed its application to several areas of human activity and concern. Other topics could be explored in similar ways, and I have written at length elsewhere about Christian attitudes toward education and toward war. But the overriding impact remains the same: the coherence, vitality, and relevance of a Christian world view.

Serious doubts arise, however, about both the assumptions of secular humanism and the direction it would lead us. Naturalism and anthropocentricity provide little if any basis for unchanging values in a world groping for direction, and no firm hope in a driving sea of dark uncertainties. They seem sadly uninviting, at times even dehumanizing, yet still a last resort for those who will not think and live in relation to the living God revealed in Jesus Christ.

The contrast is now plain, and the result we anticipated at the beginning is now in sight. It is not a logically proven conclusion, to be sure, that Christian theism is true and naturalistic humanism false, although I firmly believe that to be the case. It is, rather, a proposal as to the shape Christian thought and life should take, and an invitation to the reader to pursue its implications further because of its intellectual credibility and human appeal.

As Simon Peter said to Jesus, "Lord, to whom shall we go? You have the words of eternal life" (John 6:68).

INDEX OF NAMES

Adams, M.   158
Addison, Joseph   201
Allport, Gordon   82
Anscombe, Elizabeth   29, 85, 157
Anselm   89
Aquinas   10, 16, 37, 40, 43, 68, 73-75, 89-90, 109, 159, 169, 220, 231-32
Aristotle   3, 42-43, 48, 73-75, 78-79, 85, 89, 93-95, 114, 120, 154, 169, 177, 179, 216, 228
Armstrong, D. M.   22
Arnold, Matthew   11, 12
Augustine   4, 10, 16, 37, 43, 68, 72-73, 94, 131, 149, 159, 194
Ayer, A. J.   50

Bacon, Francis   17, 21, 207, 209
Baier, Kurt   212
Barbour, Ian   209, 211-12
Barth, Karl   13, 61, 64, 67, 84, 109
Baumer, F. L.   30
Bebbington, D. W.   196
Beck, Lewis   85, 118
Beckett, Samuel   12, 225
Bergson, Henri   79
Berkeley, George   45, 76, 83, 153
Berkhof, Hendrikus   187, 196
Berkhof, Louis   57
Berkouwer, G. C.   109
Bertocci, Peter   82-84, 100, 170, 205

Blackstone, W. T.   212
Blaikie, Robert   85
Blamires, Harry   viii
Bloh, Ernst   26
Bonino, José   174
Brightman, E. S.   40, 82-84
Brunner, Emil   6, 11, 13, 59, 67, 85, 135, 150, 161, 192, 202
Buber, Martin   84-85
Bultmann, Rudolph   41
Butler, Joseph   43, 159, 168
Butterfield, Herbert   196

Calvin, John   10, 131, 220
Campbell, C. A.   96
Camus, Albert   25, 105-106
Carey, G.   109
Carnell, E. J.   129
Casserley, J. V. L.   34, 196
Cerillo, Augustus   189
Chardin, Teilhard de   13, 43, 77, 164
Chesterton, G. K.   102
Chisholm, Roderick   50
Cicero   50
Clark, Gordon H.   14
Clement of Alexandria   109
Clines, D. J. A.   109
Cobb, John   77
Coleridge, S. T.   97, 102
Commoner, Barry   211
Comte, Auguste   21, 162, 192, 207

Connell, Francis   215
Cox, Harvey   30, 226

Dante   42
Davies, W. H.   230
Defoe, Daniel   112, 176
deGrazia, Sebastian   223, 226
Demant, V. A.   188, 217
Democritus   95
Descartes, Rene   42-43, 50, 75, 120, 130, 143-44, 212
Dewey, John   19, 21, 28, 43, 143-44
Dewich, E. C.   61
Dilthey, Wilhelm   32
Donagan, Alan   157, 166
Dooyeweerd, Herman   32, 65-66, 109
Dostoevsky   25
Dworkin, Gerold   96

Ehrenfeld, David   211
Ehrlich, Paul   211
Einstein, Albert   42
Eliot, T. S.   12
Ellul, Jacques   6, 37, 189, 211
Emerson, Ralph Waldo   76
Emmet, Dorothy   33
Erasmus   225
Erickson, Joyce   215
Evans, C. S.   149

Feyeraband, Paul   146
Ferre, Frederick   211
Feuerbach, Ludwig   27-28
Foster, M. B.   208-209
Frankena, William   161
Frankfort, Henry   59
Freud, Sigmund   23, 98, 146, 225

Ghiselin, B.   200
Gide, Andre   25
Gilkey, J. Langdon   8, 57
Gill, Jerry   129
Gilson, Etienne   62-63
Goffman, Erving   225
Gustafson, James   158

Haley, Bruce   227
Hartshorne, Charles   77-79, 81, 212
Hegel, G. W. F.   27, 32, 43, 77, 81, 94, 98-99, 106, 177, 192, 195
Heidegger, Martin   116
Helm, Paul   159
Henry, Carl F. H.   14, 66, 134
Heroditus   66
Hesse, Herman   25, 225
Hick, John   68
Hobbes, Thomas   75, 95, 145, 157
Holbach, Baron d'   95
Holmes, A. F.   8, 39, 46, 51, 53, 128-29, 150
Hook, Stanley   29
Hooykaas, R.   209
Hort, H. J. A.   185
Houston, James   57
Huizinga, Jehan   225
Hume, David   90, 140, 143, 146, 157
Husserl, Edmund   47
Ibsen, H. J.   12
Idziak, J. M.   159
Jaki, Stephen   209
James, William   140-41
Jefferson, Thomas   29, 75
Jonas, Hans   79

Kant, Immanuel   28, 32, 48, 81, 85, 90, 93, 100, 102, 140, 143, 146, 166, 192, 201
Kauffman, Gordon   85
Keen, Sam   228
Kierkegaard, Soren   78, 84-85, 100, 141-42
King, Martin Luther   191
Kirk, J. Andrew   174
Kraemer, Hendrik   61
Krikorian, Y. H.   19-20
Kuhn, Thomas   42, 44, 146, 210
Kümmel, Werner   109
Kurtz, Paul   17-21
Kuyper, Abraham   13, 135, 186, 188, 194, 196, 202, 217

Ladd, John   165

Lamond, Corliss   19
Lamprecht, S. P.   28
Lasch, Christopher   114
Latourette, K. S.   179, 194
Lazerowitz, Morris   46, 146
Lee, Robert   227
Leibniz, G. W.   76
Lewis, C. S.   6, 45, 68, 103, 187, 208
Locke, John   43, 75, 138, 145, 159, 169, 176, 183, 191-92, 216-17
Lombardi, Vince   5, 227
Luther, Martin   10, 37, 153, 187

MacGregor, Geddes   17
Machiavelli   187
MacIntyre, Alasdair   208
MacMurray, John   85, 145
Malik, Charles   14
Mann, Thomas   25
Marcuse, Herbert   6, 26, 99, 220-21
Maritain, Jacques   13, 17, 200
Marx, Karl   vii, 26-27, 30-33, 49, 98-100, 105, 116, 121, 127, 138, 144, 146, 151, 163, 174, 177, 191-92, 195
Maslow, Abraham   23, 28
Mavrodes, George   51, 91
May, Rollo   199
McIntyre, John   195-96
Melden, A. I.   96
Menninger, Karl   103, 121
Mill, John Stuart   125, 146, 162, 192
Miller, David L.   226, 228
Moltmann, Jorgen   163, 228
More, Sir Thomas   225
Morris, Herbert   103
Mott, Stephen   124, 187
Moule, C. F. D.   110
Mozart   43, 201
Munby, Dennis   221
Murray, John Courtney   vii, 55, 63

Nash, Arnold   vii
Newman, J. H.   141
Newton, Isaac   42, 75-76

Niebuhr, H. Richard   36-37
Niebuhr, Reinhold   13, 98, 115, 123, 176, 187, 191-93, 196, 202
Nielsen, Kai   28-29
Nietzsche, Friedrich   25, 46, 98, 104, 116, 146, 187, 226
Novak, M. E.   176

O'Brien, Richard   viii
Occam, William of   74, 167
O'Connor, Elizabeth   203
Origen   109
Orr, James   13, 132
Outka, Gene   161

Pelagins   101, 122-23
Pepper, Stephen   33
Piaget, Jean   226
Pike, Nelson   89
Pieper, Joseph   226
Plantinga, Alvin   68, 88-89
Plato   8, 16-17, 32, 40, 42-43, 58, 67, 71-75, 86-90, 101, 111, 114, 120-21, 139-44, 155-56, 161, 177, 217, 233
Plotinus   43, 58, 73
Polanyi, Michael   44, 149-50, 210
Pope, Alexander   11, 42
Protagoras   17

Quinn, Philip   158

Rahner, Hugh   228
Ramsey, Ian   33, 158
Ramsey, Paul   29
Randall, J. H.   19, 33
Rawls, John   157
Reid, Thomas   4, 40, 145, 159
Ringgren, Helmer   59
Ross, W. D.   166
Rousseau, Jean-Jacques   23
Ruskin   227
Russell, Bertrand   12, 50
Rust, Eric   212

Sagan, Carl   22
Sartre, Jean-Paul   12, 25, 84, 98, 105-106, 225

Sayers, Dorothy   203
Schaff, Adam   26, 99
Schelling, F. W. J.   202
Schleiermacher, F.   76
Schneider, H. W.   19
Schopenhauer, Arthur   146
Scotus, Duns   88
Sellars, Wilfred   21, 33
Shaffer, Jerome   118
Shakespeare, William   106, 116, 225
Shaw, Bernard   227
Shedd, Russell   124, 176
Sire, James   viii
Skinner, B. F.   43, 95-97, 102
Smedes, Lewis   170, 228
Smith, Adam   188, 217
Socrates   16
Spiegelberg, Herbert   47
Spinoza, Benedict   43, 50
Spykman, Gordon J.   188, 217
Stob, Henry   161
Swinburne, Richard   91
Sylvester, Hugh   68
Szasz, Thomas   103

Tawney, R. L.   219
Taylor, Paul   165
Taylor, Richard   96, 118
Temple, William   13, 43, 222

Tennyson, Alfred   11-12
Tertullian   37
Thielicke, Helmut   85
Tillich, Paul   81
Toffler, Alvin   211, 222
Torrance, Thomas   85
Toulmin, Stephen   51, 210
Toynbee, Arnold   193
Tucker, Robert C.   27
Tuveson, E.   201

Vitz, Paul   24
Voltaire   75
Vree, Dale   174

Wagner, R.   201
Warnock, Mary   201
Whitehead, A. N.   42-43, 77-78, 209
Wilde, Oscar   104
Wilkinson, Lauren   212
Wisdom, J. O.   45
Wittgenstein, Ludwig   22, 225
Wolff, H.   109
Wolterstorff, Nicholas   4, 51, 88-89, 145, 204-205, 226
Wootton, Barbara   102
Wordsworth, William   23

Yoder, J. H.   187